SMITH, Alan Gordon Rae. Servant of the Cecils: the life of Sir Michael Hickes, 1543–1612. Rowman and Littlefield, 1977. 221p ill index. 15.00 ISBN 0-87471-933-X

CHOICE   SEPT. '77

History, Geography &
Travel

Europe

Sir Michael Hickes was one of those many lesser-known figures who played a vital role in the government of Elizabethan England. He was the patronage secretary of William Cecil from 1580 to 1590; in addition, he served actively in five different branches of local government between 1598 and 1612. His friends and acquaintances included some of the leading personages of Elizabethan and early Stuart England. His biography also provides an excellent example of how a man of reasonably humble birth could amass a large fortune through the shrewd use of the prerogatives of office, money lending, and a fortunate marriage. Normally it is difficult to find sufficient source material to write a detailed biography of lesser figures but fortunately nearly 800 of Hickes's letters have survived. Smith, who has an excellent knowledge of Elizabethan government, has used these materials with great skill to write both a readable biography and an important case study in Elizabethan government and society. Although a book of this nature would normally be directed to specialized historians, Smith has supplied such clear explanations of administrative procedures that the

work can be read profitably by undergraduates. Contains extensive footnotes, adequate index, and eight illustrations. Recommended for all four-year college and university libraries.

Europe

Servant of the Cecils

ALAN G. R. SMITH was born in 1936 and educated at Glasgow High School, Glasgow University, and University College London. He graduated M.A. with First Class Honours in History from Glasgow in 1959 and Ph.D. from London in 1962, when he was appointed Assistant in History at Glasgow University. He became a Lecturer there in 1964 and Senior Lecturer in 1975. His publications include *The Government of Elizabethan England* (1967), *The New Europe* (1969) and *Science and Society in the Sixteenth and Seventeenth Centuries* (1973), and he has edited *The Reign of James VI and I* (1973) and, with Joel Hurstfield, *Elizabethan People: State and Society* (1972). He is a Fellow of the Royal Historical Society.

Alan G. R. Smith

Servant of the Cecils

The Life of Sir Michael Hickes, 1543-1612

ROWMAN AND LITTLEFIELD
TOTQWA, NEW JERSEY

FIRST PUBLISHED, IN THE UNITED STATES 1977
BY ROWMAN AND LITTLEFIELD, TOTOWA, N.J.

© 1977 BY ALAN G. R. SMITH

ISBN 0–87471–933–X

PRINTED IN GREAT BRITAIN

Contents

Illustrations

To Isabel

Introduction

Michael Hickes was private secretary to William Cecil, Lord Burghley, between 1580 and 1598. As such he is typical of the many personal assistants who served the great ministers and courtiers of Tudor England. In two important ways, however, he is an unusual figure. His master, Lord Burghley, was by far the most important person in the government of Elizabethan England after the Queen herself, and Hickes's work reflected the importance of Burghley's role in the state. Above all, Hickes's personal papers—nearly eight hundred letters—have survived and are now among the Lansdowne manuscripts in the British Museum. This is a unique collection of records for a man in his position in Tudor England. When taken with other documents from the Public Record Office and from the Salisbury manuscripts at Hatfield House these letters make it possible to reconstruct his life and work in detail. They give insights into the working of important aspects of the Elizabethan administrative machine. They also show that Hickes was a remarkable personality, a real 'character', and enable details of his personal life to be used to add human interest to the story of his administrative work and to build up an overall picture of the man. This involves frequent quotations from the manuscripts and in these, as well as in the much less numerous citations from printed sources, I have modernized spelling and punctuation.

In preparing this study I have accumulated many debts. Librarians and officials at the British Museum, the Public Record Office and the Institute of Historical Research in London have given me generous help. I am most grateful to the late marquess of Salisbury for allowing me to visit Hatfield House and read relevant manuscripts there and to his librarian, Miss Clare Talbot, for making my visits so pleasant. Mr Graham C. Greene and Miss Jane Berkoff of Jonathan Cape encouraged me during the preparation of the book and have been particularly helpful throughout the later stages. Two friends at Glasgow University, Mr P. J. Parish and Mr G. B. A. M. Finlayson, read the whole work in typescript and made many valuable comments and suggestions. The typescript itself was prepared, immaculately, by Miss Patricia Ferguson.

My seniors and contemporaries in the world of Tudor studies have given me considerable help. For a number of years I was a regular member of the Monday and Wednesday evening seminars at the Institute of Historical Research conducted by Professor Sir John Neale, Professor J. Hurstfield, and Professor S. T. Bindoff. My friends there, British and American, aided my work by talking about their problems as well as my own. Professor Bindoff himself earned the gratitude of yet another student of the Tudor period by providing insights and information from his own vast store of knowledge.

I owe much to the late Sir John Neale. His infectious enthusiasm for Elizabethan history and his own personal interest in Michael Hickes were a great encouragement, and I had wise advice from him about the techniques of writing a book. My greatest academic debt, however, is to Professor Joel Hurstfield. It was he who supervised my first steps in research and who, ever since, has taken a most generous interest in my work. He has been both a stern master and a kind friend. I would like to acknowledge my deep gratitude to him. The most recent of his many kindnesses has been to read this book in typescript and to offer numerous suggestions for improvements.

The friends who have helped me are largely responsible for any merits this book may have. I, of course, am responsible for errors and deficiencies which may remain.

A very special debt, to my wife, is acknowledged in the dedication.

University of Glasgow A.G.R.S.
October 1976

PART ONE

1543–1598
Secretary to the Lord Treasurer

1

Young Michael

In the sixteenth century Cheapside was the chief central artery of the city of London, running, as it still does today, between St Paul's churchyard to the west and another important street, the Poultry, to the east. In 1543, on its southern side, near the eastern end, lay the White Bear, a retail mercery owned by Robert Hickes, whose wife Juliana was a member of the Somerset family of Arthur of Clapham.[1] Her place of origin is significant because the Hickes family had a long history as yeomen in neighbouring Gloucestershire where Robert himself left lands at the time of his death.[2] It seems likely that he was born in Gloucestershire and, having married into a neighbouring family, dug up his west-country roots and set out to make a career in London. It was certainly there that his eldest son was born on October 21st, 1543 and, soon after, was christened Michael in the church of St Pancras, Soper Lane. That was only about a hundred yards from the family shop, where his parents sold silks and other fine clothing materials to the increasingly wealthy and ever more fashion-conscious citizens of London.[3]

Michael was the first of six sons born to Robert and Juliana and one of three who grew to manhood. The registers of the parish church record the births of three and the deaths of two of these younger brothers. Francis was born in January 1545, Hilary in the same month of the following year, and John, who died at or just after birth, in March 1548. That year must have been an unhappy one for the parents as, a few months later, in July, the youngest of their three surviving sons, two-year-old Hilary, also died and was buried beside his infant brother in the churchyard of St Pancras. [4] The births of the two other children, Clement and Baptist, do not appear in the parish register, but Baptist, the youngest of the family, was born late in 1550 or early in 1551. [5] The date of death of Francis, second of the six brothers, is unknown, but he certainly predeceased his father who, in his will, dated 1557, mentioned only three sons, Michael, Clement and Baptist. [6]

In that will Robert Hickes also stated that he wanted his body 'to be buried after the order of the Catholic Church', [7] but it is impossible to say whether or not this phrase implied a genuine devotion to Roman Catholicism. Robert died during Mary Tudor's persecution of Protestantism. Between 1555 and 1558 nearly 300 English men and women were burned at the stake for their opposition to the Roman Catholic faith, the great majority of them in the south-east of England, especially in London and the surrounding areas. In these circumstances it was politic for any man to use conventional religious phraseology in a will. In any event, the expression 'Catholic Church' was open to interpretation—Protestants often affirmed their belief in a true 'Catholic Church' free from Roman corruptions.

Whatever his father's beliefs, there is no doubt that Michael grew to adolescence during a period of continuous religious upheaval. During the first sixteen years of his life the nation's official religion changed from the 'national' Catholicism of Henry VIII's later years to the overt Protestantism of Edward VI's reign, then to the Roman Catholicism of Mary, and finally, in 1559, to the moderate Protestantism of the Elizabethan settlement. It was while Michael was between the ages of twelve and fifteen that the Marian burnings took place. We do not know whether or not he watched any of the 'fires of Smithfield', but the executions must have provided an important talking point in the Hickes household when he was at a highly impressionable age, and his later religious history—he became a Puritan—suggests that he probably shared the sympathy which many of his fellow Londoners felt for the victims.

Whatever Michael's precise reactions to the religious changes which marked his youth, he can hardly have been as continuously preoccupied with them as with the everyday sights and sounds of the neighbourhood in which he lived. Cheapside was one of the few wide streets in London at that time. Indeed, it

was as much a market-place as a street and during the daytime
it was usually covered with stalls displaying goods of all kinds.
The street had three notable landmarks. In the eastern part,
near the White Bear, was a small stone tower—the 'great
conduit' of Cheapside, which drew 'sweet water ... by pipes of
lead underground' from the country heights of Paddington and
served not only the market stalls but householders who came
from further afield. In the centre of the street was the market
cross, the 'standard in Cheap', which had first been built at an
unrecorded date. By the fifteenth century it had become 'very
ruinous with age' and was taken down and 'another competent
standard of stone ... builded for the commodity and honour of
the city'. The standard was one of the places where royal pro-
clamations were ceremonially read. In the western part of
Cheapside was the 'great cross', a remarkable object erected by
Edward I in 1290 in memory of his wife Eleanor of Castile. It
was surrounded by images of Christ, the Virgin, Edward the
Confessor and others, which were part of the fabric of the cross.
It was frequently renovated during the fifteenth and sixteenth
centuries, the last occasion being in 1554 when it was regilded
in celebration of the arrival of Philip of Spain for his marriage
with Queen Mary. It must have been a splendid sight, but later,
in Elizabeth's reign, it came under attack both as a popish relic
and as a hazard to the ever growing volume of traffic which
crowded into the street.[8] All in all, the Cheapside scene must
have been both colourful and noisy.

If the busy neighbourhood of Cheapside was one playground
for the youthful Michael, another was probably the banks of the
Thames—the river, with its numerous wharves serving a great
and growing assembly of shipping, lay only a few hundred yards
to the south of the White Bear. Another attraction, even nearer
to his home than the Thames, was old St Paul's, the greatest
church in Christendom apart from St Peter's in Rome. Its huge
mass rose at the west end of Cheapside, crowned by its magnificent spire, which towered over 500 feet above the ground.[9] Just
to the east of the cathedral were the buildings of St Paul's school,
founded at the beginning of Henry VIII's reign by John Colet,
one of the most notable of the early English humanists. It is
likely that Michael, Clement and Baptist Hickes all began their
education at St Paul's, which was governed by the Mercers

Company. Their father's shop was only a few hundred yards from the school and it would have been natural for him to send his sons there. It is significant that Baptist later made a munificent benefaction to the school, at the same time as he founded exhibitions to Trinity, his Cambridge college.[10] The usual age of entry to grammar school was six or seven, and if Michael did go to St Paul's he was probably able to read and write at the time of his entry. When Colet founded the school he gave instructions that the master, before admitting a pupil, should see that he could 'read and write competently, else let him not be admitted in no wise'. Pupils concentrated on the study of Latin grammar. First of all they learned parsing and construing and built up a vocabulary; then they went on to Latin composition, learning to write and speak in imitation of the classical authors whose works they read. Colet had ordered that the master of St Paul's 'be learned in Greek, if such may be found' — an understandable prescription from one of the pioneers of Greek studies in England — but his hopes were not always realized. Thomas Freeman, who was High Master from 1549 to 1559, was dismissed in the latter year largely because of his 'lack of the Greek tongue'.[11] Michael, therefore, certainly learned a great deal of Latin but probably no Greek during his schooldays.

Robert Hickes's death in 1557 did not lead to any decline in the family's fortunes. His will[12] reveals a moderate prosperity which must have allowed his sons to pass their childhood in some comfort and security and which enabled Michael himself to embark on a university education in 1559. Robert left land which he possessed in London, Bristol and Gloucestershire and the White Bear itself to his widow for her life.[13] One third of his movable property went to his wife and one third to his children, and there was money left to make a bequest to his brother Richard, to provide for servants, and to remember friends. Among these friends was Anthony Penne, who received 'one black gown, one coat ... and a ... gold ring'. Penne, however, got more than a small bequest as a result of his friend's death. Soon, probably within a year, he married the widow.[14]

In 1559 Michael left his mother, brother, and newly acquired stepfather and entered Trinity College, Cambridge.[15] The first year of Queen Elizabeth's reign was of decisive importance in his life. The accession to power of William Cecil as the new Queen's most trusted councillor, made his later career possible, and his residence at Cambridge from the autumn of 1559 onwards not only moulded his religious ideas but also enabled him to meet a number of men who became his close friends and probably obtained access for him to Cecil's circle.

Elizabeth's accession to the throne was followed by changes at Cambridge in general and at Trinity College in particular which are important in considering the influence which university life exercised on Hickes. On February 9th, 1559 the Vice-Chancellor and Senate asked William Cecil to accept the office of Chancellor in succession to Cardinal Pole. Ten days later Cecil expressed thanks for his election. He was not long in making the Crown's authority felt. At the end of May he notified the university of an impending royal visitation—a formal inspection conducted by the Queen's nominees. Commissioners were appointed on June 20th and the visitation lasted from July 7th until the 23rd.[16] The immediate effects on the life of the university were not enormous. Only two headships of colleges out of fourteen were directly affected: the Marian Regius Professor of Divinity, John Young, and George Bullock, Mary's Lady Margaret Professor, were replaced as Masters of Pembroke and St John's by Edmund Grindal and James Pilkington. There was nothing like the flood of expulsions of college fellows which had followed the death of Edward VI. The story of admissions, however, is rather different. Twenty new fellows of Trinity were elected in 1560 and the records of other colleges tell a similar story of expansion in the early years of Elizabeth's reign. In December 1558 the death of John Christopherson, Master of Trinity since 1553, brought an important change in the headship of Hickes's new college. William Bill, who had been elected Master in 1551, but forcibly expelled by Mary, returned to take up his old office once again.[17]

We can only guess at the precise motives which brought Hickes to a Cambridge University and a Trinity College thus moderately reformed by visitation and death. He and his family, following humanistic ideas, may have believed in the value of education both as an end in itself and as an avenue to and a preparation for employment in the public service; he may have hoped, in a general way, to further his career through contact with the influential men whom he would certainly meet at

Cambridge; he may have wanted to improve his social status by acquiring the rank of gentleman, which was traditionally granted to those who had studied at university — this last motivation was certainly common among the families of prosperous tradesmen who gave their sons a higher education. Whatever Hickes's hopes, he was lucky in his tutor, George Blythe, who became a fellow of Trinity in 1560. Blythe had conformed under Mary, for he had been presented to the rectory of Hungerton in Lincolnshire by the Queen and King Philip. He remained in favour when Elizabeth ascended the throne. He was a proctor at Cambridge in 1561 and became deputy Regius Professor of Greek in 1562.[18]

It is not easy to assess the *general* quality of university education at this time — modern scholars are deeply divided on the subject[19] — but in *individual* cases the interest and diligence not merely of the student but also of his tutor must often have been decisive. Blythe certainly seems to have exerted a considerable influence on Hickes — the two men later became close friends — and it was probably through Blythe's encouragement that Hickes acquired the extensive knowledge of the classics which enabled him to sprinkle his later correspondence with Latin epigrams.

It is not clear how long Hickes stayed at Cambridge. He was certainly in residence in March 1562 when his stepfather Anthony Penne wrote a letter addressed to 'Michael Hickes, with Mr Blythe in Trini[ty] College in Cambridge',[20] but he did not graduate. That this failure to take a degree, a common practice at the time, was no reflection on his abilities as a scholar is very evident from his stepfather's letter. 'Michael', wrote Penne,

> I am glad to hear that you apply your learning and profit very well therein. The book you wrote and sent to Mr Osborne is very well liked and much commended of him and all others that hath seen the same ... The continuance of your diligence must needs be to your advancement and your tutor, Mr Blythe, hath deserved by your forwardness great praise and commendation to whom I and your friends are much bound for his care over you and the pains he hath taken in your bringing up.[21]

Penne himself had received some 'verses' from his stepson and concluded his letter with thanks for these and a wish that the eighteen-year-old Hickes might increase still further in 'virtue and learning'.[22] The youthful Michael was clearly a conscientious student who believed that he had budding literary talents, but the benefit which he obtained from his studies, important though that may have been, was probably not the most significant result of his life at Cambridge.

In the 1560s Trinity College was one of the most important centres of Puritanism in the university. When Bill died in 1561 the Queen appointed as his successor Dr Robert Beaumont, a Leicestershire man who had been a Genevan exile in Mary's reign. Beaumont's part in the Vestiarian controversy, which aroused such ill-feeling in the Church in the 1560s, showed that he was essentially a moderate. He was one of those who, in November 1565, asked Cecil to secure the remission of orders for enforcing the use of the surplice. These orders had just been issued by the Queen through Archbishop Parker and the request, not unnaturally, was refused. Beaumont continued to wear the distasteful garment, being prepared in the last resort to subordinate his own feelings to the commands of the sovereign as supreme governor of the Church. In fact, his compliance was such that in 1566 sterner spirits accused him of superstition and vainglory.[23]

Beaumont was sympathetic to Puritan ideas, but his cautious and moderate approach to the problem of purging the Church of such remaining 'popish' abuses as vestments was very far from being representative of the prevalent mood in the college. In the early years of the reign Thomas Cartwright, minor fellow of Trinity from 1560 and major fellow from 1562, was a dominant influence in the whole university. In the 1570s he became the intellectual leader of those more extreme Puritans who wanted to abolish episcopacy altogether and set up a presbyterian system of church government. It is hardly surprising that the presence of such a man in college spelled trouble for Beaumont. In 1565 all the windows in the college chapel, 'wherein did appear superstition', were broken, and shortly afterwards, at Cartwright's instigation, the members of the college, with only three exceptions, appeared in chapel without surplices.[24]

Although Hickes had certainly left Cambridge before the

'revolt' of 1565, it is apparent from later evidence that he was a fervent admirer of Cartwright and it seems probable that his sympathies would have been with the extremists rather than with the moderates, of whom Beaumont may be said to have been representative. Hickes got to know Cartwright only slightly at Cambridge[25] but it seems clear that his closest friends at the university were Puritans. Analysis of the earliest surviving letters to Hickes, letters dating from the 1560s, 1570s, and 1580s, shows that most of them were written by four contemporaries at Trinity College: Blythe, Cartwright, Vincent Skinner, and John Stubbe.[26] The letters from Stubbe and Skinner are written in terms of easy familiarity which imply long friendship and it seems overwhelmingly probable that the foundations of the intimacy that they suggest were laid during the period when they were Hickes's fellow students at Cambridge.

Vincent Skinner, a future colleague of Hickes in Burghley's secretariat, was a Lincolnshire man who went up to Trinity in 1557, became a scholar in 1560, a minor fellow in 1561 and a major fellow three years later. He was a sponsor of the Puritan Bill in the Parliament of 1572 and it seems unlikely that the religious opinions which he held then were different from those of his university days.[27] John Stubbe, a Norfolk man, matriculated in 1555 and took his B.A. in 1561.[28] His Puritanism was notorious in Elizabethan England and it is very probable that his was the greatest of all the influences at Cambridge which helped to mould Hickes's mind. Hickes certainly became his devoted admirer. Edward and Nathaniel Bacon, sons of Sir Nicholas Bacon, Elizabeth's first Lord Keeper of the Great Seal, were also contemporaries of Hickes at Cambridge. Both went up to Trinity College in 1561.[29] Their father's and their own sympathies were with Puritanism and Nathaniel at least was on friendly terms with Hickes in later years.[30] It is likely that the association began during their university days.

There is also evidence that Skinner, Stubbe, and Blythe, all three closely associated with Hickes, were themselves linked in terms of friendship, perhaps even of intimacy.[31] As George Blythe, like his friends, seems to have been a religious radical[32] it looks as though there was a closely knit Puritan circle at Trinity College and later at Lincoln's Inn where the four were also students together. Three of the four friends, Blythe, Skinner, and Hickes, later became members of Burghley's secretariat, confirmation that the Queen's principal adviser, though he was certainly no extremist, tended to favour members of the 'Godly party' in the Church.

There is no evidence about Hickes's activities between March 1st, 1562, when he was still at Cambridge, and March 20th, 1565, when he was admitted to Lincoln's Inn;[33] but in 1564, whether he had by then returned to London or whether he was still at Cambridge, he must have been worried by his family's connection with a widely publicized political intrigue which touched one of the highest officers of state and involved that most delicate of all subjects, the succession to the throne.

Despite the fact that she had no generally accepted heir, Elizabeth always refused to name a successor. To do so, she believed, would merely lead to trouble during her lifetime without necessarily solving the problem on her death, when other claimants might challenge her nominee and thus bring about civil strife. The wisdom of her policy—there are powerful arguments both for and against it—does not concern us here, but it is important to note that the Queen's fury was roused by the merest suspicion that any of her subjects were meddling in the question, a matter, as she saw it, solely for the royal prerogative. In the winter of 1560 one of the principal claimants to the succession, Lady Catherine Grey, a descendant of Henry VIII's younger sister Mary, disgraced herself by secretly marrying Edward Seymour, earl of Hertford, son and heir of Protector Somerset, the man who had ruled England between 1547 and 1549 on behalf of his nephew Edward VI.[34] The secret came out in 1561 when Catherine became pregnant, and the furious Elizabeth imprisoned the young couple, both in their early twenties, in the Tower, where Catherine gave birth to a son in September. The Queen's rage is understandable. Hertford, like his wife, had royal blood in his veins—he was descended through his mother from Edward III—and Lady Catherine's marriage, both by its secrecy and by her choice of a husband, could easily be interpreted as a challenge to the royal authority. The Hickes family became involved in the affair through Anthony Penne, who, in 1561, was in Hertford's service, in charge of his financial affairs. On October 18th an order to Penne, signed by eleven Privy Councillors, noting that he had 'the receipt and payment

of the revenues of the earl of Hertford, presently in the Tower',
authorized him to 'pay of the same revenue so much as you
shall be appointed by order of the said earl unto you, for the
relief of him and his, being in the Tower'.[35] The couple remained
in prison and they were still under restraint in 1563 and 1564
when John Hales took a hand in the affair. Hales, a Puritan,
had been a prominent member of the 'Commonwealth' party
of social reformers and a notable supporter of Protector Somerset
during Edward VI's reign. He was a man of considerable abilities, but also, it seems, highly impetuous; a fellow member of the
1563 Parliament christened him 'Hales the hottest'. It was during this Parliament that Hales wrote a tract on the succession,
concluding that Lady Catherine was the rightful heiress to the
throne. This was political dynamite. The tract was not printed,
but in January 1564 Hales distributed manuscript copies in
Westminster and compounded his offence by declaring that
Lady Catherine's marriage to Hertford was valid, despite a
contrary official pronouncement, made during the previous
year by the archbishop of Canterbury.[36] Hales was arrested and
towards the end of April 1564 was closely questioned about his
activities.[37]

The ripples of the affair touched Anthony Penne on April
6th, about three weeks before Hales was interrogated. Penne,
who by this time had transferred to the service of Lady Catherine's uncle, Lord John Grey, was arrested by the marshal-at-
arms and questioned, somewhere outside the city of London, by
Lord Robert Dudley, the Queen's favourite, who was taking
part in the investigations. On the same day Dudley wrote to
Cecil, '[Penne's] wife doth remain at London ... Fain he would
have sent word of his sending for to ... [her], but the marshal
would not [let him]. Therefore, if he have any books or writings
of these matters he is to be charged with, they are to be found
there in London at his house, where you may now give order in
time for the search thereof.'[38] We do not know what happened
to Penne as a result of these inquiries, but his master, Lord John
Grey, was certainly in deep trouble as a result of the affair and
the Lord Keeper, Sir Nicholas Bacon, who was implicated, was
forbidden to attend the Court for a time.[39] The whole business
was a clear warning to the Hickes family of the dangers attached
to political intrigues in high affairs of state, a warning reinforced

by the fate of Hales, who was still under restraint as late as 1568. [40]

Michael Hickes's entry to Lincoln's Inn, a year after his stepfather's unhappy meeting with Lord Robert Dudley, must have been preceded by an interview in the hall of the Inn, so that the Bench, the governing body, could 'substantially inquire of his demeanour and conversation'. [41] This was almost certainly a formality—many students at the Inns of Court were notorious for their rowdiness—and Hickes took his place in an institution which, with the three other Inns of Court, formed what came to be called 'the third university of England', devoted to the study of the common law. Stubbe, Blythe, and Skinner all preceded him to the Inn, Stubbe in November 1562, Blythe in March 1563, and Skinner in January 1565. [42] The admission register also contains, under the year 1565, the name of Hugh Beeston, a Cheshire man who became Hickes's lifelong friend. [43] Students entered the Inns of Court, just as they went to the universities, with a variety of aims. Some wanted to acquire social status — law students, like their fellows at the universities, were entitled to the coveted rank of gentleman; some, often after a period already spent at university, regarded the Inns as finishing schools, bases from which they could sample the delights of London life while at the same time making contacts in official and court circles which might prove useful in their later careers; all probably intended to acquire at least a smattering of legal knowledge, which was very useful in a highly litigious age, when most men of substance found themselves, at some time in their lives, engaged in lawsuits with neighbours or tenants. Only a small minority of students intended to become professional lawyers, and they had to spend at least seven years preparing for a call to the bar. Those who successfully obtained that call had taken the first step in a career which brought notable Elizabethan barristers both fame and great fortune in the courts.

Learning the English common law, with its elaborate precedents and involved technicalities, was a long and tedious business. Students were expected to attend lectures and disputations conducted by senior members of the Inn as well as reading as many as possible of the growing number of law books. There were no tutors in the Inns to supervise their work and the majority of students, bored by the difficulties of the subject, attracted by the pleasures and vices of London, and in any event not intending to become professionals in the law, probably made little progress with their studies. It was a different matter for those who were reading for the bar and the latest authority on the subject concludes that although the minimum qualifications for call 'probably did not demand any highly developed legal expertise ... barristers were [generally] condemned for lacking morals, not learning'.[44]

Whatever Hickes's motives for entering Lincoln's Inn, it seems that he did not neglect his studies while he was there. He bombarded his friend Stubbe with questions about legal technicalities,[45] and maintained his interest long enough to receive a call to the bar in 1577,[46] four years after his entry into Burghley's service and long after he had ceased to be a full-time student. The summons may have given him considerable satisfaction, but there is no evidence that he ever practised as a lawyer.

Little is known of Hickes's life at the Inn. He certainly acquired a room there while he was a student and retained it long after he entered Burghley's service—as late as March 1586 a letter was addressed to him at Lincoln's Inn.[47] In view of the convivial qualities which he displayed in later life, he probably took the opportunities which the frequent 'revels' at the Inn provided to give full expression to the gaiety of his nature. These revels, which were held six times a year, were elaborate affairs with feasting, plays, and music. The two most important were those held at Christmas and on February 2nd, the feast of the Purification. The earl of Rutland supped at the Inn at the February revels of 1568, when the payment of £3. 6s. 8d. was recorded 'to Mr Hickes, for victuals for many gentlemen of the Middle Temple, who came here to dance the Post revels with the gentlemen of this Inn'.[48]

One of Hickes's contemporaries at the Inn was Edward Suliarde, who had been admitted in March 1559 and was certainly in residence in 1580.[49] By 1584 the two men were on intimate terms,[50] and it seems likely that the association was struck up at Lincoln's Inn. The land on which the Inn stood belonged to Suliarde, who sold it to the society in 1580 for £520.[51] He and Hickes kept up their friendship as they grew older—they were certainly in touch as late as 1607.[52] Here is one example of that genius which Hickes seems always to have shown in making and keeping friends.

It is not possible to say how long Hickes remained a full-time student at the Inn, but it is clear that, for some time before he entered Burghley's service in 1573, he helped his mother to run her mercer's business at the White Bear.[53] During this period his stepfather, Anthony Penne, died. Penne's will,[54] which was proved in the summer of 1572, reveals that he had no land. He left all his goods to his wife, who was soon contemplating the possibility of a third marriage. In August 1573 George Blythe wrote to her from Dover

> I pray you, commend me heartily to Mr Twitty, and since it hath pleased God to give you such grace, I do not only rejoice with you but will be bold to tell you mine opinion, as if the matter were yet in deliberation. Surely you could not have chosen better, the quality of the man considered, his age, his wealth, his reputation, his great affection, so as you, having done twice well before, may be reckoned thrice happy in this choice ... What a conquest have you made of an old captain that, though he have perhaps heretofore of his good nature and for charity loved, yet never before did yield himself to bonds of love ... As for procreation, neither is it desperate, and though it were, yet there is greater demonstration of goodwill in adopting your children, as I hear he hath done, than if you should have naturally children by him, which is a thing that happeneth as well when folks be angry as when they love. I have no leisure nor no learning nor experience in these matters, only, I pray you, if the marriage be not finished, do somewhat for your friends, provide we may be welcome and be witnesses of your joy.[55]

One wonders what Michael Hickes, then nearly thirty years old, felt about being 'adopted' by his prospective stepfather, but, despite Blythe's confidence that the marriage was imminent, if not already accomplished, it did not take place. Perhaps Mr Twitty took last-minute fright at the prospect of permanent subjection to 'bonds of love'. At any rate, we hear no more of him.

It was in the same year as this domestic drama that Hickes

entered Burghley's service.[56] It is impossible to be certain how he made contact with him in the first place, but there are several possibilities. His mother probably lent money to Burghley in 1558, just before Elizabeth's accession to the throne.[57] That favour, at a time when William Cecil was in the political wilderness, may have given Mrs Penne a claim upon him in the days of his eminence. It is much more likely, however, that Hickes was brought to Burghley's attention by either Vincent Skinner or George Blythe. In January 1570 Skinner married Audrey Man, a cousin of Burghley's second wife, Mildred Cooke. This entrée into the family circle must have been important in securing for Skinner the post which *he* later obtained in Burghley's service, and he could easily have put in a good word for his old friend. George Blythe, too, was related to Burghley by marriage, as his mother, Alice, was the sister of Burghley's first wife, Mary Cheke. Moreover, he himself was one of Burghley's secretaries between 1571 and 1574.[58] He may well have secured Hickes a place in his uncle's household. Whatever the means by which Hickes obtained his introduction, his entry into Burghley's service in 1573 was a decisive stage in his career. He was on the threshold of both political influence and personal affluence.

2

Hickes in the
Lord Treasurer's Household

Burghley's household, when Hickes joined it, was a large one. An anonymous member of it,[1] who wrote an account of Burghley's life, estimated that the latter kept a permanent staff of about eighty at Cecil House in the Strand, his main London residence, and another twenty-six or thirty at Theobalds, his great country mansion in Hertfordshire, about twenty miles from the capital.[2] As he had a third large residence, Burghley House in Northamptonshire, where he must have kept at least a skeleton staff, his entire household, when the members of his family and his wards are included, probably numbered at least 150. They were a varied lot, ranging in rank from peers of the realm to those who performed menial tasks in the gardens and the kitchens. They included, to name only some, ushers, pages, chaplains, keepers of the wardrobe and of the plate, coachmen, bailiffs, park keepers, and cooks, the whole household being presided over by Thomas Bellot, Burghley's trusted steward, who filled his office faithfully for over thirty years.[3]

From Hickes's point of view the most interesting and important members of the household were Burghley himself, his family and wards, and, after 1580, his secretaries. In 1573 Burghley was in his early fifties and already had all the *gravitas* of an elder statesman. On November 20th, 1558, only three days after Elizabeth's accession to the throne, when she held her first Privy Council meeting at Hatfield, she made William Cecil a councillor and indicated that he was to be her chief adviser. 'I give you this charge,' she said to him, 'that you shall be ... content to take pains for me and my realm. This judgment I have of you that you will not be corrupted by any manner of gift and that you will be faithful to the state; and that, without respect of my private will, you will give me that counsel which you think best, and if you shall know anything necessary to be declared to me of secrecy you shall show it to myself only. And assure yourself I will not fail to keep taciturnity therein, and therefore herewith I charge you.'[4] It was the beginning of the longest and one of the most notable political partnerships in English history.

The fundamental trust which continued to exist between Queen and minister for the remaining forty years of Cecil's life must not, however, be allowed to obscure the fact that the two had their differences, especially in the earlier years of the reign. The 1560s saw the emergence of Lord Robert Dudley—the handsome son of the duke of Northumberland who had been executed for treason in Mary's reign—first of all as the Queen's favourite and potential husband and then later in the decade as a political figure in his own right and, as such, a rival to Cecil. The climax of the Cecil–Leicester rivalry (Dudley was created earl of Leicester in 1564) came during the period 1568 to 1572, which has been aptly described as 'the crisis of the reign'. The flight of Elizabeth's rival, Mary, Queen of Scots, the Catholic claimant to the English throne to England in 1568, to escape the wrath of her Scottish subjects, marked the opening of four years of dramatic events in both domestic and foreign affairs. In December 1568 the English government seized ships on the way to the Netherlands with money to pay the Spanish troops fighting against the Dutch rebels—the beginning of a prolonged and dangerous crisis in Anglo–Spanish relations. The following year there was a plot to marry Mary, Queen of Scots to Thomas Howard, duke of Norfolk, the first peer of the realm and England's only duke; a Norfolk–Leicester intrigue to overthrow Cecil; and the 'rising of the northern earls', a revolt by conservative noblemen which was due to a combination of political, social, and economic discontents and certainly included in its aims both the restoration of Catholicism and the removal of Cecil. These three threats to Elizabeth's authority in 1569 were all defeated, but they were followed in 1570 by a Papal Bull declaring her deposed and in 1571 by the Ridolphi Plot, a Catholic conspiracy which involved both Spain and the duke of

Norfolk and aimed at her overthrow and Mary's accession. After the discovery and frustration of the plot Norfolk was executed in 1572 and in the same year England signed a defensive alliance with France, which had been her chief enemy in the early years of the reign. This 'diplomatic revolution' of 1572 marked the beginning of a calmer period in both domestic and foreign affairs and it left Cecil in a very strong position. It was with full support from the Queen that he had defeated the intrigues of 1569 aimed at removing him from the political scene. Elizabeth emphasized her confidence in him in no uncertain terms in 1571 when she raised him to the peerage as Baron Burghley and in 1572, when she appointed him to the great office of Lord Treasurer, which had become vacant by the death of the aged marquis of Winchester. As for Leicester, he retained the Queen's affection and considerable political influence, but the events of 1568 to 1572 had shown him the limits of his power. In 1572, in Professor MacCaffrey's words, 'Burghley ... stood pre-eminent.'[5]

His political success does not seem to have affected his domestic virtues, and Hickes must soon have become aware of the commendable personal qualities of his new master. Burghley, if we are to believe his household biographer, was a pious, good-natured man of simple tastes, devoted to his family. He 'most precisely duly observed his exercise of prayer, morning and evening. He would never miss sermon if he were able ... nor ever failed the communion day every first day of the month.'[6] John Clapham, who was a member of Burghley's secretariat during the 1590s and wrote a valuable account of his character, confirmed this picture of piety when he noted that every morning and evening his master 'used ordinarily to read or hear some part of Holy Writ in Latin read unto him'.[7] The biographer wrote that Burghley was 'of the sweetest, kind and most tractable nature that ever I found in any man, gentle and courteous in speech, sweet in countenance, and pleasingly sociable with such as he conversed', and Clapham painted a somewhat similar picture when he reported that Burghley 'carried himself so temperately as he seldom or never showed any outward sign of temper or discontentment'.[8] It seems, however, that his normally equable temperament became soured during the 1590s when, according to the biographer, 'age, the mother of morosity, and continuance of sickness altered even the course of his nature, with pains in his body [and] griefs and cares in his mind'.[9] There is plenty of evidence about Burghley's bodily weakness during his later years. In April 1595, for example, Clapham wrote to Sir Robert Cecil about pains in his master's right foot and hand which kept him awake at night.[10] It is clear from this and other evidence that the gout from which Burghley had suffered since the 1550s became much more severe during the 1590s and, on occasion, even interfered with his usually formidable powers of work. In September 1594 Hickes himself wrote 'truly me thinks he is nothing sprighted, but lying upon his couch he museth or slumbreth. And being a little before supper at the fire, I offered him some letters and other papers, and he was soon weary of them and told me he was unfit to hear suits.'[11]

Despite his ailments, however, Burghley did live to be nearly seventy-eight and it is not unlikely that, in an age when over-eating was common, his longevity was connected with his simple tastes in food. His biographer commented that he never ate 'but of two or three dishes, drinking never above thrice at a meal, and very seldom wine. He would many times forbear suppers if he found his stomach offended.' His pleasures were as modest as his diet: 'if he might ride privately in his garden upon his little mule or lie a day or two at his little lodge at Theobalds retired from business or too much company, he thought it ... his only happiness.'[12]

The biographer also praised Burghley's love for his children 'to whom there was never man more loving nor tender hearted, and yet with so wise moderation and temper as he was inwardly more kind than outwardly fond of them'.[13] This is an accurate enough picture of his feelings for his son Robert and his daughters Anne and Elizabeth, the children of his second marriage to Mildred Cooke, but it is almost certainly an idealization of his attitude to his elder son, Thomas, born in 1542 to his first wife, Mary Cheke. Thomas showed little interest in or aptitude for the intellectual and political affairs which were his father's passion, and was a bitter disappointment to the latter, who admitted in May 1561 that 'to this hour I never showed any fatherly favour to him but in teaching and correcting'.[14] It is hardly surprising that the young Thomas, cold-shouldered by

1 Michael Hickes

2 Baptist Hickes

his contemptuous father, indulged himself in the pleasures of dicing and women. By the time Hickes entered Burghley's service he had long ceased to be a member of his father's household, having married in 1564 and set up his own establishment. Burghley's elder daughter Anne, born in 1556, had also married by 1573, but her wedding to Edward Vere, the 17th earl of Oxford, in December of 1571, brought her only unhappiness. Oxford, the heir of one of the oldest noble families in the land, was a great social catch, but personally he was impossible, a mercurial and irresponsible young man who treated his wife abominably. As a result Anne spent much time with her parents and Hickes must have got to know her well before her death in June 1588. Burghley had cherished her dearly and when she died he assumed the guardianship of her three young daughters, the Ladies Elizabeth, Bridget, and Susan Vere, born in 1575, 1584, and 1587 respectively. These girls did much to brighten his old age, and he lavished affection upon them. His second daughter, Elizabeth, born in 1564, was only nine when Hickes entered the household. She married in 1582 and died the following year, seven years before her formidably learned mother, who provided Burghley with loyalty and companionship, though probably not with much passion, during the forty-four years of their married life.

As Mildred was a devout Protestant, with strong leanings towards Puritanism, she and Hickes must have thoroughly approved of each other's religious views. There is no doubt, however, that much the most important member of the household from Hickes's point of view —apart, of course, from Burghley himself—was Robert Cecil. Robert had been born in June 1563 and was therefore only ten years old when Hickes first got to know him. He was a tiny, delicate boy, completely different from his elder half-brother. He shared his father's intellectual gifts and it was on him that Burghley pinned his political hopes. By the 1580s Robert and Michael Hickes had become close friends, and they remained on intimate terms in the 1590s, when the former began to wield authority in affairs of state.

Burghley's political hopes for members of his household extended, besides his ambitions for Robert Cecil, to the noble wards who were under his care. As Master of the Court of Wards, an office to which he had been appointed in 1561,

Burghley among other things undertook during his lifetime the guardianship of eight noblemen who succeeded to their titles while still minors. He thus became responsible for their upbringing and marriages. One of these wards was the young earl of Oxford, who made such a disastrous husband to Anne Cecil, but it would be wrong to suppose that Burghley's principal concern was with their marriages. He was probably much more interested in their general training, and tried, within his household, both to give them a good academic education, and to inculcate into them his own political ideas and aptitudes. He may indeed have seen them as the nucleus of a group around Robert Cecil which would carry his own principles of statecraft into a later age. If this was his aim, he failed lamentably. Two of the eight were already out of wardship when Hickes entered the household. One of these was Oxford, whose general conduct had already marked him down as totally unstable and untrustworthy. The other, Edward Manners, third earl of Rutland, who attained his majority in 1570, showed considerable legal aptitude, but his death in 1587 at the age of thirty-eight cut short what might have been a distinguished career. Of the three who were in wardship in 1573, Edward, Lord Zouche, then seventeen years of age, won some reputation in the course of a long lifetime as an administrator and diplomat, but he never became a leading political figure; Philip, Lord Wharton, eighteen in 1573, never played any role on the national stage; and Philip Howard, earl of Surrey, the sixteen-year-old son and heir of the executed duke of Norfolk, became a Catholic and died in the Tower in 1595. The three remaining wards came into Burghley's care during Hickes's time in his service. Robert Devereux, second earl of Essex, succeeded to the title in 1576 at the age of ten. He, of course, became Queen Elizabeth's last favourite, the stormy petrel of the Elizabethan court in the 1590s and the implacable opponent of Burghley's ambition to secure high political office and authority for Robert Cecil. Devereux's failure in this and in other schemes led in 1601 to the armed revolt which brought him to the block and in which he involved the last two of Burghley's noble wards, Henry Wriothesley, who succeeded as third earl of Southampton in 1581 at the age of eight, and Roger Manners, who became fifth earl of Rutland in 1588, when he was twelve. These two did escape execution, but the fact remains that three of Burghley's wards engaged, within a few years of his death, in an uprising against the Crown which was also a challenge to his own political system as personified by his heir Robert Cecil.[15]

Hickes, who must have watched with interest the education of six of these young noblemen, may not have had many direct dealings with them. His closest contacts in the household—at least after 1580, when he became one of Burghley's secretaries —were doubtless with his colleagues in the secretariat. Between 1580 and his death in 1598 Burghley seems to have had five secretarial assistants, though not all of them were in service at the same time. Two, Barnard Dewhurst and John Clapham, do not seem to have become personal intimates of Hickes, but the others, Vincent Skinner and Henry Maynard, were among his greatest friends.

Dewhurst, a man of Lancashire origins, may have had family connections with Burghley which helped to secure his entry into the latter's service. He was certainly in the household by 1572 and by 1580 was acting as a secretary.[16] John Clapham, who came of Yorkshire yeoman or minor gentry stock, tells us that he was associated with Burghley from a 'tender age' and that he spent 'about seven years in attendance upon his own person'. The last three of these years, at least, from 1595 to 1598, were spent as a member of the secretariat.[17] Vincent Skinner, Hickes's old friend of Trinity College and Lincoln's Inn days, was the son of John Skinner, a Lincolnshire gentleman, receiver of duchy of Lancaster lands in that county. After he finished his education Vincent too became involved in local administration, first of all as escheator of Lincolnshire in 1573–74. In 1575 he was granted the reversion of his father's receivership, but by that time he may already have entered Burghley's service. Certainly, he was listed as one of his secretaries by 1576.[18] Henry Maynard, Hickes's most important colleague in the secretariat in the 1580s and 1590s, was descended from a long established family of Kent and Devonshire. While still a young man he entered the service of Sir Nicholas Bacon, Lord Keeper of the Great Seal, and at the time of Bacon's death in 1579 was his secretary. By October 1581 he was filling a similar role in Burghley's service.[19]

Hickes and his colleagues, like all Burghley's servants, worked in splendid surroundings —Burghley was one of the great builders of his day. His town residence, Cecil House, stood on the north side of the Strand, between London and Westminster. At one time it had belonged to the incumbent of St Martin-in-the-Fields, but in the reign of Edward VI it came to Sir Thomas Palmer, who was executed in Mary's reign because of his support for Lady Jane Grey. John Stow, the historian of Elizabethan London, tells us that Palmer 'began to re[build] the same of brick and timber, very large and spacious, but of later time it hath been far more beautifully increased by ... Sir William Cecil, Baron of Burghley.' It was nearly finished by the early 1560s and Burghley, though he preferred the countryside to town life, probably spent the greater part of his time there, because of its convenience for Westminster, where he performed so many of his official duties. He also rebuilt the family seat at Stamford Baron in Northamptonshire, beginning in Mary's reign in 1553 and finishing in 1589. The result, Burghley House, was a huge edifice which is one of the most impressive of all surviving Elizabethan houses. His third great mansion, Theobalds, is no longer standing, but it was the greatest of all his houses, one of the wonders of the age. He began building it in 1564, at a site in Hertfordshire, conveniently close to the capital. It was virtually complete by 1585, when it stood in a magnificent park, eight miles in circumference. Its enormous size —it was one of the largest buildings in England —can be explained largely by Burghley's determination to provide adequate accommodation and a fitting setting for the Queen's visits to him. Elizabeth took full advantage of his consideration. She came to Theobalds twelve times in all, and on each occasion the honour cost Burghley a small fortune. All his houses were noted for the splendour of their interiors, but Theobalds, as the awestruck reports of foreigners make clear, had especially impressive internal decorations. It was certainly Burghley's favourite house, and he escaped to it as often as possible from the crowds and bustle of London and Westminster.[20]

For seven years Hickes served in these magnificent settings as a humble member of the household. We do not know what his duties were during this period, but promotion came in 1580, when he was admitted to the secretariat. He himself has left an account of the circumstances. 'I desired to be in your lordship's presence by the occasion of my service,' he told Burghley in 1581, 'yet I never made suit for the place [of secretary]. Albeit, I do not but think, and also acknowledge it with my most dutiful thanks, that the good report given by some of me to your lordship did the rather move your lordship both to conceive the better of me and to do me so special a favour.'[21] One of the favourable reports probably came from Vincent Skinner, who had already been in the secretariat for at least four years, but Hickes seems to have had genuine doubts about his suitability for the job and he hastened to make these clear to Skinner. 'Help of nature I have none', he told him, 'and, to my great shame may I speak it, in many matters of course and ordinary experience very raw and ignorant. My hand is ... not very swift and my French neither good nor ready.' He went on to assure Skinner that he only took on the duties because it was Burghley's express wish that he should, and concluded, 'My chiefest hope and comfort is that my sincere and dutiful affection towards his lordship in this service, accompanied with a careful endeavour and diligence to perform as much as shall lie in my power, shall serve ... in some part to excuse or at the least to cover my manifold wants and imperfections.'[22]

He soon found out that the inadequacies which he feared were real enough. After just one year as secretary he expected dismissal and wrote to his master about his tribulations.[23] 'I observed sometimes but of late especially,' he told Burghley,

that your lordship had a hard conceit of me, as of one that neither conceiveth with that dexterity nor yet dispatcheth with that celerity as is required in the execution of that service; for the which cause, though not forbidden by your lordship, yet have I forborne, to my great grief, to enter into your lordship's chamber or to offer or to intermeddle in suits according to my accustomed manner ... I think it a hard matter for a man of good pregnancy and otherwise well qualified, in such a multitude and multiplicity of causes to keep stroke with the sharpness of your lordship's conceit ... except it please your lordship to vouchsafe to allow unto him some reasonable time to acquaint himself with the course and sundry natures of your lordship's affairs.

He went on to affirm that at least one comfort remained to him. That was that

> neither your lordship hath noted, neither yet ... hath [it] been informed to your lordship that I have behaved myself undutifully towards your lordship or insolently towards suitors, either by a careless neglecting, or a needless protracting, or by any ... unhonest exactions for their dispatch, whereby I might give offence to them [or] bring slander to the place or dishonour to your lordship.

He then conjured up a pitiful picture of the effect his dismissal would have on his 'poor old mother, who, in her natural love and care, foretasting and peradventure accounting of the profit and prefermen[t] that might befall me by the example of others that have gone befo[re] me, when she shall find her expectation frustrate in both, it can not but make a very deep impression of grief in her heart'. He concluded with an appeal that, if Burghley had irrevocably decided to discharge him from the position of secretary, he might be allowed to remain temporarily in his service in another capacity, 'until I may apprehend some good occasion ... to retire myself like a hurt deer out of the herd and betake myself to some private life in the country more answerable, I confess, with my unstirring disposition than either the Court or public causes.'

Burghley seems to have made no reply to this missive for Hickes soon drew up another long letter[24] admitting that, as his inadequacies in the job might be 'prejudicial and hurtful to ... all sorts of persons ... I may not think myself hardly dealt withal by your lordship to be put from it, albeit I can not but think my fortune to be very hard that I ever entered into it.'

We can perhaps sympathize with Hickes, who not only had problems in trying to master the complexities of the job itself, but who must also have had difficulties in even approaching the standards of diligence and endurance which Burghley himself set in his work. Burghley's overwhelming devotion to duty was a source of wonder to his servants. His household biographer wrote that he

> drew upon him such multitude of suits as was incredible but to us that saw it, for, besides all business in Council or

other weighty causes, and such as were answered by word of mouth, there was not a day in a term wherein he received not threescore, fourscore and an hundred petitions, which he commonly read that night, and gave every man answer himself the next morning as he went to the hall ... But after he grew impotent and weak and could not go abroad, as his nature was ever prone to do good, he neglected no means to perform it. For then he devised a new way, which others may imitate, that, by age and infirmities being forced to keep his chamber and sometimes his bed, he took order that poor suitors should send in their petitions sealed up, whereby the poorest man's bill came to him as soon as the rich. Upon every petition he caused his answer to be written on the back side and subscribed it with his own name, or else they had his letter or other answer as the cause required.

His 'labour and care' in the service of the state were so great that

in cases of necessity, he cared neither for meat, sleep or rest, till his business was brought to some end. And when he was in never so great pain, or sickly, if he could but be carried abroad, he would go to dispatch business ... His industry in times of necessity very great and his diligent and studious course of life continually no less, as caused all his friends to pity him and his very servants to admire him. And myself as an eye witness can testify [that] I never saw him half an hour idle in four and twenty years together.[25]

John Clapham painted a similar picture in his account of a typical day in Burghley's life. Apart from time spent at religious devotions and at meals he was occupied

for the most part either in writing with his own hand or else in dictating to his secretaries when, by reason of the gout in his hand, he could not write, though he would ofttimes with much pain enforce himself thereto. And it was observed by divers that, albeit many weeks together his arms and legs were grievously tormented with that disease, yet his right hand was seldom or never so possessed with it, but that, within two or three days he was able to write.[26]

His preference for doing his own writing whenever possible is certainly obvious to anyone who has worked among the Elizabethan state papers. His unmistakable angular handwriting appears on a very large proportion of the documents. He was plainly afraid of delegating too much authority and liked, whenever possible, to do things for himself. Burghley, in fact, was the very epitome of those of whom Francis Bacon wrote: 'men in great places are thrice servants: servants of the sovereign or state; servants of fame; and servants of business. So as they have no freedom, neither in their persons, nor in their actions, nor in their times.'[27]

Burghley does not seem to have complained too much about his life of drudgery; for him it was an honour and privilege to enjoy the Queen's confidence and serve the state. He may not have expected his subordinates to reach his own standards, but he certainly demanded a high level of competence from them and when Hickes failed to meet expectations in 1580 and 1581 he was left in no doubt as to his master's displeasure. His fears of dismissal, as expressed in his letters, must, however, have been exaggerated. He survived the crisis and continued to serve as secretary until Burghley's death in 1598. There is no evidence to suggest that he fell into real disgrace again.

During the period 1580 to 1598 Burghley seems to have had, at any one time, either three or four secretarial assistants.[28] His policy of keeping his secretariat small won the approval of knowledgeable contemporaries, such as Robert Beale and Nicholas Faunt, both of them private secretaries to Sir Francis Walsingham, who was Secretary of State from 1573 to 1590. In 1592, two years after Walsingham's death, Beale advised Sir Edward Wotton, then a prospective Secretary of State, not to burden himself with 'too many clerks or servants as S[i]r Fra[ncis] Walsingham did'. He held Burghley up as an example. When Secretary of State between 1558 and 1572 Burghley 'had not [had] above two or three [secretaries]'. Faunt shared Beale's ideas. '*Frustra fit per plura quod fieri potest per pauciora*', he wrote, also in 1592, when he stated that Walsingham's multitude of confidential assistants had 'bred much confusion with want of secrecy'.[29]

Some comments on the quality rather than the size of Burghley's secretariat were less favourable. Thomas Wilson had harsh words to say in 1601 about the great politicians, who, he complained, 'will not have about them other than base pen clerks, that can do nothing but write as they are bidden, or some mechanical dunce that cannot conceive his master's drifts and policies, for if they had lynces' [i.e. lynxes'] eyes they must look into their actions. This was first brought by the old Treasurer ... and it is well followed by his son at this day.'[30] Wilson made these remarks four years before he himself became Robert Cecil's secretary. Doubtless he would have revised them drastically if his account had been written a few years later! In 1601, however, he was still an outsider and his appraisal should be balanced against that of John Clapham, certainly not an unprejudiced witness, but one who knew Burghley's secretariat from within. Burghley, wrote Clapham, admitted into his service only 'men of honest and civil behaviour ... whom he should not have cause to change ... and those that of themselves were not so well disposed, either regard of their own profit or reverence of the master retained in order and obedience. By his bounty he advanced divers of his servants, who now [in 1603] live and enjoy good places in the commonwealth.'[31]

The secretaries, of course, did not always give satisfaction. Hickes's troubles in 1580 and 1581, immediately after his appointment as secretary, can be compared with the rather different type of disgrace which befell Henry Maynard in the early 1590s, when he had already spent a decade in the secretariat. In July 1593 Maynard wrote a long letter to Burghley in which he expressed 'exceeding grief' at his master's 'hard opinion' of him. During the previous two or three years he had found Burghley's accustomed favour withdrawn. The rupture in the relationship had stemmed from reports, which had come to Burghley's ears, that Maynard had boasted that he could 'rule or govern' his master. He vehemently denied these charges and asked for the renewal of Burghley's good opinion.[32] His request was probably granted in due course—he certainly retained his position as secretary until Burghley's death—but it may be significant that he was out of favour during the period 1590 to 1593, the very years when Burghley began to suffer increasingly from ill health;[33] consciousness of failing powers may have made him especially susceptible to any hint that he was losing his grip on affairs.

If the rumours about Maynard's boasts were true, then his behaviour was not always as 'honest and civil' as Clapham would have us believe. On the other hand, the importance of the work which he did makes it plain that he was not one of Wilson's 'base pen clerks' or 'mechanical dunces'. He was one of three secretaries — Hickes and Dewhurst were the other two — who performed specialized functions. The others, Skinner and Clapham, undertook more general duties. Nicholas Faunt stated that, ideally, a statesman should have two personal secretaries, and he provided a detailed account of how their work should be divided. One should serve his master as 'his own pen, his mouth, his eye, his ear, and keeper of his most secret cabinet'. This principal assistant should be concerned chiefly 'with foreign matters, and others that may more nearly [touch] ... the state, both to keep his letters of negotiations that daily come in from foreign parts, and to answer them when need shall be'. The second assistant was to be concerned with the dispatch of 'ordinary matters'.[34] Burghley, of course, had always at least three secretaries during the 1580s and 1590s, but Maynard and Hickes were much the most important. Hickes dealt with the 'ordinary' but for him very profitable business of domestic patronage. He can be equated with Faunt's 'second' secretary. Maynard, on the other hand, dealt with matters of state, especially foreign affairs, and was sometimes actually addressed as 'principal' or 'chief' secretary.[35] His duties involved him in the business of countries which ranged from Scotland to Germany, and he was concerned with naval, military, and diplomatic problems — a reflection of the fact that Burghley, though he had ceased to be Secretary of State in 1572, was, as the Crown's principal minister, intimately concerned with the whole field of the country's foreign relations.[36] Barnard Dewhurst had special responsibilities for wardship,[37] but he, like Maynard and Hickes, was also available to share in the wide range of general duties which occupied the time of Skinner and Clapham, the 'men of all work' in Burghley's secretariat. These general duties included, to take just four examples, transmitting messages to Burghley,[38] reminding him of business which needed attention,[39] writing miscellaneous memoranda and letters,[40] and looking after his papers.

This last responsibility was an important one, as the course of official business might be interrupted if a secretary was unwilling to search among these papers for relevant documents. In 1592 Thomas Windebank spoke to Burghley on behalf of the signet and council clerks who believed that their rights were being invaded. Burghley, however, was in a hurry and did not remember the details of the affair. He told Windebank to come back at some other time. The latter then asked Maynard if he had seen the memorandum which had previously been delivered to Burghley about the matter. Maynard promptly snubbed him, saying that he had seen the document but did not know where it was and did not propose to spend time looking for it. As a result, a new memorandum had to be drawn up.[41] The importance of Burghley's papers is further illustrated by events which followed his death. Soon afterwards, when Maynard asked Sir Robert Cecil for permission to go to his house in Essex for a time, he made it clear that he did so only because he knew that Clapham, who was acquainted with most of Burghley's papers, would be remaining in London. Even so, during August and September 1598 there was a good deal of correspondence between Maynard and Cecil about the papers.[42] Moreover, in October 1599, when Hickes went through them, he found many letters from Sir Robert Sidney, which he offered to the latter to burn.[43] We do not know how much further this purge went, but it may have cost historians much interesting information.

The fact that Hickes and Maynard both undertook general duties suggests that it would be a mistake to over-emphasize the extent to which they concentrated on specialized tasks. Moreover, they were each allowed spells of leave during their time in Burghley's service, and when one was on holiday the other must have been able to take over his absent colleague's responsibilities on a temporary basis. In July 1589, when Maynard was 'infinitely toiled' with naval matters, Hickes was more fortunate, as he was able to 'follow his pleasure'.[44] On August 25th, 1591, Robert Cecil referred to the fact that Hickes was then engaged in 'idle journeys and sports' and assured him that Maynard had agreed 'to stay [on duty] till the tenth of the next month and then to tarry one day or two only, to acquaint you with that which, I assure you, will infinitely trouble you as things stand at this time'.[45] In September 1595 Hickes was enjoying another holiday. Maynard wrote to him on the 20th of the month, when he told him that he had been very busy the previous day dealing with Irish business, which had kept him from playing bowls. He proposed to set off for Essex the following Friday and told Hickes that he expected him to take his place at Burghley's side at least two days before then.[46] In January 1596 Hickes was again on leave of absence, this time to attend the birth of his eldest son. On January 18th, the baby having been born, Maynard sent his congratulations from the Court. He also informed Hickes that he would 'license' him to take his own time for his 'coming hither'.[47] In September 1596 it was Maynard's turn to enjoy a well-earned rest. Richard Webster, a clergyman, bewailed Maynard's absence at that time as the latter had taken 'pains' on his behalf in a suit with Burghley. Webster, however, did not forget to ask Hickes to act as his patron in Maynard's place,[48] a request which Hickes would have found it difficult to refuse as it was Webster who had christened his infant son earlier in the year. In August 1597 Maynard was again on holiday and impatient for court news and gossip which he expected Hickes, who was on duty, to supply.[49] Burghley's secretariat during the 1580s and 1590s was clearly a flexible organization. Its two leading members, Maynard and Hickes — despite the fact that they specialized, respectively, in foreign and domestic business — were capable of undertaking a wide variety of duties, which reflected the extensive responsibilities of their master as principal minister of the Crown.

One of Burghley's main concerns throughout the reign was the management of Parliament and particularly of the House of Commons which, as Sir John Neale has shown, provided difficulties for the government. After his elevation to the peerage in 1571 Burghley himself sat in the House of Lords, but he was kept abreast of proceedings in the Lower House by reports from relatives, friends, and fellow councillors who sat there. Several of his secretaries also obtained seats and they too must have been useful sources of information. At least two secretaries sat in each of the Parliaments between 1584 and 1597.[50] Only Dewhurst never obtained a seat. It would be wrong, however, to suppose that Burghley obtained seats for his secretaries simply in order to use their presence in the Commons for his own purposes — that would be an oversimplification of the position.[51] By Elizabeth's reign, a place in the Commons was a social distinction, a mark of success in some walk of life, and the secretaries themselves would certainly have wanted to sit in Parliament. Burghley probably felt it proper that their services should receive due recognition in this way, though the fact that they could normally be expected to support his policies and watch over his interests was no doubt an added recommendation.

There is no indication that any of the secretaries played a prominent role in the Commons. This is hardly surprising in the case of Clapham, who sat in only one Parliament, in 1597, but it is more remarkable that Skinner, Maynard, and Hickes, each of whom sat in at least four Parliaments during the 1580s and 1590s, did not make a greater mark. Skinner and Maynard both sat on committees, but there is no evidence that either spoke in the House. In 1593 Hickes did prepare notes for a speech—we do not know whether it was actually delivered—on a Bill for the relief of soldiers maimed whilst fighting on the Continent against Spain. These men often had the greatest difficulty obtaining either work or relief at home after their discharge from the army, and Hickes's speech was an impassioned plea for the passing of the Bill, which had not been making progress. It had, he maintained, 'brought forth nothing but a few fair leaves and blossoms of conceit and speech and now in the end is become speechless, lying as it were in a trance, given over of the physicians as past recovery'. Maimed soldiers slept 'upon the boards or bare grounds, whilst we drink wine in bowls [and], lying upon beds of down, sleep soundly and safely in whole skins'. He ended with a contemptuous reference to those members who 'say they would be very sorry that some provision should not be made ... but sleep never the worse nor eat never the less'.[52] The bill, which provided for relief through local assessments, was revived and passed.[53] In January 1598, on the one occasion on which there is definite evidence of Hickes speaking in the Commons, he was involved in an incident with members 'in the rebellious corner in the right hand of the House', furthest away from the Speaker. He had been speaking on a point of order connected with a Bill in which Burghley may have had an interest. The interrupters were finally silenced and he was allowed to continue.[54]

At the time Hickes was involved in this minor fracas Burghley had less than a year to live and was leaning very heavily, in the performance of his official duties, on his son, Robert Cecil, who, as the 1590s progressed, took over more and more of the work for which his father bore formal responsibility. Letters between Maynard and Cecil and Hickes and Cecil illustrate this process as well as showing how dependent Burghley had become on his secretaries during the last years of his life.[55] In September 1594, for example, at the end of a letter to Cecil dealing with foreign business, Hickes added, 'My lord hath had but ill rest tonight, is now abed and I know not whether he will rise or no'.[56] In the 1590s Burghley often seems to have been unable to get up in the mornings. On May 12th, 1595, Maynard, who had not even been able to see him until eleven o'clock, informed Cecil that his pain the previous night had been 'so great and the gout possessing so many places, as he is not able to come out of his bed, neither hopeth of better ease until the weather may be more constant'.[57] On September 3rd of the same year Burghley spent the whole day in bed and on December 29th was 'sick in his stomach' and unable to write letters.[58] It is clear, indeed, that throughout the 1590s Hickes and Maynard played important roles as channels of communication between the failing Burghley and his brilliant, up-and-coming son.

These communications were part of Hickes's duties, but Cecil was his close friend as well as his master's son and potential political successor. Hickes's role as Burghley's patronage secretary can only be seen in its full significance in the light of that friendship with Cecil, which had fully developed by the 1580s and continued throughout the 1590s. In the summer and early autumn of 1584 Cecil was in France,[59] and on September 28th he wrote from Paris a letter[60] which shows that, at the age of twenty-one, he was already on friendly terms with Hickes, who was twenty years his senior.

By the beginning of 1588, when Cecil accompanied Lord Cobham's unsuccessful peace mission to the Netherlands, the friendship had ripened and the two men were on terms of intimacy. 'Good Michael', wrote Cecil to Hickes in February before setting out,

> To tell you I love you still were but to remember you of that you are, I hope, assured of ... Mr Arundel [an interpreter in Burghley's service] at my departure entreated

46

me to solicit my lord that he might come over if his lordship had occasion to send over. It is a thing I am loath to
do, and therefore, good Michael, make this lie for me; that
you have seen some private letter of mine to my lord, wherein I have performed his request to recommend his desire;
which done he is satisfied and the thing will never more be
thought of ... Wish me as often well as I will wish you with
me ... God save my house ... from thieves, and so good
night to your flat cap![61]

Youthful gaiety and mocking affection are even clearer in a
second letter, written from Ostend on February 29th. 'Mr
Hickes', began Cecil,

Lest you might think Ostend hath altered my disposition,
though it may chance to change my complexion, I have
written these few lines. You live ... in safety and pleasure,
both which I never wanted till now; the soldiers every day
disposed to mutinies; nothing to be had but what we
brought with us, and that spoiled with lying shipped a
month for want of wind and waftage ... I desire to hear
answer of my letter from Dover. I can not see in what
sense I can be looked for till midsummer, as I dare to you
confess in private ... My health was never so good, I praise
God. Honesty is a goodly jewel. Many things I could be
merry with in my letter to you ... but *literae scriptae manent*
and *vivat* the good earl of Derby, whose muttons die, his
hens starve, and we are fain nevertheless to eat them. My
house is all my riches with which I trust you. From Ostend,
where I shall learn what becomes a soldier, though I must
say *cedant arma togae* ... Your nose would drop, i'faith, don
Michael, if you were as cold as we have been. Not a fair
woman nor an honest.[62]

The letter was addressed to 'Mr Michael Hickes, my friend by
the fire side, I believe'.[63]

It is clear that by 1588 Hickes filled the triple role of crony,
factotum, and confidant of Cecil who, during the 1590s, continued to find the greatest pleasure in the company of 'lusty Mr
Michael'.[64] On occasion, he asked Hickes to accompany him
on a journey, as when he suggested a meeting at two o'clock

47

one afternoon, so that they might travel together to Theobalds, where Burghley was in residence. He added that they could travel back the next day, which would give them a further opportunity to have a friendly talk.[65] One of Burghley's illnesses provided another opportunity for the friends to meet. Cecil wrote, 'If my lord be sick, I see no reason why you may not come tomorrow to dinner, where you shall find them that before you missed, and all charges shall be borne.'[66] One day, in July 1597, he told Hickes, 'I would gladly have your company tomorrow by three of clock at furthest, for I must go to sup where you shall be welcome. And so I leave you this Sunday night, having sent you a piece of venison for your dinner.' He added that, if the supper lasted until late, 'you and I will lie at Cecil House'.[67]

Cecil also sent his friend court and foreign news. 'All is well,' he wrote on one occasion in 1591, 'My lord holds on his progress. The Queen hunts and is merry. You shall do well to come to Portsmouth, and you shall do as well to leave all your reckonings behind you.' He concluded by prophesying that the French king would besiege Rouen.[68] In March 1591 Cecil asked Hickes to 'thank my Lord Cobham for his remembrance of me, in requital whereof I can promise nothing certain but my love and service, and ... I hope to be the cause that his daughter shall make my lady a grandmother'.[69] That letter was written less than three weeks before the birth of Cecil's son and heir William, which took place on March 28th, 1591.[70]

Hickes and Cecil certainly exchanged frequent letters when they were apart. 'I must needs confess with acknowledgment your kindness, knowing that letters are the means for friends' conference and so causeth absence to be the less grievous,' wrote Cecil in an undated letter which certainly belongs to the years before 1598. 'For your doublet,' he went on, 'I have not yet spoken with my tenants, but I mean to press them, if not to black satin yet to green taffeta for a shooting doublet, or at the least a bow and shafts.'[71] It is likely that the last part of the letter is in code. Hickes and Cecil certainly engaged in plenty of dubious intrigues in the 1590s, and 'black satin' and 'green taffeta' may have concealed matters which they were anxious to keep confidential.

Cecil and Hickes, who found such pleasure in each other's

company, also liked, in the early 1590s, to form part of a convivial and merry circle in which the witty Hickes, with his gift
of repartee, occupied a prominent place. Two letters from Cecil
reveal the type of entertainment which went on. 'Mr Michael',
he began in one,

I have not leisure to answer the fruits of your idle, bald
pate, which hath been read by those you left together, till
our bellies burst almost with laughing, for, more cogging
[i.e. jesting] descriptions, more knavish constructions, more
wicked interpretations or ungrateful acceptations of our
honest, manly and friendly entertainment could no pen
express. Your mother ... sends me word ... [that if you]
will not marry ... she will then make me a conveyance of
her house and her stuff. This [offer] I swear to you ... I
received this day and I believe you will swear that I am not
like to refuse such an offer for foolish, baby kindness to you,
my friend. Neither is there any here that doth advise me to
reject the kindness.[72]

On another occasion Cecil wrote in similar vein. 'Your cogging
letter I have showed [to our friends],' he told Hickes,

and of the word cony [i.e. rabbit] straight was made such
an argument as the phrase was by them held not so bald
as your bald crown. The whoreson Papist they would fain
change for your Puritan's company, and I can assure you
that we are merry and would be the better if you were
here. All this I write you may take for a favour, for I have
well supped and am almost asleep.[73]

These letters reveal, amidst all the humour, the warmth of
Cecil's affection for his friend. His relationship with Hickes in
the 1590s dispels beyond doubt the legend that he was, outside
his immediate family circle, a cold, humourless man.

Cecil was knighted in May 1591 and was admitted to the
Privy Council in August of the same year. Early in 1592 he was
a commissioner at the trial for treason of Sir John Perrot, a
former Lord Deputy of Ireland, and late in the same year he was
sent to watch over the royal interest in the captured Spanish
treasure carrack *Madre De Dios*. From then onwards evidence of
his activity in state affairs multiplies. He acted as unofficial

assistant to his father, although he himself was not appointed to high office until July 1596, when he was made Secretary of State.[74] Hickes, the intimate of his leisure hours, was also the confidant of the rising politician and administrator. Their intrigues, during the political climacteric of Elizabeth's last decade, were linked with and add extra interest to Hickes's work as Burghley's patronage secretary.

3

The Patronage Secretary

In the Elizabethan period the control and distribution of patronage were crucial elements in the political system. The Queen herself exercised supreme authority in both domestic and foreign affairs, deciding policy and superintending its execution. She consulted members of the Privy Council, her most trusted advisers, when she thought fit, and then either accepted or rejected the advice they gave. In this system of personal monarchy, where there could be no political parties in the modern sense, ministers' political standing depended, to some extent, on the offices they held, but, above all, on the Queen's confidence in them. She demonstrated that confidence by allowing each a greater or lesser role in the distribution of patronage. The amount of patronage under a minister's control, therefore, reflected his standing in the state, and the greater the patronage the larger the number of clients and suitors who swarmed about him, anxious to secure a share in the benefits which he was able to bestow.

The Crown's patronage was extensive: grants of honour, notably peerages and knighthoods; appointments to offices in the Church, Court, judiciary, central, regional, and local administrations, and in the military and naval services; pensions and annuities; leases, on favourable terms, or gifts of royal lands; grants of economic privileges, such as export licences, which exempted recipients from statutes forbidding certain kinds of exports. This is not an exhaustive list, but it does include the main categories. The Queen distributed the greatest offices and gifts personally; for example, it was she and she alone who decided to make Burghley Master of the Court of Wards in 1561 and Lord Treasurer in 1572 and to confer upon Leicester and later, after his death, upon Essex the right to the customs duties which were paid upon sweet wines entering the country. The latter privilege, granted in return for a fixed annual payment to the Crown, was highly profitable to the recipients — indeed it came to form the mainstay of Essex's finances — but lesser men could not hope to obtain such privileges and the vast majority of suits were for minor jobs and favours. This was where ministers came in. They could sometimes grant these benefits themselves by virtue of their offices — Burghley, for example, controlled a great deal of patronage through the Lord Treasurership and the Mastership of the Wards — or else they might influence the Queen on a suitor's behalf. In the 1580s leading figures in court and official circles, men like Lord Chancellor Hatton, Secretary of State Sir Francis Walsingham, and Chancellor of the Exchequer Sir Walter Mildmay, had their own circles of suitors, but only Leicester rivalled, though he could not match, Burghley in the number and eminence of his clients. Burghley and Leicester, the Queen's principal political confidant and her leading favourite, were the two lynchpins on which the patronage system depended during the high Elizabethan period, the 1570s and 1580s.

The workings of the patronage system benefited a large proportion of the two or three thousand men who, at any one time during Elizabeth's reign, took a direct and intelligent interest in politics. They were the men who either thronged the Court, seeking a patron to help them secure profit or office, or else pursued their suits more cautiously by letter from afar. Each patron, surrounded by his cluster of clients, stood, in effect, at the head of a faction, endeavouring to secure as many benefits as possible for his followers in return for their loyalty and support. This system worked reasonably well until the 1590s because until then, despite Leicester's occasional extravagant gestures, no one seriously challenged the basic premise necessary for its success — the axiom that no single favourite or minister should monopolize the Queen's confidence and with it the disposal of patronage.[1] Elizabeth herself was determined to keep open a number of channels through which the Crown's favour could be obtained. It was one of the secrets of her political

success, a fact recognized by Sir Robert Naunton, an Elizabethan courtier, who wrote in the early years of Charles I's
reign an account of his late mistress and her favourites and
ministers. 'The principal note of ... [Queen Elizabeth's] reign,'
he affirmed, 'will be that she ruled much by faction and parties
which herself both made, upheld, and weakened, as her own
great judgment advised.' He went on to relate how the Queen,
on one notable occasion, humbled Leicester when the latter
presumed too far, saying 'God's death, my lord, I have wished
you well, but my favour is not so locked up for you that others
shall not partake thereof; for I have many servants unto whom
I have and will at my pleasure bequeath my favour and like-
wise resume the same. And if you think to rule here I will take
a course to see you forthcoming. I will have but one mistress
and no master.'[2] If the story is true these were salutary words
and Leicester appears to have remembered them; he resigned
himself to sharing the Queen's goodwill with others.

In fact, he had a lesser say in the distribution of patronage
than Burghley. He never obtained one of the great offices of
state which gave its holder independent control over lesser jobs
and benefits. He was, therefore, very largely dependent on the
Queen's day-to-day indulgence for his ability to gratify suitors.
Burghley, despite, or perhaps because of, the semi-independent
position he enjoyed through his high political offices, never
presumed on the Queen's favour. This was one of the reasons
for her fundamental confidence in him and it helps to explain
the leading role which he played in the patronage system even
before Leicester's death in 1588. Some contemporaries, indeed,
argued that Burghley, first of all alone and later in conjunction
with his son, engrossed virtually all of Elizabeth's favour and
prevented other able men from rising in the royal service.
Edmund Spenser made the point in his poem 'The Ruines of
Time', published in 1591.

> O grief of griefs, O gall of all good hearts,
> To see that virtue should despised be
> Of him, that first was raised for virtuous parts,
> And now broad spreading like an aged tree,
> Lets none shoot up that nigh him planted be.[3]

Francis Bacon returned to the charge in 1616 when he recommended to James I's favourite, George Villiers, newly raised to the rank of viscount, 'that you countenance and encourage and advance able men and virtuous men and meriting men in all kinds, degrees and professions. For in the time of the Cecils, the father and the son, able men were by design and of purpose suppressed.'[4]

Spenser and Bacon were not impartial witnesses—both had axes to grind—and Burghley did not monopolize the Queen's confidence; he had too much sense to try and in any event she would not have allowed it. His influence did, however, increase with the years, and after the deaths of Leicester, Mildmay, Walsingham, and Hatton between 1588 and 1591, 'old Saturnus' as Burghley came to be called, held a unique position at the centre of power. Next to the Queen he was outstandingly the most important person in the distribution of favours. In this situation Hickes, as his patronage secretary, exercised great influence.

Suitors, at all levels, might have a difficult, protracted, and humiliating task in their search for favour. This was recognized by Bacon and Spenser, who knew from personal experience what they were talking about. 'The rising unto place', wrote Bacon, 'is laborious, and by pains men come to greater pains; and it is sometimes base, and by indignities men come to dignities.'[5] Spenser lamented in his poem 'Mother Hubbard's Tale',[6]

> Full little knowest thou that hast not tried,
> What hell it is, in suing long to bide:
> To lose good days, that might be better spent;
> To waste long nights in pensive discontent;
> To speed today, to be put back tomorrow;
> To feed on hope, to pine with fear and sorrow,
> To have thy Prince's grace, yet want her Peer's;
> To have thy asking, yet wait many years;
> To fret thy soul with crosses and with cares;
> To eat thy heart through comfortless despairs;
> To fawn, to crouch, to wait, to ride, to run,
> To spend, to give, to want, to be undone ...

Those are very different pictures from that given by Burghley's household biographer when he wrote of his master's courtesy and dispatch in dealing with clients. The truth doubtless lies somewhere between the two extremes, but it is certain that Burghley was overwhelmed with suits and he could not possibly have given detailed attention to them all. It is not surprising that a large number of clients worked through his secretary.

Many of the letters which Hickes received about suits were from men of high rank or official position. The greatest noblemen of the realm, such as the earls of Oxford, Huntingdon, Southampton, Sussex, Lincoln, Cumberland, and Derby, did not think it beneath their dignity to transmit their suits through Hickes, and of 173 surviving letters addressed to him in his capacity as secretary, thirty-six were from peers of the realm.[7] The bulk of the others were from men of established social position, knights and gentlemen, many of them government officials, university dons, mayors of towns, judges and serjeants-at-law. There were also a number from ecclesiastical dignitaries, whose knowledge of the benefits to be obtained from Burghley's patronage was at least as highly developed as that of their lay colleagues.

The place of origin of these letters is significant. Many clients did not indicate from where they wrote, but in 101 cases there is clear evidence. Forty-seven of these letters were from the London area or the Court; another eleven came from the six Home Counties of Middlesex, Surrey, Kent, Essex, Hertfordshire, and Sussex. The remaining letters came from every part of the country. Twelve were from three northern counties, Cheshire, Yorkshire, and Northumberland. It would be unwise to place too much significance on the geographical origin of letters, but some tentative conclusions seem possible. The attractive power of London is very evident. Most of those who had business with the government, particularly those who had suits to pursue, naturally tended to congregate at or about the Court. It is nevertheless true that correspondence came to Hickes from much further afield. This indicates that his reputation had penetrated to most corners of the country, and suggests that, although distance from the Court may have made a suitor's task more difficult, it neither blinded him to the enchantments of contact with the Court circle nor lessened his comprehension of the magic which Burghley's influence might work.

The methods by which suitors approached Hickes and through him Burghley throw light on the workings of the patronage system. Most suitors who wanted Hickes's mediation on their behalf wrote directly to him, but a substantial minority —over a third—employed an intermediary who wrote for them. Those who wrote directly either placed their whole trust in Hickes's personal furtherance of their causes or else they asked him to deliver letters which they had written to Burghley about their suits. Clients who relied solely on Hickes's help usually asked him to approach his master when the latter was in a receptive mood and then to expound and press their suits. Those who asked him to deliver letters nearly always also requested his word in Burghley's ear on their behalf. Suitors who had letters from sponsors usually presented themselves in person to Hickes, armed with their introductions. Sometimes, however, sponsors sent letters directly to Hickes and the clients themselves merely awaited results. In the small world of the Elizabethan Court and administration the personal touch could be all important. In this situation it paid to secure an introduction to Burghley's influential secretary.

These methods of approach reveal the great influence which Hickes must have wielded. He could, as we shall see, do much to help clients to obtain their desires. On the other hand, by neglecting to deliver letters, by refusing to admit suitors to Burghley's presence, by bringing suits to Burghley's notice at inopportune moments, he could effectively torpedo clients' hopes. He guarded the door to his master's inner sanctum and his goodwill had to be secured.

Each time that he did help a suitor he added another to the wide circle of those who were in his debt, and many grateful clients were or became men of considerable influence, well placed to return favours. One such client was George Carew, who, in October 1594, asked Hickes to support a suit of one of his kinsmen.[8] That suit was unsuccessful, but Carew's disappointment did not discourage him from turning to Hickes for help on other occasions, and it is clear that he was not always unlucky. By April 1597 he was indebted to Hickes for numerous favours.[9] Carew was knighted in 1603 and became ambassador to France two years later, retaining the post until 1609. Early in his embassy, on Hickes's recommendation, he took William Beecher junior, the son of a prominent London businessman, into his service.[10] The life of the younger Beecher has been studied in some detail,[11] and it seems that Hickes's recommendation was a decisive step in furthering his career. He was left as agent in Paris when Carew was recalled to London and, after the appointment of Sir Thomas Edmondes as the new ambassador, became tutor to Lord Clifford. He was knighted in 1619, and in 1623 was made a clerk of the Privy Council, an office which he held for eighteen years.[12]

Hickes dealt with suits of a very varied nature. Many concerned wardship, a reflection of the fact that Burghley, as Master of the Court of Wards, was responsible for all minor tenants-in-chief; that is, men under twenty-one and women under fourteen who held lands directly from the Crown. During the Middle Ages, when tenants-in-chief were required to perform military service, it was considered essential that the Crown should control both their persons and their lands while they were under age. Otherwise, they might make unsuitable marriages or fall under the influence of the king's enemies, which could pose serious military problems for the government. By the sixteenth century the required military service had become nominal and wardship was a fiscal device: Burghley as Master sold wardships to courtiers and officials as well as to relatives of the wards and these sales brought in a regular revenue for the Crown as well as substantial profits for Burghley, who frequently received gratuities from grateful or hopeful suitors for wardships. Those who bought wardships gained the right to arrange the ward's marriage and, if they leased some of the ward's lands as well, the right to exploit these until their charge came of age. These could be most valuable privileges and there was intense competition for wardships, with courtiers and officials often outbidding relatives in the unseemly scrambles which took place.[13] Hickes dealt with requests for wardships and also with other aspects of the multifarious business thrown up by the activities of the Court of Wards. He frequently received appeals for assistance from men of the highest rank. In June 1592 Hickes received a letter from Henry Wriothesley, earl of Southampton, a royal ward under the guardianship of Burghley. Southampton, who was then eighteen years old, was worried about his manor house at Beaulieu, having heard that it was falling into decay through want of money to bear the cost of repairs. He asked Hickes to persuade Burghley to take appropriate action and ended his letter with a hint that he would give Hickes a gratuity for his trouble in the matter.[14]

In 1591 Henry Hastings, the Puritan earl of Huntingdon, one of the most important noblemen in the realm, sent Hickes a letter which illustrates the complicated and devious paths which sixteenth-century wardship negotiations often took. He wanted to inform Burghley, through Hickes, that he was quite content that Sir Thomas Gerrard should get a certain wardship which was then up for sale. Huntingdon had become interested in it when he had been requested by Mrs Lee, mother of the ward, to obtain Sir Robert Cecil's favour on her behalf. Cecil, in other words, was to act as intermediary between Huntingdon and Burghley in securing the wardship for Mrs Lee. Huntingdon stated that Cecil 'did promise his furtherance ... upon my letters written to him'. Mrs Lee clearly had very powerful backing, but it was of no avail. Burghley had promised the wardship to Gerrard, and he got it.[15]

When Henry Hastings died in 1595 he was succeeded by his brother George, and the new earl made it his business to keep on good terms with Hickes. The tone of his letters is interesting —despite the social gulf which separated the two men they were written as if to an equal. The explanation seems to be that Hickes proved useful to the earl who hoped for and expected further services. He wrote to Hickes in the winter of 1597, 'I have been beholding to you for your travail and pains taken in soliciting my causes for me to my good lord [Burghley] for which I hold myself in your debt ... and amongst the rest for this of Waterton's wardship.' The financial negotiations attending the grant of the wardship had been causing trouble and Huntingdon had set down his suggestions on the matter in a petition. He required Hickes's help 'to prefer the same and get his lordship's direction thereupon'. In acknowledging his debt to Hickes for services rendered he gave a very broad hint that a gratuity would soon be paid.[16] In May 1598 Huntingdon was again interested in a wardship and once more it was Hickes to whom he turned for assistance. Mr Justice Beaumont, Huntingdon's cousin, had just died and the earl wanted the wardship of the heir. His reasons, he affirmed, were disinterested. He would be sorry to see his cousin's son 'receive any hard measure, either in bringing up or matching of him in marriage, who, if he be committed to me, by God's grace shall that way receive no disparagement'. He asked Hickes to 'solicit my honourable good lord for me in this suit'. Huntingdon did not trouble, on this occasion, to cloak his promise of a gratuity in a euphemistic phrase. He offered Hickes 'twenty angels' — an angel was a coin worth ten shillings — to bring the suit to a successful conclusion.[17]

Other members of the aristocracy and gentry also asked Hickes to further their requests for wardships. In May 1594 Lady St John, through Richard Frampton, asked Hickes to deliver to Burghley a letter of thanks for the portion assigned to her 'out of Sir George Trencher's ward'. Her ladyship believed that it paid to be quick off the mark, for, Frampton informed Hickes, 'She is a suitor for another ward, if his father happen to die shortly, which may be some better help unto her [and] whereof yesterday, I perceive, by a friend she had advertisement.' She expected Hickes's help in this latest quest for profit. 'I hope she will be able to requite it,' observed Frampton.[18]

Another correspondent who believed in the efficacy of speed was George, earl of Cumberland, notable for his privateering exploits at sea, a man whose need for money was as great as his love for adventure was strong. He wanted the wardship of a boy whose father had died only the previous night. Even so, Cumberland was afraid that the wardship might already have been disposed of. He asked Hickes to give Burghley a letter containing his bid and promised that any help that Hickes himself might supply in the suit would not go unrewarded.[19]

It might be expected that rather than use Hickes's help peers would have made direct approaches to Burghley or perhaps even to the Queen herself when suing for wardships. George Hastings did take one of his suits directly to Elizabeth. When he wrote to Hickes in May 1598 about the wardship of his cousin Beaumont's heir, he specifically stated that he had obtained the Queen's approval of his request. Even on that occasion he felt it best to secure dispatch of the Queen's pleasure by obtaining Hickes's mediation with Burghley.

Hickes may have received many requests from men of lesser rank to use his influence on their behalf in wardship matters, but little evidence of such suits survives among his papers. There is, however, an interesting letter relating to one case. It was written in December 1594 by John Sedley to his cousin, Mr Marston. 'I pray you, deal with Mr Hickes for the obtaining of the wardship of young Henry Crisp,' wrote Sedley.

> I am a stranger to him [i.e. Hickes]. Nevertheless, upon the report of his honesty and gentlemanlike dealing and proceeding in the causes he entertaineth, I had rather commit my friend's cause to him than to any other ... If Mr Hickes will procure him if he be found a ward, the mother will give him £60. If ... Mr Hickes will not deal in so small a suit, pray him to direct you to some other that will entertain it.[20]

Sedley certainly had a high conception of Hickes's influence and importance, and his comment on his reputation for honesty is of considerable interest. It is clear that some people at least held the view that if one dealt fairly by Hickes — and 'fairly' no doubt meant providing him with a gratuity — then one would get fair treatment from him.

Hickes's services could clearly be of great value in wardship matters. He could also do much to aid towns, which often had suits at Court. In April 1590 the mayor of Hull wrote to thank him for his help in furthering the town's causes and petitions to Burghley.[21] Seven years later the mayor and aldermen of Newcastle asked for his help against the intrigues of Henry Sanderson, an enemy of the town.[22] Hickes aided the merchants of Chester on several occasions in their suits to Burghley,[23] and agents of Berwick also sought his help in their town's affairs.[24] The problems of one town seem to have engaged his special attention. The great port of Bristol was in Gloucestershire, the county where his father was born, and his 'good affection'[25] for the town was probably an example of the local patriotism which was so strong in the sixteenth century. He certainly spent a lot of time and trouble helping Bristol's representatives in London to further their causes with Burghley.[26] He even concerned himself with the sale of the city's pepper.[27]

Hickes also dealt with letters from heads of Oxford and Cambridge colleges, a reflection of Burghley's interest in and concern with university business. Whitaker of St John's, Cambridge, wrote about alleged misdemeanours by members of his college;[28] Holland, of Exeter College, Oxford, expressed his gratitude for favours which he had received from Hickes during the Queen's visit to Oxford in September 1592;[29] and James, of Christ Church, Oxford, expressed gratitude for Hickes's help in college business.[30] Hickes also dealt, on one occasion, with aggrieved representatives of Cambridge University who were anxious to interview Burghley,[31] and, at another time, in 1595, he busied himself with problems attending the appointment of a new master of St John's, Cambridge.[32]

Officers of state and others engaged in government business often sought Hickes's aid in the course of their official duties. Lord Deputy Fitzwilliam of Ireland wrote in March 1592 seeking his help in the furtherance of Irish business,[33] and two years later Robert Newcomen, as representative of the Lord Deputy, wrote with a similar request.[34] Maurice Berkley, a tax collector, sought Hickes's help with Burghley in case his payments should 'chance to be behind hand'.[35] Morris Pickering, keeper of the Gatehouse prison, informed Hickes in May 1596 of the escape of a captive who had been in his charge, asked him to inform Burghley, and earnestly implored him to put the matter in the best possible light.[36] Peregrine Bertie, Lord Willoughby d'Eresby, who succeeded Leicester in 1587 as commander of the English forces in the Netherlands, sought his help in obtaining formal permission to set off for the Low Countries.[37]

Hickes's services were also in demand in matters connected with the country's customs administration, for which Burghley held responsibility by virtue of his office as Lord Treasurer. Suitors seeking appointments to customerships and controllerships at the ports often sent their requests for office through Hickes's hands,[38] and he also dealt with other business, such as obtaining a warrant to the customs authorities at Southampton to allow the passage of ordnance; dealing with a dispute about the rating of imports from the West Indies; and furthering a suit of the townsmen of Portsmouth about their customs house.[39]

He dealt too with business which had legal connotations. Sir John Stanhope, a prominent courtier, asked him to further the suit of Mr Johnson of the Temple for a place as one of the judges in the Court of Exchequer.[40] Another client was Matthew Dale, nominated in 1593 as a serjeant-at-law. Although the right of confirmation nominally belonged to the Lord Chancellor, Dale requested Hickes's mediation with Burghley to secure approval of the appointment[41] — a striking example of the value which suitors placed upon the elder Cecil's influence, even in appointments over which he had theoretically no control. Humphrey Glaseour, a Cheshire gentleman, was another who sought Hickes's help; he wanted to be made a justice of the peace.[42] Other suitors, with more pressing problems, were debtors who were anxious to secure mitigation of the rigours of the law and asked Hickes to obtain Burghley's help for them.[43]

Hickes was also concerned with a variety of ecclesiastical causes. In 1596, on the death of Hugh Bellot, bishop of Chester, he was asked to further the prospects of one of the candidates for the vacant episcopal throne.[44] In May 1593 Nathaniel Bacon asked him to secure the abandonment of a proposed visitation of the diocese of Norwich.[45] The dean of York sought his help in 1595 in the dispatch of business with Burghley.[46] Francis Thomson, a recusant, who asked for help against the attentions of the notorious anti-Catholic informer Topcliff, baited his request to the Puritan Hickes with the promise of a gelding worth £12.[47]

Hickes also dealt with many suits which are not easily classified. In June 1594 the earl of Huntingdon asked him to sponsor a poor man's suit with Burghley.[48] In November 1589 Lord Cobham sought a warrant to obtain particulars of lands in which he was interested.[49] In 1595 the earl of Derby wanted letters from Burghley to the Lord Deputy of Ireland on behalf of his relative John Salisbury.[50] In August 1597 Sir Anthony Paulet, governor of Jersey, asked Hickes's help in securing his recall on health grounds.[51] In October 1595 the impecunious and intemperate Sir John Smith — a man with a military background — informed Hickes that he wanted to be allowed to muster the local armed levies in Essex and Hertfordshire. In view of Smith's known character we may safely assume that even Hickes's silver tongue could not have obtained a successful conclusion to that suit. Smith's disappointment may well have had something to do with his dramatic intervention at the Essex musters some time later. He harangued the troops, called Burghley a traitor, and was imprisoned for his pains.[52]

Sometimes eccentrics wrote to Hickes. Robert Anderson, for

example, wrote on behalf of the bearer of his letter who sought 'to remove a brood of devils'. Anderson asked Hickes to 'be a means to my lord [Burghley]' on his behalf.[53] Burghley was expected to act as a marriage counsellor as well as an exorcist, as Roger Manners made clear in a letter to Hickes on behalf of his friend Mr Brudenell, who required help in his suit with Burghley. Brudenell was 'well affected in religion, an earnest Protestant ... but, alas, his wife will not be ruled by him ... She will not come to the church. He would fain have her reformed, but [is] loath to have her imprisoned.'[54] Hickes and Burghley must have sympathized with Brudenell, but whether they had either the time or the ability to persuade the recalcitrant lady to obey him is another matter.

Other suits reflected more important problems. In July 1590 Robert, Lord Rich, informed Hickes that orders from the Privy Council for a stay of all building operations in London had halted rebuilding, on old foundations, which was being undertaken by one of his tenants within the liberty of St Bartholomew. He sought permission for building to recommence. His request draws attention to the grave social problems caused by the rapid growth of London in the sixteenth century. The Council's orders are merely one illustration of a policy of restriction on building pursued by both national and municipal authorities in the fifty years after 1580. The Rich family was, after 1590, in frequent conflict with the authorities over its rights within the liberty of St Bartholomew.[55] Another suitor, the dean of Windsor, wrote about a very different type of problem in October 1589, when he described and bewailed the continuous trouble and excessive charges to which the canons were put in maintaining the possessions of the poor knights of Windsor. He asked Hickes to further their request for relief.[56]

Some indication of the pressure to which Hickes was subjected by suitors can be gained by examining a list of replies which he drew up as possible 'answers' to clients' importunities. 'You are a simple fellow'; 'thus it is to deal with ignorant fellows'; 'you understand it not'; 'before God I never spake it ... '; 'you are a lying knave'; 'I will not do it'; 'hold you contented, you hear mine answer ... take it for an answer'; 'I will hear you, but I will believe never [a] word you say till I hear the other party'.[57] These examples indicate that many clients must have had unrewarding interviews with him, but it must be significant that a great variety of people continued to address a multitude of suits to him over a long period of time. These clients, many of them important members of Court and official circles, recognized his great influence, and it is likely that his 'answers' were reserved for less prominent and influential people.

He certainly had no doubts about his own powers. In August 1594 the impoverished Lord Willoughby d'Eresby, a former commander in the Low Countries, asked the Privy Council for compensation for 'horse lost in service'. His agent, Captain John Buck, reported the Council's refusal, attributing it either to unwillingness or to pressure of other business. Their lordships insisted that special suit to the Queen was necessary before payment could be made. 'Mr Hickes hopeth better,' reported Buck, 'and promiseth his best help'.[58] Hickes's respect for a Council decision—in an admittedly minor matter—was evidently limited.

It is often impossible to discover the results of suits with which Hickes dealt. The surviving evidence, while making it very clear that a suit was in progress, usually fails to supply sufficient details to make further investigation possible. Sometimes, when the result is known, it is clear that the suit was unsuccessful. Bishop Scambler's visitation of the diocese of Norwich, which Nathaniel Bacon tried to get cancelled in May 1593, took place as arranged.[59] Matthew Dale's request, in the same year, that Hickes should secure approval of his nomination as a serjeant-at-law, was not successful.[60] Solicitor-General Egerton wrote to Hickes in the spring of 1594 on behalf of his servant Thomas Ravenscroft, who wanted the controllership of the port of Chester. Ravenscroft was disappointed.[61] Humphrey Glaseour's request to be put into the commission of the peace in Cheshire was unsuccessful.[62] Glaseour, however, was a persistent suitor, and it is clear that he was not always so unfortunate. When he wrote asking to be made a justice of the peace he enclosed a gratuity for Hickes's favour in a former suit and, a year later, in May 1597, he thanked Hickes for other services rendered.[63] The request to Hickes in 1596 to secure the promotion of the nephew of Sir Gilbert Gerrard, former Master of the Rolls, to the bishopric of Chester, was unsuccessful. Richard Vaughan was transferred from Bangor to fill the vacant see.[64] Sir Anthony

3 William Cecil, Lord Burleigh, after 1585
(*attributed to Marcus Gheeraerts the Younger*)

SERO, SED SERIO

4 Robert Cecil, earl of Salisbury, 1602
(by John de Critz the Elder)

Paulet, governor of Jersey, who wanted to be allowed to return to England in 1597 for reasons of health died in Jersey in July 1600, still in office.[65] Johnson did not get the vacant judgeship in the Exchequer Court which he so ardently desired.[66]

These were some of the unlucky ones. Many clients who sought Hickes's patronage did obtain their desires. Evidence about some of these successful suits is to be found in letters of thanks in which, although the nature of Hickes's services is not usually explained, the fulsome expressions of gratitude and the accompanying gratuities made it clear that the suitors had secured the favours which they had sought.[67] In some cases in which Hickes obtained or helped to obtain clients' wishes there is more evidence. Nine such suits involved appointments to escheatorships, local offices dealing with land tenure, which were in the gift of Burghley as Lord Treasurer. Five were successful.[68] In 1593, in another suit, John Jegon, master of Corpus Christi College, Cambridge, obtained by Hickes's 'good means' Burghley's letters recommending his brother Thomas for a proctorship in the university. When Thomas Jegon's subsequent election was challenged Hickes helped to obtain its confirmation.[69] William Mount owed his preferment in 1594 to the mastership of the Savoy, in some measure at least, to Hickes's efforts on his behalf.[70] In May 1597 Lord Thomas Howard asked Hickes to help Samuel Thompson, suitor for a pursuivant's place. Thompson got the job.[71] On April 12th, 1597 William Stanley, earl of Derby, wrote to Hickes on behalf of John Salisbury, who was awaiting appointment as one of the deputy-lieutenants for Denbighshire. A warrant had already been drawn up conferring the office and Derby asked Hickes to obtain Burghley's signature. Hickes can have wasted little time in doing so, as the very next day a Council letter was issued to the Lord Keeper of the Great Seal, instructing him to renew the earl of Pembroke's commission as Lord-Lieutenant, and naming Salisbury as one of his deputies.[72] In the spring and summer of 1597 Serjeant Warburton corresponded with Hickes about his coat of arms. Warburton was of illegitimate descent and wanted an ermine mark, part of his mother's coat of arms, as a distinction on his own. His case was complicated by differences of opinion between two of the officers of the College of Arms, Garter King-of-Arms and York Herald. Hickes obtained

Burghley's approval of the desired distinction and received a delighted letter of thanks and a 'token' from Warburton.[73] In 1597 Richard Pitts, a merchant, was suitor for a customership at Newcastle. He had to satisfy Burghley as to his qualifications for the post and obtained a sponsor in Baptist Hickes, who asked his brother Michael to further the matter. 'What pleasure you shall herein perform in his behalf', stated Baptist, 'I make no doubt that you shall find him a man not unthankful unto you'. Pitts was appointed.[74]

The appointments which Hickes helped to secure, the words of satisfied suitors, the high rank of many of his clients: such evidence, fitful, fragmentary, and tantalizing as it often is, takes us some way in an attempt to assess the influence which Hickes wielded. The favours which he distributed had to be paid for, and most suitors were well aware of that fact. The gratuities which they offered were an accepted part of the rewards of all ranks of officials, from the very highest officers of state to minor officials in local government. One of the reasons for this was the low salaries paid to government officers. It has been estimated that only about four hundred officials and royal household servants all told received salaries of £20 per annum or above, and of these only a tiny minority, about twenty, had more than £200.[75] Such salaries hardly began to keep officials and courtiers in the style of life which they expected to maintain in an increasingly extravagant age, and they obtained additional payments—fees and gratuities—from people using their services. Fees, which were paid for the performance of specific administrative tasks, tended to be fixed or limited, but gratuities—tips as we might call them—were restricted only by the ability of suitors to pay and the willingness of patrons to accept such payments. Patrons, virtually without exception, did accept and any client who expected to bring his suit to a speedy and successful conclusion had to reckon the cost of gratuities to officials and others who helped him on his way. Burghley himself must have received vast sums. His office of Master of the Wards alone was highly profitable. John Clapham stated baldly that 'after Sir Thomas Parry's death he was made master of the wards and liveries, by means whereof he grew rich and ofttimes gratified his friends and servants that depended and waited on him'.[76] Modern research has confirmed his picture. During the

last two and a half years of Burghley's life he received at least
£3,000 from suitors for wardships at a time when his official
salary as Master was only £133 a year.[77] As for the private
assistants to great officers of state—men like Hickes and Maynard—they might be almost wholly dependent on gratuities.
There is no evidence that Burghley paid either of his two leading
secretaries any salary at all, but they more than made up for
that by the gratuities which they received. One episode involving Maynard throws considerable light on contemporary attitudes to these unofficial payments. In 1593 Sir Thomas Sherley,
Treasurer at War, was subjected to a series of charges, among
which was one of misappropriation of funds. It was asserted
that of the £120,000 a year allowed by the Queen for campaigns
in the Low Countries Sherley detained £30,000. Burghley, it
was admitted, disapproved of such actions but Sherley 'infinitely
bribed' Henry Maynard to secure his ends. Sherley did not deny
having paid Maynard for services rendered, but stated 'I do
swear by the living God that to my remembrance I have not
given to Mr Maynard above ten pounds in one year for all his
pains, being ashamed to make it known that I have used so
small gratuity for so great pains as I have continually put him
to'.[78] Sherley obviously regarded £10 a year as a sum to which
even the most censorious could not object. His attitude confirms
the view that 'reasonable' gratuities were regarded as entirely
normal and necessary.

Sherley's misappropriations were made possible by the war
against Spain which began in 1585. Its enormous cost, coupled
perhaps with the Queen's growing meanness in old age, caused
a reduction in royal favours and gifts to courtiers and officials
as the 1590s progressed. 'What little gain there is gotten in this
time,' wailed one man in 1594.[79] In this situation such pieces of
patronage as remained were especially valuable and the rewards
of unscrupulous and influential middlemen potentially very
great. Hickes was clearly in a most favourable position to exploit
the ambitions of suitors for his own profit. We have seen that he
received gratuities for his help in wardship matters and he made
his views on the subject clear in a letter to his friend Roger
Manners, whom he assured of his 'honest, true affection', and
remarked that he was able to give proof of this now and again
'in these petty kind of offices ... which I know are as welcome

and acceptable to you as twenty fair angels laid in the hands of us poor bribers here in Court'.[80] There is evidence that Hickes's idea of a fair recompense for his assistance was not always shared by suitors. The reports which John Sedley heard about his honesty certainly did not come from the unnamed lady who made her dissatisfaction plain through the earl of Cumberland. 'She hath twice been sent for,' wrote Cumberland, 'and by the messengers assured that, if she will give the sum you know of, her suit shall presently be dispatched; but she refused to harken to it, resting upon me. Wherefore, I pray you, send me word what you will do. If you will dispatch it what I said shall be performed. If not, give her liberty to seek [an] other [patron], which I wish she should not need.'[81] Humphrey Glaseour, writing in May 1596, also complained of Hickes's demands. £6 10s. was the sum involved, a 'very large allowance' as Glaseour remarked.[82]

Some suitors were convinced that it was little use asking Hickes for help without the promise of a concrete return for his services. John Linewraye wrote in 1593, 'I am bold to send unto you bare handed, yet do I well know that papers can in no sort recompense your pains ... but, I protest, I will be thankful unto you upon the ending of this my honest, humble suit ... to that most of my poor ability.'[83] William Nevill, who wrote to Hickes from York in October 1595, had been a suitor to Burghley on several occasions, each time without success. Reflecting on his failures he was convinced that the crux of the matter was that he had never tried to requite Hickes's favours, 'no, not with the least thankfulness'. He had resolved to turn over a new leaf. 'This last suit which you have me[n]tioned unto my lord is the only thing I hope of,' he told Hickes and asked his help in obtaining it. In return Hickes could name his own 'composition'.[84] We do not know the result, but Nevill's promise can have done his cause no harm.

It is possible to discuss the gratuities which Hickes received on a statistical basis by considering 158 cases in which his assistance was in demand.[85] In twenty-nine there is evidence that gratuities were either given or clearly promised. Sometimes money was sent to Hickes for services which he had already performed. In October 1592 Maurice Berkley paid £20.[86] Other satisfied suitors gave five or six angels.[87] The Lord Deputy

of Ireland sent twenty 'royals' (a royal or rose noble was worth
15*s.*) in March 1591 to buy 'a good English nag for [the]
summer'.[88] Some evidence relates to money offered for services
to be rendered by Hickes. These promised gratuities were sometimes considerable: £100, 20 angels, 100 angels are examples.[89]
An acceptable reward did not have to be money. Sir Walter
Raleigh, when he acknowledged Hickes's favours in July 1594,
promised him a pearl and added that the more Hickes helped
the bearer of his letter in a suit, 'the bigger the pearl will be
found'.[90] Alexander Nowell, dean of St Paul's, sent a statue of
Edward VI, 'the Josias of England',[91] a gift which may have
pleased Hickes the Puritan more than Hickes the patron. A
buck, a gelding, and a 'Welsh nag' worth £5 were other induce-
ments offered.[92]

In thirty-nine cases there is no evidence in the letters to Hickes
that gratuities were either given or promised but this is not to
say that they were not paid on some of these occasions—in the
nature of things, promises of financial rewards or other induce-
ments for expected favours must often have been conveyed by
word of mouth. It is only fair, however, to note that some suitors
made it quite clear that they were not prepared to provide
Hickes with a concrete reward. Thomas Egerton, Master of the
Rolls, apologized in April 1594 for frequently troubling him
with 'poor suits' in which his only reward was the prayers of the
clients.[93] Nathaniel Bacon, in May 1593, remarked that 'divers
times a year' Hickes moved Burghley in suits 'without any particular profit sought thereby'.[94] Giles Wigginton, a notorious
Puritan, asked Hickes's help in October 1594 for two poor
friends of his, who were trying to secure some property rights.
He admitted that Hickes could not expect any worldly recom-
pense for his services, but assured him that he would win the
higher blessing of the suitors' Christian gratitude[95]—an admirable sentiment to which Hickes's reaction is unknown. William
Hubbock, chaplain of the Tower of London, fortified his suit by
reminding Hickes of a passage from the Book of Proverbs. He
quoted Solomon's mother, who had said to her son, 'open thy
mouth for the dumb', and then asked God to open Hickes's
mouth 'to speak' and Burghley's heart 'to do'. He was worried
about his house in the Tower, which was in serious disrepair.
The weather had been very bad, he himself had been ill, and

his wife was pregnant — a pitiful story. He ended by stressing that the quotation from the Bible was the only reward which Hickes could expect from him; God, he affirmed, would provide the rest. [96]

In the remaining ninety cases clients veiled their promises of gratuities in hints and euphemisms. William Day, dean of Windsor, informed Hickes in October 1589 that he would make sure that his help would be 'considered as this bringer shall show you'. [97] John Stubbe, writing in September 1589 on behalf of his friend Charles Calthorp, Attorney-General in Ireland, told Hickes, 'your pains and goodwill in this behalf shall be well considered over and above thanks'. [98] Peter Whetcombe told Hickes in September 1593, when he asked him to further his suit with Burghley, 'I hope you shall not have cause to say that you have dealt for an ungrateful person.' [99] The earl of Huntingdon, after receiving Hickes's help in a suit to Burghley in December 1597 assured him, 'I hold myself in your debt and will come out of it ere it be long.' [100]

It seems likely, then, that Hickes received some kind of reward for his help in the majority of suits with which he dealt. Given the immense number which passed through his hands it seems probable, as was suggested over twenty years ago, that during the 1590s he 'received more gratuities than any other servant in England'. [101] He certainly obtained some through his work in connection with escheatorships. These important local offices were distributed annually and there was always a scramble among members of the gentry class to secure them. Hickes took over responsibility for the appointments in September 1593, succeeding Vincent Skinner, who left Burghley's personal service at that time on being given a job in the Exchequer. [102]

There is evidence about nine negotiations for escheatorships in which Hickes was involved between 1593 and 1596. It is striking that all of the candidates sought his help through intermediaries, relatives or influential friends who were acquainted either with Hickes or with the subtleties of negotiating for offices, and who were prepared to exert themselves on the applicants' behalf. One of the cases deserves detailed attention later. The other eight candidates applied through two peers of the realm, the earl of Essex and Lord Cobham; Chancellor of the Exchequer Sir John Fortescue; Baron Ewens, one of the Exchequer judges;

Chief Justice Anderson of the Court of Common Pleas; John Glanvile, a serjeant-at-law; the noted antiquary, William Lambarde; and Sir George Carew, who later became ambassador to France. In every case except one it was indicated that Hickes could expect to profit from his services; only Chief Justice Anderson did not hint at a forthcoming gratuity. Lambarde affirmed that his friend and candidate, Kitchill, 'shall be thankful for it [i.e. Hickes's help] and I will add it to the heap of your manifold favours towards me, for all which I must be debtor and leave payment till God vouchsafe ability'.[103] Fortescue gave no indication in the body of his letter on behalf of Griffith Payne that Hickes might expect to gain from his assistance. He then had second thoughts and added the footnote, 'I will think myself beholding unto you and requite it where I may.'[104] Glanvile's hint was rather broader. He promised Hickes that his candidate Dunriche 'shall content you for your kindness in such reasonable sort as I hope you shall be pleased. What this bearer doth promise, I will see performed.'[105] Sir George Carew decently cloaked his promise of a gratuity in Latin. 'I shall reckon myself beholding unto you,' he wrote, and promised not to omit 'that which others do in such cases, according to the saying *hoc fac et illud non omittas*'.[106] Baron Ewens stated that his candidate, Burgis, would not be unmindful of Hickes's assistance, and Cobham and Essex also affirmed that their protégés would requite Hickes's favour.[107]

The correspondents, however, did not as a rule rely merely on promises of gratuities to help their candidates' causes. They also laid stress on the suitability of the men whom they suggested for office. Anderson wrote that his nominee was 'able and meet to be escheator, as well for understanding and honesty as also for ability'.[108] Lambarde wrote of Kitchill, 'Touching his skill and sufficiency of living, I know the one and the other to be answerable, the first by long education and practice and the latter by his marriage with a landed wife.'[109] Glanvile merely stated that Dunriche was 'an honest man and very sufficient and hath married my wife's sister',[110] but Baron Ewens pointed out that Burgis brought the commendations of the justices of assize.[111] Essex stated that his candidate Frothingham had already been escheator of Yorkshire and was known for his loyalty and sufficiency.[112]

Four of the eight applicants got the escheatorships which they wanted namely Ewens, Kitchill, Payne and Heath, the candidates of Anderson, Lambarde, Fortescue and Cobham.[113] It is tempting, in the last decade of Elizabeth's reign, to search in all appointments for reflections of the feud between Robert Cecil and the earl of Essex which created such a stir in Court and official circles at that time. This approach has its dangers, but it is at least worth noting that the candidate of the 'Cecilian' Cobham, Cecil's father-in-law, was appointed, whereas the nominee of Essex, despite his previous experience, was rejected.

In the 1590s, with the emergence of Essex, the classic Elizabethan patronage system that had depended for its successful working on no one man attempting to monopolize the royal confidence came to an end. The Queen may have hoped, during the last decade of her reign, for the development of the kind of situation which had prevailed in the 1570s and 1580s when Leicester and Burghley had been the two main channels for the distribution of patronage. If that was her ambition —with Essex succeeding to the role of Leicester and Robert Cecil inheriting the mantle of his father Burghley —it was rendered impossible by the attitude of Essex. He scorned the idea of sharing power and wanted everything for himself and his followers. Even he could not hope to achieve his aims while Burghley was alive, but his whole policy during the 1590s was directed towards securing a reversionary interest in the political authority which would lapse into the Queen's hands when Burghley died. Throughout the last decade of the reign he constantly tried to secure offices for himself and his followers while opposing grants to Robert Cecil and his supporters. His frequent failures merely made him redouble his efforts. Much of the correspondence between Hickes and Cecil during the 1590s, though not necessarily directly related to this Essex–Cecil conflict, should be seen against the feverish political background which it produced, with every significant appointment a prize to be won —or lost — by the rival factions. In that atmosphere Cecil and Hickes were prepared to engage in intrigues of which Burghley was almost certainly unaware and of which he would probably have disapproved.

During the years 1590 to 1596 the very important job of Secretary of State, with responsibility for much of the country's foreign policy and internal administration, remained vacant, with Cecil doing more and more of the work under his father's general supervision. It is clear that Cecil soon had his eyes on the office itself. In an undated letter he expressed his anxieties to Hickes. 'If you can conjecture ... whether my lord had been thinking of secretaries or no, or speaking with the Queen, seeing I hear nothing, I pray you ... write unto me.'[114] When he was finally appointed to the Secretaryship in 1596 he wrote jocularly to Hickes about his good fortune.[115] Cecil was an obvious target for suitors of all kinds, but he often displayed impatience with or indifference to the demands of unimportant clients, whose support could not add significant weight to his side of the scales in his rivalry with Essex. 'You may thank God you have not been here,' he wrote wearily to Hickes in August 1591, 'for I assure you, on my faith, I never saw more troublesome nor more importunate, tedious suits and suitors'.[116] On another occasion he wrote enclosing a letter for Burghley from a client, with a copy for Hickes's own information. 'So you procure him an answer,' he affirmed, 'I care not what it be.'[117] He displayed similar indifference in July 1594. 'Mr Wroth had much importuned me,' he told Hickes, 'to speak somewhat in the behalf of his nephew ... If you please only to say that I wrote to you to further his dispatch with my lord I shall have performed part of that courtesy I promised Mr Wroth, and, for the matter, I leave it to my lord's own pleasure.'[118] Cecil was a good deal more interested when there was an obvious chance of making a profit for himself. During the 1580s and early 1590s, when he had no official source of income, he must have found gratuities from clients especially welcome. In 1589, for example, he and Hickes were interested in the suit of a certain Mr Portington. The details of the affair are obscure, but Cecil made it quite clear that he expected a monetary reward for his services.[119]

Sometimes Cecil and Hickes resorted to dubious practices. In June 1590 Cecil, who had been asked to recommend a Mr Fortescue to his father for an office wrote to Hickes,

Do not deliver ... [the enclosed letter to Burghley] till Mr Manners come to you with a letter unsealed, which is the letter I make him believe I do send [on Fortescue's behalf]. But I would have you only deliver this I send you sealed. But that would I not have him know and, therefore, when

c*   73

he gives it you, seem not to know thereof, but say it shall be delivered, and deliver you the other and keep that for me.

Having instructed his friend to perpetrate this ingenious bit of trickery, Cecil added sarcastically, 'This is no knavery, for, if it were, I know your upright conscience.'[120] It is difficult to imagine Burghley, even in his early years, stooping to such practices.

In June 1592 Sir John Popham became Chief Justice of the Queen's Bench and Sir Thomas Egerton replaced him as Attorney-General. Egerton himself was succeeded as Solicitor-General by Sir Edward Coke.[121] Two cryptic letters suggest that Hickes and Cecil were deeply involved in intrigues about these important appointments. 'I will assure nothing,' wrote Cecil to Hickes in one letter, 'but believe it upon my word, whosoever tell you otherwise, that this day of Mr Solicitor's sending for [by the Queen] and his coming hath not done any halfpennyworth of harm to your friend, for I was by at every word ... For my part I must tell you still, but use it discreetly, [that] I am in constant hope of your friend and mine.'[122] The second letter, also from Cecil to Hickes, is even more suggestive. 'If not now never,' began Cecil, 'for Mr Solicitor doubt him not on my word, and on the other she [i.e. the Queen] doth and hath resolved, and I hope tomorrow my lord [Burghley] shall have order for it. Mr Attorney removeth and Mr Solicitor with him. Believe it, this is as certain as any resolution can be. Burn this.'[123] The evidence about Hickes's activities in these and most other individual incidents during the 1590s is tantalizingly slight. There is, however, much fuller information about two episodes which throw narrow but vivid shafts of light on important aspects of the late Elizabethan political scene. The first is a devious ecclesiastical intrigue in which Cecil was involved with Hickes; the second an appointment to office which, among other things, shows Hickes obtaining his pound of flesh for services rendered.

Even before his elevation to the Secretaryship of State in 1596 Robert Cecil was playing a major part in the business of ecclesiastical appointments. The closing months of 1594 and the first part of 1595 saw considerable changes in the upper ranks of the ecclesiastical hierarchy. Some thirty letters, written to or by

Cecil about these transactions survive and reveal that he was the recipient of much fulsome episcopal gratitude.[124] One of the changes involved the promotion to a bishopric of Toby Matthew, dean of Durham, who was angling for preferment as early as August 1594. At the end of the month he laid his request for promotion before Burghley, writing to the latter through Hickes, whom he promised 'due consideration' if he would further the suit.[125] Hickes delivered Matthew's letter to Burghley, who read it and gave it back to him. Hickes promised Matthew that he would keep it from 'any common eye, or any eye besides', and added,

> I doubt not but my lord doth well apprehend the matter therein contained, and doth so well conceive of the writer as there will not want his good furtherance, as he hath already [given] his good word. For myself, I am but as one that giveth aim, and can but wish well and hope well where preferment is so well deserved ... I know you have a very honourable friend, though not mentioned yet I think meant in your letter, and of me you shall have a poor friend, ready to hold the candle to give light to the game whilst others play it.[126]

Matthew replied to Hickes's letter on the day he received it, September 1st, when he thanked him for his trouble and added, 'Indeed I know I have been and am exceedingly beholden and bounden to that honourable councillor whom both you and I do mean, but I would not doubt to increase his favour and furtherance by your own good and friendly solicitation.'[127] Other evidence leaves little doubt that the councillor was Robert Cecil. These letters suggest, indeed, that as soon as Matthew approached Burghley in his quest for promotion he got in touch with Robert Cecil as well. Hickes seems to have been the channel of communication with both father and son.

As a result of his negotiations with Burghley, Matthew was offered the bishopric of Worcester. It was also arranged, about the same time, that the see of Durham should go to William Day, dean of Windsor, and in mid-October Day accepted.[128] By November 14th these plans had been altered. On that date Matthew thanked Burghley for securing his nomination to

Worcester, but added that he had heard that the Queen intended to appoint him to Durham. He insisted that her decision came from 'her own princely consideration rather than upon any suit of mine or solicitation of my friends',[129] but it is probable that he owed his elevation to Durham mainly to the efforts of Robert Cecil. On the same day that he wrote to Burghley he also sent a letter of thanks to Hickes in which he mentioned Sir Robert Cecil, 'my most honourable and assured good friend and favourer, and the better a great deal affected I doubt not toward me by your good means'.[130] Cecil himself was terrified that his father or worse still, the Queen might get to know of his scheming on Matthew's behalf. He used his access to Elizabeth, he told Hickes, in such a way that she could not suspect that he 'looked to anything but [her] service'[131] – a tacit admission that he was at least equally concerned with his own schemes. Cecil's fears would explain not only the absence of any direct correspondence between Matthew and himself, but also the cryptic allusions to 'the honourable councillor' in the letters between Hickes and Matthew and Matthew's protestations to Burghley that the Queen's decision was entirely her own.

The likelihood that Cecil did play a crucial role is reinforced by a letter which his aunt, the dowager Lady Russell, wrote to him in February 1595, long after the matter had been settled. She told him that she had hoped that Day, a grave and worthy man, might get the see of London. As this was not possible, Burghley had been wise enough to put his name down for Durham. Lady Russell did not think that Matthew was a very upright man and told Cecil that when his father nominated Day he should have considered the matter settled. But, she lamented, *'quae supra nos nihil ad nos'*.[132] The whole letter is a scolding from an affectionate old aunt to a wayward nephew. There is no doubt that Lady Russell was convinced that Cecil was primarily responsible for Matthew getting Durham. Poor Dr Day was offered Worcester! In December 1594 he accepted, but by the following January he had found out that he had been seriously misinformed about the value of the bishopric and begged to be allowed to stay where he was. Worcester remained vacant until April 1596 – the see was so poor that no one would accept it.[133] It had clearly been to Matthew's advantage to get the much wealthier bishopric of Durham and he had reason to be grateful for Cecil's and Hickes's efforts on his behalf. It is likely that he expressed his gratitude in concrete terms. We have already seen that Hickes received a hint that his services would not go un-rewarded, and Burghley, who had finally agreed to Matthew's promotion to Durham,[134] but was certainly less of a moving spirit than Cecil, was offered a substantial gratuity. In April 1595 Matthew told him that he could not,

> Without great note of ingratitude, the monster of nature, but yield your lordship some signification of a thankful mind ... Seeking by all good means but, contrary to mine expectation, not finding any office or other particular pres-ently void, either fit for me to offer your lordship or sure for your lordship to receive at my hand, I have presumed, in lieu thereof, to present your good lordship with an hun-dred pounds in gold, which this bearer will deliver to your lordship.

We do not know whether or not Burghley accepted the money, but it is worth noting that Matthew made an effort to soothe any pangs of conscience which he may have had. 'It is no recom-pense any way proportionable, I confess, to your lordship's great goodness toward me,' Matthew affirmed, 'but only a slender token of my duty most bounden ... which I beseech your lordship to accept in such part as it is simply and faithfully meant.'[135] If Matthew really considered £100 a 'slender token' for Burghley's minor part in securing his promotion, one won-ders what he considered suitable gratuities for Hickes and Cecil. Matthew obviously owed his bishopric to the Cecilian interest, but in the highly charged political atmosphere of the 1590s it was wise to have a foot in the Essex camp as well. In December 1594, when he knew that he was going to get Durham, he thanked Essex for his favourable attitude in the Privy Council.[136]

The details of Matthew's promotion allow us a choice glimpse into the intrigues of the late Elizabethan age. The ambitious dean, 'on the make', achieved his aims through the Cecils but took care to safeguard his standing with the other faction. Burgh-ley, old and failing, saw his original wishes thwarted and his son and secretary seem to have acted largely behind his back, work-ing hand in glove together in an affair which did little credit to either.

In the autumn of 1595, about a year after the beginning of the Toby Matthew episode, Hickes was deeply involved in the appointment of Richard Putto, a London man, to the escheatorship of Kent. In June 1600 Putto took legal action, arising from the appointment, against William Smith who, in 1595, had been seal bearer to Sir John Puckering, then Lord Keeper of the Great Seal. Putto claimed that Smith refused to pay him £5 which was his by right and asked the Court of Requests to order Smith to appear before it and explain his refusal to pay up. The existing evidence consists of Putto's bill of complaint,[137] and Smith's answer to it.[138] The two men told very different stories and, lacking further evidence or the verdict of the Court, it is impossible to say which, if either, of them told the truth. It is plain, however, that intricate negotiations attended the appointment of Putto, who was granted the office of escheator in November 1595.[139]

Putto asserted that in the autumn of 1595, when his suit for the escheatorship was before Burghley, he had occasion to 'use the help and friendship of Michael Hickes ... and for and in respect of the pains and friendship of the said Mr Hickes in and about the said suit to be by him ... solicited and speedily effected ... promised to give and bestow on him ... the sum of twenty pounds ... to be paid ... immediately upon the effecting of the said suit.' As he was not personally acquainted with Hickes, Putto thought it best to employ an intermediary, William Smith, a servant of Sir John Puckering, and promised Smith £5 for his mediation. After the suit had been brought to a successful conclusion, Smith, 'meaning as did appear afterwards to deceive and wrong' Putto, asked the latter to hand over the £20 promised to Hickes and the £5 promised to himself, 'alleging and saying that it would be best and most fit for him, the said Mr Smith, to pay the ... twenty pounds unto ... Mr Hickes'. Putto handed over the money but Smith paid only £15 to Hickes, retaining an additional £5 for himself, 'contrary to the true intent and meaning' of Putto. Later, however, Hickes encountered Putto and demanded his extra £5. Putto paid up as he was 'not willing that speeches and contention should be and arise for the same between ... Mr Hickes and Mr Smith, as well as for divers other reasons'. When Putto, in his turn, demanded repayment of the £5 from Smith the latter 'did deny and yet doth deny repayment thereof, and contrary to all equity and good conscience doth still retain the same'.

Smith, in his story, confirmed that in 1595 he was seal bearer to Sir John Puckering and stated that Putto himself was then an 'extraordinary servant' in the Lord Keeper's service. Putto, knowing Smith's 'credit and interest' with Puckering and wanting to be escheator of Kent for the following year, asked Smith to obtain 'his lordship's letter to ... Lord Burghley ... for the procuring of the said escheatorship'. Putto promised to give Smith for his trouble 'twenty and five pounds of lawful money of England, which, shortly after, he paid ... And hereupon [Smith] earnestly and humbly besought the said ... Lord Keeper that his lordship would vouchsafe to direct ... his letters to the ... Lord Treasurer'. Puckering signed a letter on behalf of the suit, it was sent to Burghley,

and the suit ... [was] immediately granted by the ... Lord Treasurer, and order given by his lordship to Michael Hickes, esquire ... for the dispatch thereof ... [That] grant notwithstanding, to the end the same might with more speed be dispatched ... [Smith] went to the said Mr Hickes ... and promised unto ... [him] the sum of ten pounds forthwith upon the dispatch of the patent; to be paid unto him so he might have speed therein.

Delay ensued, however, and Smith, urged on by Putto's importunities, asked Puckering to mention the matter when he next met Burghley. This Puckering did 'in the dining room of the Star Chamber. Whereupon, the ... Lord Treasurer, calling for Mr Hickes, seemed to be angry that the matter was not dispatched, holding it unfit, as he then said, that the ... Lord Keeper should be driven to move his lordship twice for so small a matter'. Smith, 'doubting how Mr Hickes would like of this proceeding [and] being very desirous of the continuance of his love and good opinion ... went again to ... [him] and, entreating still his friendship for the speedy procuring his lord's hand to the ... patent or writing and desiring expedition therein, promised, over and above the ten pounds aforesaid, the sum of five pounds more.' Hickes shortly after delivered the required patent and Smith handed over the £5. Smith concluded by denying all accusations in Putto's account contrary to his own statements.

Several points of common ground appear in both accounts. The escheatorship of Kent for one year cost Putto at least £25 and Hickes got a minimum of £15 for his services. Smith got £10. A comparatively minor suit involved Burghley and at least two intermediaries—Hickes and Smith[140]—as well as the client himself. The fact that money changed hands was obviously regarded as normal and necessary. Favours had to be paid for and it was not thought incongruous that a court of law should be asked to enforce the payment of money connected with a gratuity. Gratuities, of course, were supposed to be 'reasonable'; that is to say, they should not be used to pervert the course of justice, to secure the diversion of large sums of public money into private pockets, or to obtain the advancement of men to offices for which they were manifestly unfit or for which conspicuously better candidates were available.[141] Seen in this context the £15 or £20 which Hickes received for helping Putto on his way to the escheatorship of Kent was an unofficial fee for administrative services—a perfectly proper payment—and it would be quite wrong to brand him as 'corrupt' simply for accepting this and similar gratuities. Some of his intrigues with Robert Cecil, however, do seem to have been of dubious propriety and the Toby Matthew episode was certainly an unsavoury affair in which Hickes and Cecil were concerned with their own schemes rather than with what was desirable for the Queen's service. At all events, whatever the moral verdict on Hickes's activities during the 1590s, it is clear that, as Burghley's patronage secretary and the intimate of Robert Cecil, he received large sums of money from grateful clients. He seems to have invested a good deal of that capital in money-lending activities.

4

The Money-Lender

In sixteenth-century England, as in most ages and places, money-lenders were both indispensable and unpopular. The extent of borrowing, just as in the Middle Ages, was very great, and most classes in the community, from peasants and small masters at one end of the scale to great aristocrats at the other, were involved in the perennial search for credit. The great majority of such transactions involved insubstantial men in the localities who borrowed to tide themselves over those periods of hardship which came to most of the English peasantry in the course of a lifetime. This type of money-lending was, in the words of Professor Tawney, 'spasmodic, irregular, unorganized, a series of individual, and sometimes surreptitious, transactions between neighbours' in which the security was usually some form of personal property.[1] It was different when it came to the upper classes, the men with whom Hickes was involved in his money-lending activities. Even the largest landowners, men with vast capital wealth in their estates, frequently resorted to borrowing. This was partly because their expenditure fluctuated greatly from year to year — the costly marriages of a couple of daughters might upset the finances of even the greatest nobleman for a time — partly because, once they had got themselves into debt, they generally preferred to undertake further borrowing to service the debt rather than sell land to pay it off, and partly because their rents, generally the main source of their income, were usually paid only twice a year, in September and March, with a consequent need for short-term credit to tide them over as a new rent day approached.[2] Courtiers, of course, depended to a great extent upon the favours which they received from the Crown as well as upon their rents, and there seems to have been a period of particularly serious indebtedness in Court circles at the end of Elizabeth's reign when, burdened by the expenses of the Spanish war, the Queen cut off many of her rewards to her servants. This period of royal parsimony co-incided with increasingly extravagant living among the upper classes, with courtiers laying out vast sums of money on building, gambling, clothes and other forms of conspicuous consumption. James I's open-handed generosity, together with the general raising of rents which was characteristic of the early seventeenth century, did much, in due course, to restore the position, but it seems that the period from 1590 to 1610 was one when the English aristocracy and courtiers generally were even shorter than usual of ready cash.[3] Those, then, were golden years for money-lenders, and it was fortunate for Hickes that it was just at this time that he began to amass a substantial amount of capital for lending purposes.

Since both lenders and borrowers came from all sections of the community, it is clear that at this time money-lending was not the specialized profession it was to become in the seventeenth century, but rather a subsidiary occupation taken up by many of those who were fortunate enough to have some spare capital. Setting aside the smaller transactions which were characteristic of village life, it does, however, seem possible to distinguish three main groups in the community who lent substantial sums of money to upper-class borrowers. One of these consisted of government officials, men like Hickes, whose work often gave them access either to public funds, which they sometimes lent out in their own names, or else to substantial gratuities. Then there were the lawyers, who were notoriously prosperous in a litigious age which brought them substantial fees, some of which they were not averse to lending out at interest. Most important of all were the great London merchants who, having made for-tunes in overseas or domestic trade, increased their capital by advancing loans. That last activity was usually subordinate to their other business, but it was from among them that, by the early seventeenth century, the first specialist money-lenders had emerged, men for whom usury was becoming the principal and most profitable activity. One of this tiny but enormously wealthy group of specialists was Michael's brother, Baptist Hickes, who made a huge fortune and was able to buy his way into the peerage in the early years of Charles I's reign.[4]

The reason why so many men were anxious to lend their surplus capital was that loans brought in a high and usually safe return for money invested. During the Elizabethan period land could generally be bought for between sixteen and twenty times its annual value. This meant a return of 5 per cent or 6 per cent upon capital, whereas, in the later years of the reign, the return on money lent was 10 per cent. Of course, the ownership of land brought high prestige in society, whereas money-lending tended to carry something of a stigma. In view of the profits to be made in the latter operation, however, there were plenty who were prepared to accept the sneers and dislike of their fellows, as typified by Francis Bacon, who knew only too well about the burdens of debt when he wrote, 'Usury is the certainest means of gain, though one of the worst; as that whereby a man doth eat his bread *in sudore vultus alieni*'[5] (i.e. in the sweat of another man's brow). The available sources of loans in London, the centre of the money market, varied from month to month and indeed sometimes from day to day as eager borrowers obtained capital first from one lender and then from another. It was important, therefore, that those seeking money should be directed to lenders who had funds in hand. This was where the loan-broker—the man who brought borrowers and lenders together—came in. In early seventeenth-century London scriveners began to undertake this job, but their work still left plenty of room for private brokers, whose role was perhaps at its most important at the end of the sixteenth century.[6] The ideal man for the job was one with extensive contacts in both the Court and the city—a man, in fact, like Michael Hickes. As secretary to Burghley he was well acquainted with most leading courtiers and officials, and he had extensive city contacts through his mother and brother, both of whom were money-lenders and mercers, and through his wife, who was the widow of a prosperous merchant.

Throughout the Middle Ages and the sixteenth century high interest rates were almost invariably charged for loans, despite the disapproval of the Church and, for most of the time, of the state as well. Bacon recognized the inevitability of this when he wrote, 'It is a vanity to conceive that there would be ordinary borrowing without profit; and it is impossible to conceive the number of inconveniences that will ensue if borrowing be cramped. Therefore, to speak of the abolishing of usury is idle. All states have ever had it, in one kind or rate or other. So as that opinion must be sent to Utopia.'[7] This was a recognition of the hard facts of life, but at a time when economic activities were still judged, in theory at least, in terms of a Christian morality which frowned upon usury, the state was very reluctant to give explicit legal sanction to the taking of interest. The sixteenth century inherited from the Middle Ages a legal tradition which totally prohibited the taking of 'pure' interest — interest laid down in advance for a loan of goods or money without any risk to the lender. The essence of the matter was that the lender's gain was certain, whether or not the borrower profited from the loan. This was held to be fundamentally inequitable, a challenge to Christian moral principles. It was a different matter if both lender and borrower ran a risk. Thus, the sale of annuities was perfectly legal — there was a chance of profit to either party in view of the uncertainty of the length of the buyer's life. During the sixteenth century official attitudes towards lending and borrowing continued in theory to be based on ethical standards, but two schools of thought emerged on the definition of 'usury'. The stricter opinion continued to argue that all 'pure' interest was morally wrong and should be prohibited, but more liberal thinking, anxious to reconcile Christian morality with business practice, argued that the legitimacy of interest depended on the circumstances of the parties involved. It was not immoral, they argued, to charge 'reasonable' rates of interest to large landowners who were willing enough to pay in order to get their hands on ready cash. This school of thought, therefore, made a distinction between usury, which it defined as 'excessive' interest, and the charging of legitimate interest rates.[8] Its views can be seen reflected in the laws which were passed on the subject during the sixteenth century. All of them — including those which allowed the taking of 'reasonable' interest — were described as Acts 'against usury'.

An Act of 1545,[9] the first to give official sanction to the taking of any interest, permitted a rate of up to 10 per cent. The Act was drawn up in the hope of stopping the previously very common, if totally illegal, practice of charging much higher rates, and provided severe penalties, including imprisonment at the king's pleasure, for offenders. This act was repealed in Edward VI's reign, in 1552, by a statute[10] which forbade the taking of any interest whatever under pain of imprisonment together with forfeiture of the principal and interest. This return to a more traditional policy may have reflected the influence in Edward's reign of the 'commonwealth' party of social reformers with their strongly conservative attitudes to economic problems,[11] but it did not, of course, end the taking of interest, which continued to be charged by means of underhand devices, enabling lenders to obtain up to 15 per cent.[12] This was recognized in 1571, when the 1552 Act was repealed on the grounds that it had 'not done so much good as was hoped it should, but rather the said vice of usury ... hath much more exceedingly abounded'. Interest up to 10 per cent was once more allowed, although lenders were not given legal security for their gains. Any debtor could sue in the courts for the return of interest charged, however small.[13] This provision remained, in effect, a dead letter. Any debtor who sued for the return of his interest would never have been able to obtain another loan, and in the years after 1571 10 per cent became the normal rate of interest, charged and paid largely as a matter of course. This remained the position into the early seventeenth century when an excess in the supply of loanable funds led to a drop in interest rates, first of all to 8 per cent in 1624 and then to 6 per cent in 1651.[14]

Lenders naturally demanded security and by the end of the sixteenth century, when Hickes was active in the loan market, they had four main types of security instruments to which they could turn: bonds, recognizances, statutes and mortgages. These devices could be used for enforcing any kind of legal contract, and their existence does not necessarily imply a monetary debt. Very often, however, they were securities for debts, normally valid only for short periods — usually six months — a reflection of the general suspicion of debtors' trustworthiness and also, at the end of the sixteenth century, of the intensity of the competition for available funds. Renewals could generally be obtained at the cost of a good deal of trouble and expense and their frequency helps to explain the vast number of references to debts in contemporary letters and other documents. From the point of view of lenders and borrowers, the main differences among the securities were the relative ease or difficulty with which they could be enforced in the event of failure to pay the debt. Bonds were enforced by the Court of Common Pleas, which could order the arrest of the person or the goods or half the landed property of the debtor, and recognizances by the court in which they were enrolled, which could order the imprisonment of the debtor and the confiscation of his goods or the seizure of his goods and lands, though not the arrest of his person and possession of his lands at the same time. Recognizances, therefore, carried stiffer penalties than bonds, but the enforcement of both could be a slow and expensive business in notoriously dilatory courts against cunning debtors who could convey their real estate out of the reach of creditors and hide their goods and even themselves for long periods. Lenders, therefore, were generally reluctant to part with large sums without the better security of a statute or a mortgage.

The statute was a credit instrument which had been developed by the merchant community in the later Middle Ages to ensure the swift and effective enforcement of debts, and in 1532 it was made available to the community at large when a central registration office was set up under a clerk of recognizances. Creditors who held statutes from defaulting debtors did not have to go to law to obtain redress, as bond and recognizance holders did. They could automatically obtain a writ which enabled the quick seizure of the lands of the debtor, whose goods and body could also be arrested if necessary. Statutes were obviously much more satisfactory securities than bonds or recognizances, but all three instruments had one weakness in common when debtors were members of the peerage: they depended for their ultimate sanction on the arrest of the person of the debtor, and noblemen were immune from arrest in such civil suits. In these circumstances creditors often insisted that a nobleman's friends or servants should be associated with him in a bond, recognizance or statute—they, at least, could be arrested if need arose.

The fourth form of security was the mortgage of land. Debtors disliked mortgages and avoided them whenever possible because, at the end of the sixteenth century, failure to pay the debt at the stipulated time might lead to the complete forfeiture of the land, which was usually worth a great deal more than the debt for which it stood security. Forfeiture was by no means automatic—mortgages were frequently renewed and the Court of Chancery was already beginning to intervene to impose equitable settlements upon greedy creditors—but the possibility was there, and mortgages were often a last resort of borrowers who had already tried and failed to obtain credit upon other security.[15]

We have seen that an important aspect of a money-lender's security was the threat of imprisonment that he could hold over the head of a recalcitrant debtor who was not lucky enough to be a peer of the realm. That threat, given the dreadful conditions in most sixteenth-century jails, was a dire one, and Hickes's mother, Juliana Penne, who seems to have begun the family money-lending tradition, was well aware of its potentialities. She began lending money before Elizabeth's accession to the throne, and one of her early clients was William Cecil, who wrote during the concluding months of Mary's reign, 'to crave a favour which I never deserved; that is, to lend me fifty pound[s], which I will take as kindly as ever I did any courtesy done unto me of any friend I have, considering how hardly it is to be gotten in this troublesome time and how much pleasure it will do me now in respect of a great occasion I have to use it'. This was, of course, at a time when all interest charges were theoretically forbidden, but Cecil hastened to promise that he would 'give more than ordinary interest'[16]—probably an indication that he was prepared to pay 15 per cent. Another debtor, a Mr Hardwick, obtained a loan in 1563 and borrowed again in 1570. Mrs Penne seems to have renewed his debts frequently; but in due course she lost patience and took legal proceedings against him, affirming that she 'had never nothing [sic] of Mr Hardwick but fair promises', instead of the £400 which he owed her. Hardwick went to prison, but in 1577 Mrs Penne had to write off the debt.[17] In the same year she drew up, in her uneducated but vigorous and distinctive handwriting, a statement of her assets, which, besides mentioning plate, jewels, tapestry, linen and furniture, noted debts worth £1,800.[18] In the years just before her death she was making loans to members of the nobility. One debtor was the untrustworthy earl of Oxford, who was such a trial as a son-in-law to the long-suffering Burghley. Oxford owed her money in 1591, and when he refused to pay up, she wrote to him of 'the great grief and sorrow' which he was causing her, and asked that he should deal with her 'in courtesy, for that you and I shall come at that dreadful day [of Judgment] and give account for all our doing'.[19] She could not, of course, get Oxford arrested for the debt, but she had taken the precaution of getting a bond from Thomas Churchyard as the earl's security. Churchyard, terrified of imprisonment, fled to sanctuary, from which he wrote in bitter terms to Mrs Penne.[20] Another aristocratic debtor was Henry Fitzgerald, 12th earl of Kildare, an Irish peer who succeeded to the title in 1585. In the summer of 1591 he defaulted on the repayment of his debt and Mrs Penne wrote to him in violent terms, accusing him of being one in whom there was 'no truth nor honour'. She reminded him of his 'great swearing and oaths, denying God if you did break one of them with me', and warned him that the Almighty would 'perform every word that he hath spoken upon the just and the wicked'.[21] Mrs Penne was clearly a very formidable old lady, and the earl, who was then at Greenwich, hastened to reply, apologizing profusely for the delay and promising repayment as soon as his man returned 'with money out of Ireland, which will be within this fortnight'.[22]

Mrs Penne's example must have suggested to her sons Michael and Baptist Hickes the possibility of making loans on their own behalf, and from the 1580s onwards Michael's contacts with needy members of the Court circle brought him a large clientele only too anxious to obtain loans from him personally or else to use his knowledge of the financial world to help them to borrow or to service their debts elsewhere. He was also in a position, through his government contacts, to help large creditors of the Crown to obtain their dues from a never overfull Exchequer. Most of the evidence about these activities comes from the period after 1598, but there is some material for the earlier years. As early as 1571 he acted as a loan broker for his friend Vincent Skinner, obtaining money for him from his brother, Baptist Hickes. The delighted Skinner thanked him 'a thousand times' for his friendship. His wife had used the money to make payments 'which without your help I know she could not', and he asked Michael to obtain another loan from Baptist so that his wife could pay off other debts.[23] Another man who badly needed a loan was Richard Rich, who confessed that he did not know where to turn to obtain the money, and asked Hickes to get it for him.[24] Henry Beaumont, a Leicestershire friend, sought Hickes's aid in 1595. He was worried about a debt which was in dispute and asked Hickes to help him settle the matter.[25] Another friend in need of assistance was Francis Bacon's brother Anthony who, in the summer of 1593, owed Baptist Hickes £500. He wanted six months to pay and successfully asked Michael to obtain forebearance for him from his brother.[26]

Michael himself was already lending money by the 1560s, but the great majority of his loans were made from the 1590s onwards. His capital probably came from a number of sources. During the 1580s and 1590s as secretary to Burghley he received, as we have seen, many gratuities from grateful or hopeful clients. Some of these were for substantial amounts and the total in any one year must have come to a largish sum in ready cash, ideal for lending purposes. His mother's death in 1592 and his own marriage in 1594 to the widow of a prosperous London merchant must also have put a considerable amount of money at his disposal—his wife had received at least £5,000 on the death of her first husband in 1593.[27]

Hickes lent on all the main types of security—bonds, recognizances, statutes and mortgages—during his career, but we do not know the security used in every loan, and in the pre-1598 period there is no definite indication of his lending on bonds or mortgages. There is evidence for five possible and six definite loans by Hickes in the years up to 1598. Three of the five possible loans turn on the existence of statutes, dated 1595 and 1596, in which landed gentlemen acknowledged themselves under an obligation to Hickes. As statutes could be used to enforce any kind of contract it must not be automatically assumed that these represent loans by Hickes, but it is very probable that they did. If so, the sums lent were substantial, totalling probably £2,000 in all.[28] A fourth possible borrower was Lord Stafford, one of the poorest peers in England. Sometime before 1598 he asked for a loan of £10, but we do not know whether he got it.[29] The fifth, Francis Bacon, needed a much larger sum in March 1596, when he asked Hickes and Henry Maynard to lend him £1,000 to pay off a mortgage which had to be redeemed later that month.[30] There is no further information about his request but, as he successfully asked Hickes for other loans in the years after 1598, it is probable that he was not disappointed.

One man who definitely obtained a loan—we do not know the amount—was Hickes's cousin, Gregory Sprint, who lived in Bristol. In February 1582 Hickes wrote a sharp letter of reproof to him about his failure to repay the debt, dismissing his excuse that others had failed to meet their commitments to him. 'What's it to me?' asked Hickes, 'you have rather cause to complain of their ill dealing towards you than by their example to deal so with others'.[31] Lord Henry Howard also borrowed money in the period before 1598,[32] and another debtor was Anthony Holborne, who asked for and got £2 in 1594,[33] evidence that Hickes was prepared to lend tiny sums. The security which he obtained from Sprint, Howard and Holborne is not known, but his first recorded loan, in 1565, was on a recognizance. The borrower, Nicholas Beaumont, father of the Henry Beaumont who turned to Hickes for help with his financial problems in the 1590s, was probably a close friend, but this did not prevent Hickes from driving a hard and shrewd bargain. He advanced £220 and in return obtained an 'annuity' of £40 per annum out of the Beaumont manor of Coleorton in Leicestershire—this was really an interest payment concealed in the form of an annuity in order to circumvent the prohibition on the taking of 'pure' interest which was then in force by the terms of the Act of 1552. It was to be paid four times a year, and each time Beaumont failed to pay the £10 as stipulated he was to forfeit £5, this penalty to be paid within ten days of default. In the event of further failure to pay, Hickes was to distrain upon the lands of the manor for both annuity and penalty. The annuity was to cease if Beaumont repaid the £220 in 1568 or 1570, three or five years after the date of the agreement.[34] In effect, Beaumont was paying interest at a rate of 18 per cent. Good business by Hickes! Another debtor was Anthony Bacon who obtained loans from Michael as well as from Baptist Hickes. In 1593 Michael advanced £200 on the security of a statute, and in 1598 Anthony still owed him money.[35] Sir Henry Lee, Master of the Armoury, was also a debtor, the first really large borrower from Hickes of whom we have record. He obtained £2,000, secured by a statute, in April 1598.[36]

By 1598 Hickes was beginning to establish himself as a money-lender and also, in his other capacity as a loan-broker, to acquire a reputation as a financial expert, a useful mediator between Court circles and the London money market. He greatly developed both these roles in the first decade of the seventeenth century. The official voice of the Church remained deeply suspicious of such financial activities, but despite this Hickes, like so many of his fellow money-lenders, seems to have had little difficulty in reconciling them with deep and sincere religious feelings.

5

The Puritan Amidst
his Family and Friends

Michael Hickes's religious views were formed during the 1560s at Trinity College and Lincoln's Inn where he became a member of a circle of religious radicals which included his Cambridge tutor George Blythe; his future colleague in Burghley's secretariat, Vincent Skinner; and his close friend John Stubbe. These men and others who saw the 1559 religious settlement, with its quasi Catholic liturgy, as only the beginning of a more radical reformation began to be called Puritans during the first decade of the reign, and the name stuck. Elizabethan Puritans wanted to purge the Church of its remaining 'Romish' characteristics, such as 'excessive' ceremonial and the wearing of vestments. During the 1560s the great majority of Puritans were moderates, who were prepared to accept episcopacy, but the hierarchy's attempts to enforce the use of the surplice in church services in the 'vestiarian controversy' of 1563–7 turned many of them against the idea of bishops. During the 1570s and 1580s the movement developed a powerful extremist wing, which wanted to abolish episcopal government of the Church and substitute a presbyterian system. The presbyterians, under the intellectual leadership of Thomas Cartwright, who was Lady Margaret Professor of Divinity at Cambridge in 1569–70, and organized by John Field, a propagandist of genius, conducted, during the 1570s and 1580s, a formidable campaign in pamphlets, pulpit and Parliament directed at subverting the established Church. In 1588, however, Puritanism was seriously weakened by the death of its most powerful patron at Court, the earl of Leicester, and the vituperative Marprelate Tracts of 1588–9, with their coarse and vulgar abuse of the bishops, went far towards alienating opinion in the country at large. In this situation John Whitgift, who became archbishop of Canterbury in 1583, was able to mount a successful frontal assault on the organized presbyterian movement during the years 1589 to 1592. As a result, presbyterianism went underground for the rest of the reign, although a more moderate Puritanism, which stressed the virtues of sabbatarianism and of religious observances centred on the household, continued to be very strong among the laity.[1] Hickes's relationships with Stubbe and Cartwright, which provide the main evidence about the Puritan influences in his life, should be seen against this general background.

By 1570, the year of the first surviving letters from Stubbe to Hickes, the two men had long been intimates, and it is clear that Hickes was deeply devoted to his friend. He complained from London in the spring of 1570 that Stubbe, who was in Cambridge, had recently written to several of their mutual acquaintances but not to him. This was particularly hurtful because he had recently been seriously ill. He had, indeed, been '*semimortus*' and had hastened to draw up a will in which he had not forgotten to mention Stubbe. Stubbe replied on March 21st. 'All your life hath been ... an evident proof of your goodwill toward me,' he wrote, and he said that he was particularly touched by Hickes's remembrance of him during his illness. He made light of his failure to write before, endeavouring to explain that this in some ways implied a compliment: 'letters between absent friends', he told Hickes, 'are the principal food and nurriture whereby the life of their amity is sustained. Such nurriture to young and newly entertained friends ... to weak friends, is necessary ... but our friendship is ... strong and ... able enough to last the whole day through without such childish supporting.'[2] These words seem transparently hypocritical and even if they did soothe Hickes's injured feelings for a time, which is doubtful, he soon had other complaints. Four months later Stubbe, still in Cambridge, was replying to accusations that he had greater affection for John Drury, a former fellow student of their Lincoln's Inn days, than for Hickes himself. Stubbe seems to have been embarrassed by the whole business. He told Hickes that he found such comparisons 'odious, for, I promise you, I can not readily tell which of you I would have to love me better'.[3] It is clear, indeed, that in 1570 Hickes was writing frequent letters to Stubbe.[4] His devotion and his jealous desire to be first in his friend's affections are evidence of the influence which Stubbe exercised over him.

Five years later he had still not got over his resentment at Stubbe's friendship for John Drury. In October 1575 Drury was staying with Stubbe at Norwich and when the latter wrote to Hickes thanking him for his letters he mentioned a rueful complaint by Drury that Hickes would never write to *him*.[5] Two and a half years later, in March 1578, Stubbe informed Hickes of the marriage of his sister Alice to Thomas Cartwright. He was delighted and asked Hickes to tell anybody who disliked the match, 'that I contented myself with such an husband for her whose livelihood was learning, who should endow his wife with wisdom, and who might leave to his children the rich portion of Godliness by Christian careful education ... esteeming these things as precious stones, while ... the worldly commended things ... I deem less worth than a barley corn.'[6]

As this letter suggests, Stubbe believed in expressing his principles forthrightly, and he got into serious trouble in 1579, when he published his notorious *Gaping Gulf*, a pamphlet denouncing the possible marriage, then under discussion, between the Queen and the duke of Alençon, heir to the French throne. This aroused in Stubbe's mind the nightmare possibility of the subjection of Protestant England to Catholic France and, although he wrote of the Queen herself in terms of great loyalty and affection, he did not hesitate to denounce Alençon in intemperate terms. The duke, he said, was rotten with debauchery, 'the old serpent himself in the form of a man, come a second time to seduce the English Eve and ruin the English paradise'. By publishing this tract Stubbe interfered in foreign policy, a 'matter of state' which belonged to the royal prerogative. The Queen was furious at the implied challenge to her authority and at the insult to a foreign power. Her resentment was increased by Stubbe's tactless suggestion that she was too old to marry and bear children. In October Stubbe, together with his publisher and printer, was tried at Westminster on a charge of disseminating seditious writings. All three men were sentenced to have their right hands cut off. Elizabeth pardoned the printer, but she refused Stubbe's pathetic plea for clemency and on November 3rd the sentence on him and on Page, the publisher, was carried out. They were brought from the Tower, where they had been imprisoned, to a scaffold set up in the market-place at Westminster. Stubbe addressed the onlookers, asking them to pray 'that God will strengthen me to endure and abide the pain that I am to suffer and [will] grant me this grace: that the loss of my hand do not withdraw any part of my duty and affection towards her majesty'. After this brave speech his right hand was struck off 'with a cleaver driven through the wrist by ... a mallet'. His agony did not prevent him from taking off his hat with his left hand and crying in a loud voice, 'God save the Queen'. He then fainted and had to be carried back to the Tower. The throng of spectators was 'deeply silent' during the proceedings, a sign, perhaps, that they disapproved of the punishment.[7]

Stubbe remained in prison in the Tower but he was allowed to correspond with his friends and he wrote to Hickes who hastened to draft a reply. 'I have received from you since our first acquaintance,' he reminded Stubbe

many good and friendly letters which bear testimony of the goodwill you bear me. These I retain and many times do read to recall that long and mutual goodwill betwixt us. But I assure you, these few lines in this ragged piece of paper and written with the left hand ... do more truly d[e]clare you to love me than those many sheets, albeit I remember I have good lessons in some of them and am beloved in them all.

He asked Stubbe to continue to give him good advice and not to fail to criticize him openly if need should arise:

albeit I have a weak and a froward stomach and so much abhorring physic that I either do very unwillingly receive or very hardly retain any bitter potions, yet, when any wholesome medicine is ministered unto my soul, I thank God ... I do receive it readily and do brook it very well, albeit it be as bitter as aloes, so that I never need to have my pills put in a golden forell. [i.e. covering]

He concluded by asking Stubbe to pray for him.[8] These pious sentiments were reciprocated in December 1580 when Stubbe,

95

still in the Tower, prayed God to make Hickes 'increase in ability and hearty will to serve the Lord and his Church'.[9]

Stubbe was released in 1581 and in the summer of 1582, when he was in his home county of Norfolk, he wrote to Hickes in London deploring the 'folly and idleness' of their misspent youth together and urging that they should redeem it 'by spending the rest with more conscience to our building up in faith and faithful conversation, whereby we may in some godly vocation glorify our God and benefit our brethren and withall live like Adam's children, as we are, upon our own sweat. Let us pray one for another that we may thus live to the comforting and joy one of another.' He also asked Hickes for a strong knife with a good handle, 'that I may hold it the more steadily'.[10] Hickes sent the knife.[11] The last information we have of contact between the two is a letter of 1589 in which Stubbe wrote on behalf of a mutual friend who had a suit with Burghley. He concluded, 'The Lord Jesus keep you ever his',[12] a suitably pious ending to our record of the relationship. Two years later Stubbe died in France.

Whether a predilection for Puritan ideas drew Hickes into Stubbe's circle at Cambridge and Lincoln's Inn, or whether his admiration for and friendship with Stubbe turned him towards Puritanism, the result was the same. He became a Puritan and Stubbe's devoted friend.

His relationship with Thomas Cartwright was on a different plane.[13] The two men were never intimates and Hickes's attitude seems to have been that of an admiring disciple. He got to know Cartwright only slightly at Trinity College,[14] where the latter was a fellow from 1560 onwards, but in 1573 eagerly seized an opportunity to do him a major service. In the summer of 1572 John Field and another leading Puritan minister, Thomas Wilcox, produced their *Admonition to Parliament*, a direct presbyterian attack on the Elizabethan Church Settlement. In November Whitgift, then master of Trinity College, wrote an *Answer* to the *Admonition*, and in the spring of 1573 Cartwright entered the lists with his *Reply* to Whitgift's *Answer*. In June 1573 both the *Admonition* and the *Reply* were suppressed by royal proclamation, and in December Cartwright, afraid of arrest, was in hiding in London. On the 9th of that month it was reported that

5 Elizabeth I, *c.* 1592 (*by Marcus Gheeraerts the Younger*)

6 Francis Bacon (*by Van Somer*)

he was lodging in Cheapside, at the house of Martin, a gold-smith. He had certainly stayed for some time before that at the White Bear, the Hickes home in Cheapside, as, on the very day of the report that he was at Martin's, he wrote to thank Hickes for hospitality. Hickes had given him money when he left and he protested that 'with many such lodgings I might soon grow to the riches of an English bishop. But, because you were so earnest with me, and because you should perceive that I was not unwilling to be further bound unto you, I received it.' He asked to be allowed to return some part of the favours he had received in the gift of a book, 'wherein are laid up the riches and treasures which last for ever'.[15] Two days later, on December 11th, the Privy Council ordered his arrest and he fled abroad, where he remained for eleven years, returning to England in the spring of 1585. In 1586 the earl of Leicester made him master of his hospital for the poor at Warwick, but after Leicester's death in 1588 he found himself in grave financial difficulties, unable to obtain the money necessary for the upkeep of the hospital or even to obtain payment of the annuity which Leicester had granted him. In 1590 he asked for and received help from Hickes and Burghley in these troubles. In his letter to Hickes, written in August, he referred to their 'fellowship in one university and one college ... accompanied with profession of the same faith'.[16]

By 1590 the organized presbyterian movement was being threatened by Archbishop Whitgift's determined campaign against it, which culminated with the arrest of the leading Puritan ministers and their trial before the Courts of High Commission and Star Chamber. Cartwright himself was arrested in October 1590 and in February 1592, still in the Fleet prison, requested Hickes's mediation with Burghley to secure his release, reminding him of 'the love you bore to my brother Stubbe, which would have poured all the ointment of the interest of his friendship with you upon my head if he had lived'.[17] We do not know how far Hickes was able to help, but three months later Cartwright was released. It is clear, indeed, that the passage of years did not diminish Hickes's admiration and respect for Cartwright. In September 1595 he asked him for a form of prayer for his own use. Cartwright obliged, accompanying the prayer he drew up with a letter full of pious sentiments.[18] This is the last recorded contact between the two men. Cartwright died eight years later.

Hickes's Puritan fervour during the Elizabethan period was reflected in his devotion to Stubbe and his services to Cartwright. It seems likely that by the early years of James I's reign his ardour had cooled. Presbyterianism was no longer the force that it had been and the ageing Hickes, the friend of some of the greatest in the land, may have become something of a politique in religion, content with listening to sermons and practising pious exercises within his household. The decade of the 1590s was probably the vital period in this transformation, both for Puritanism generally and for Hickes personally. Whitgift's violent attack on the more extreme Puritans showed just how far the Queen and he were prepared to go in enforcing conformity, and after 1592 even Cartwright gave no more trouble. Hickes too may have seen that discretion was the better part of valour. Changing circumstances as well as the growing conservatism of old age probably explain the decline in his religious radicalism that can be seen by the early years of the seventeenth century.

Whatever the precise shade of Hickes's religious views during the 1590s it is certain that these years were of great importance in his family life, as they saw both the death of his mother and his own marriage. His mother, Juliana Penne, lived for nearly twenty years after she abandoned the idea of a third marriage in 1573. During these last two decades of her life her main interests were probably her mercery business, her money-lending activities, and her family. She seems to have been in poor health for much of the time. References to her illnesses are scattered throughout Hickes's papers, and in the summer of 1582 John Stubbe wished her 'a sound and strong mind to bear the infirmities of her diseased body'.[19] Despite her physical disabilities, however, she clearly remained a woman of spirit. She became acquainted with Robert Cecil, doubtless through her son Michael, and a real friendship seems to have developed between the elderly lady, with her forceful personality, and the rising young statesman. In October 1588 Cecil thanked her for the 'many kindnesses' he had received at her hands and told her that he wanted to acquire a silver bell, which belonged to Lady Gorges. 'If you of yourself would ... buy it,' he went on, 'I would willingly pay whatsoever she will ask, so that it might not be known to her that I am to have it, for I would not be beholding unto her. You see how bold I am with you.' He ended his letter by wishing her 'health and long life for my friend's good, your eldest son'. [20]

Cecil himself was prepared to act energetically on Mrs Penne's behalf. On one occasion—the date is not known—he examined buildings which her enemies were erecting in London against her protests but evidently with Burghley's sanction. During his tour of inspection Cecil, violently partisan on Mrs Penne's behalf, exchanged heated words with a Mr Symmons, who owned some of the buildings. [21] On another occasion he exerted his influence with his father to secure the latter's support in the Privy Council for the release of an imprisoned friend of Mrs Penne. [22] In June 1592, however, relations between Cecil and Mrs Penne were strained. The cause of the breach was the latter's friendship with Charles Chester, who was arrested on June 19th on the orders of Cecil and Lord Admiral Nottingham. Chester was suspected of conspiring with foreigners, Jesuits, and other 'evilly disposed' persons against the state and was committed close prisoner to the Gatehouse. His rooms were searched and about twenty 'vain and papistical' books, mainly in Spanish, were found, as well as 'pictures, beads, mass-book, pax, shirt of hair, whips, and other trumpery'. Chester was a widely travelled man—he had been to Russia, the Ottoman Empire and the Canary Islands—and no doubt he had plenty of colourful stories to tell Mrs Penne. [23] At any rate he had certainly been a frequent visitor at her house, and the day after his arrest Cecil wrote her a friendly warning. 'I have thought to make a difference between your house and others in like case,' he told her,

> presuming so much upon your discretion as that you will as surely deliver up all such papers, books, caskets or other things belonging to Charles Chester ... upon this my private letter, as if I had sent a pursuivant to make search, which I will not offer unto you, although it be credibly informed that your house hath been of long time his chief receptacle ... You shall do well to deal clearly in the discovery of such things as be in your house, for his confession will otherwise discredit your denial. [24]

Mrs Penne does not seem to have replied and the tone of Cecil's next letter was much sharper. He warned her that if he did not get a satisfactory answer at once he would send a pursuivant to search her house. The old lady took the point and hastened to write a disarming letter, telling him that she had put all Chester's things together 'until your honour send to view or search them, when I trust that you will find that I will not wittingly conceal anything of his, nor will be found, I hope, to have fostered him to any ill purpose'.[25] Cecil seems to have been well satisfied with this reply and took pains to point out that no suspicion had arisen of her having been an accomplice in Chester's designs.[26] The resumption of friendly relations was sealed by a visit by Mrs Penne to Burghley's house, but soon afterwards she became 'extreme sick'. Cecil wrote to commiserate with her, hoping that 'discreet and warm keeping' would soon lead to a complete recovery.[27] The illness, however, proved fatal. Mrs Penne died on November 14th, 1592.[28]

On her death Michael, as the eldest son, inherited the lands in Bristol and Gloucestershire and in the parish of St Katherine Colman in London which had been left to her for life in Robert Hickes's will in 1557. Michael also got a London house on St Peter's hill, about a hundred yards north of the Thames, which she had bought in 1559, and probably a substantial proportion of her movable property as well, but he agreed that the White Bear, the family mercery business in Cheapside, should pass to his youngest brother, Baptist.[29] Baptist and he kept in touch during the 1590s but the bulk of the surviving correspondence between them—mainly about Baptist's financial affairs—belongs to the early years of the seventeenth century. The second of the three brothers, Clement Hickes, became searcher of customs at Chester during the 1590s. He seems to have obtained the post through Michael's influence with Burghley, but was by no means satisfied with his lot. He constantly complained that it involved him in financial losses and asked for an official allowance, in addition to his ordinary fees, to cover them.[30]

In January 1595 Clement and his wife sent their regards[31] to Elizabeth Hickes, the widow whom Michael had married only a month before, when he was fifty-one.[32] She was by no means his first choice. He had previously proposed marriage to at least three other widows. His suit to Mrs Heyd,[33] probably about

1570, seems to have made some progress. Unfortunately, however, her friends did not consider him a good bargain, saying that he was nine or ten years her junior and implying that he was more interested in her money than in the lady herself. Hickes replied gallantly that nobody 'that hath but half an eye' could think that he was younger; 'for your wealth', he added discreetly, 'as it is not that I seek after, so it hath not been the thing that I have inquired after'. He insisted that he would make a good, loyal, and true husband, but Mrs Heyd turned him down. In 1584 he was pursuing another suit, but his friend Edward Suliarde told him that if the widow was 'as hard to be won as you are slow to woo what a goodly time are you like to live a bachelor still'.[34] Suliarde's advice was to 'give the assault'. The lady in question was probably Mrs Woodcock, who had been twice widowed. On the death of her first husband, as Hickes told her,[35]

> albeit ... you were a woman unknown to me but by sight only, yet such was the good report which was generally given of you, as I was not only moved to love and desire you but was minded also to have been a suitor to you. But my wavering hope being thwarted and overthrown with the view and weight of mine own unworthiness, I gave over my determination in seeking you for a wife, though I could not leave to love you, as such a woman doth deserve.

When, however, her second husband died, Hickes, emboldened perhaps by Suliarde's words, decided to press his claims. He freely admitted his unworthiness. 'When I look into mine own manifold wants and imperfections and consider withal what a number of good parts and virtues there be in you,' he told her, 'I see plainly the more cause I have to love you, the less hope I have to enjoy you.' He wanted her, he protested, 'for yourself and not for that which you have', and added, 'Of myself I will say nothing, though peradventure I could say somewhat. They are not always the deepest waters that make the greatest noise, nor yet the best fruit that bear the fairest blossom ... a barque that bears a low sail above board may carry a heavy burden under the hatches, and though I myself wear not a coat of scarlet, yet I shall be able and will maintain my wife in a gown of silk.' Alas, even this final inducement was not enough and Hickes, who maintained that he was hers 'without change and without end', in due course looked elsewhere. In his third suit,[36] to Mrs Loftus, he maintained fervently, 'I cannot leave to love you, nor will not leave to sue to you.' Despite these stirring sentiments he was once again unsuccessful.

These rebuffs did not prevent his giving what he clearly considered to be sage words of advice to married women who were having difficulties with their husbands. He told one estranged lady that 'an unjust peace is better than a just war, and that commonwealth ... better which hath a tyrant than that which hath no king', and advised a reconciliation despite 'hard and froward conditions' on her husband's part.[37] Another friend in distress was the earl of Oxford's sister, Lady Mary Vere, who had married Lord Willoughby d'Eresby in 1577. Husband and wife were on poor terms as early as the autumn of 1578 and Lord Willoughby's financial difficulties in subsequent years can hardly have improved the situation. By 1589 he had pawned his wife's jewels. Hickes's advice to Lady Willoughby, which he probably gave during the 1590s, was to 'commit your unhappy case to God by your prayers and commend your honest cause to the world by your patience'. He told her sententiously that she should 'subdue and submit' her will to that of her husband 'in all honest and lawful things, seeking ... to win his goodwill with covering his faults and bearing with his infirmities ... the which, although it may seem hard to flesh and blood, yet is it fully warranted by the word of God, which binds all women, of what birth or calling soever they be, to yield due benevolence and obedience to their husbands.' This was unexceptionable in terms of sixteenth-century attitudes to marriage, but hardly, perhaps, valuable practical advice! In any event, Lady Willoughby does not seem to have taken it. By 1600 she and her husband were completely estranged and had separated.[38]

Hickes himself got married at last in December 1594 to Elizabeth Parvish, the widow of a prominent London merchant. He must have been delighted to secure such a rich prize. By the custom of London the widow of a merchant could claim at least a third of his movable property, and when Henry Parvish died in August 1593 her share of his goods came to over £5,000. In addition she got a life interest in his lands in Surrey and in the country house at Ruckholt in Essex which he had bought in

1592. Hickes inherited all this with the lady, though he may have had more mixed feelings about the family of nine stepchildren—four boys and five girls—that she also brought with her.[39] Gabriel, the eldest son, was fourteen when his father died, and in December 1593 his mother got the wardship, which was regranted to her, jointly with Hickes, in March 1596.[40] Besides looking after this large ready-made family Hickes also became involved with their late father's business affairs. Henry Parvish and another prominent London merchant, William Beecher senior, had business dealings together and each stood security by bond for the other's debts. After Parvish's death there was dispute between his widow and Beecher as to liability for these bonds. Hickes became a party in the quarrel after his marriage and in March 1597 Beecher complained bitterly to Burghley about the abuse he had received from Hickes, whose 'revile and threatenings' were, he said, beyond endurance. The rights and wrongs of the matter are obscure but it certainly dragged on for years. In August 1607 Hickes paid Beecher £400 in settlement of the affair, and by then the latter had also obtained 'other valuable considerations', which no doubt included Hickes's recommendation of his son, William junior, to Sir George Carew, ambassador to France.[41] Parvish had extensive trading interests in Italy and when he died was engaged in a dispute with the Venetian authorities about £6,000 worth of his goods which they had confiscated. Hickes tried for several years to recover them, using as his agent Paul Pindar, who had been Parvish's factor in Venice since the 1580s and had remained there after the latter's death. We do not know whether or not Hickes got the goods, but Pindar, who also worked for himself, certainly prospered and in James I's reign became successively consul at Aleppo and Ambassador at Constantinople, returning to England in 1623 a very rich man, to become one of the greatest customs farmers and money-lenders of the reign of Charles I. In 1639 his estate was valued at £236,000.[42]

Hickes's marriage in no way weakened his friendship with Robert Cecil, who had himself got married in 1589 to Elizabeth Brooke, daughter of his father's old friend Lord Cobham. Each of the two men seems to have got on well with the other's wife. Cecil was a considerate friend, quick to think of Mrs Hickes's comfort and convenience. On one occasion he told one of his household staff to 'let Mr Hickes have my horses and my bigger coach to bring his wife from her house to London. Let mine own coachman go with it, and let her use it as she pleaseth.'[43] Although Cecil was fond of Elizabeth Hickes he did not hesitate to involve her, at times, in the coarse humour which he exchanged with his friend. 'I wonder not that your matrimony dulls you,' he wrote to Hickes sometime in the 1590s, 'for such a belly as I believe she hath will mar a better back than you have.' He concluded by protesting mockingly that he was Hickes's 'sincere and most constant religious friend'.[44]

The Hickes family was not without means of returning the kindnesses which they received from Cecil. 'Sir Walter Raleigh and I dining in London,' wrote Cecil to Michael Hickes, 'we went to your brother's shop, where your brother desired me to write to my wife ... [to ask her] not to let anybody know that she paid under £3:10:0 a yard for her cloth of silver. I marvel she is so simple as to tell anybody what she pays for everything.'[45] Michael seems to have been a great favourite with Elizabeth Cecil. She called herself his 'landlady', and sometimes Cecil and she wrote joint letters to him.[46]

Hickes's first child was born in January 1596 and his colleague Henry Maynard, congratulating him on the happy event, added, 'you deserve so much the more commendation as you have gotten a son, where others have had but girls'. Maynard had told Robert and Elizabeth Cecil the good news. Both were 'exceeding glad' and Elizabeth 'willed me to let you understand from her that now you have an heir of your own a friend of yours in Cheapside who expected that fortune from you will sell his velvet 2 shillings a yard dearer. Thus you see she is merry with you, which she knoweth cometh not in an unseasonable time.'[47] Shortly afterwards Cecil himself wrote to offer congratulations. 'I and Bess do send to you to kn[ow] how your wife and your jewel do,' he said, adding that he did not know whether to be more pleased at God's blessing to his friend or envious of Hickes's good fortune.[48] Burghley agreed to stand godfather and the baby, named William in his honour, was christened in Hickes's house on St Peter's hill. A delightful description has survived of an incident which followed the ceremony. Burghley, then seventy-five years old, pulled out his purse to give some gold to the servants. One or two pieces dropped from his gouty fingers and rolled under the bed, but he would not allow them to be picked up, saying that the sweepers could have them.[49] Young William Hickes seems to have prospered. At the age of seven months he was a 'fat, jolly' baby.[50] A second child, a daughter, was born in 1598 and christened Elizabeth on July 17th, in the parish church of St Mary the Virgin, Leyton, which was near Ruckholt.[51] Cecil attended the ceremony, which, Hickes told him, was 'an argument of your love towards me ... a comfort to my wife, and an honour to her house'.[52]

Hickes's friendship with Cecil, though it was of exceptional importance to him, was only one of many. Throughout his life he seems to have had little difficulty in making and keeping friends and would no doubt have agreed with Francis Bacon's dictum 'that it is a mere and miserable solitude to want true friends, without which the world is but a wilderness'.[53] Many of his friends were men whom he first met during his Cambridge and Lincoln's Inn days. His old tutor George Blythe and he remained on friendly terms until Blythe's death in 1581,[54] and his friendship with Vincent Skinner continued until his own death in 1612. Robert Southwell, a member of a distinguished Kentish family, was another Trinity College contemporary who consolidated his friendship with Hickes at Lincoln's Inn. In 1575 Southwell, then in Venice, recalled nostalgically the pleasant times he had spent in Hickes's rooms at the Inn. This friendship was doubtless strengthened by the great regard which both men had for John Stubbe.[55] Edward Suliarde of Flemings in Suffolk, the man who took such an interest in Hickes's pursuit of Mrs Woodcock in 1584, was another Lincoln's Inn man who became a lifelong friend.[56] By the 1560s Hickes was also friendly with Lord Henry Howard, who, as earl of Northampton, was to play such a sinister role in the politics of James I's reign. Sometime between 1565 and 1570 Howard wrote from Cambridge to Hickes at Lincoln's Inn asking if he could recommend a good teacher of the lute and arranging to have a gown made in the latest fashion, with short hanging sleeves.[57] Many years later, unable, owing to Burghley's death, to obtain his annuity from the Exchequer, Howard turned to his old crony Hickes for help.[58]

One of Hickes's closest friends was certainly Henry Maynard, his colleague in Burghley's secretariat. The long hours when the two men worked together cemented an intimacy to which their correspondence bears witness,[59] and Maynard and his wife and children paid visits to Ruckholt, returning the hospitality by entertaining the Hickes family at Easton, Maynard's fine Essex seat.[60] Sir Robert Wroth, also an Essex neighbour, was a man with whom Hickes shared a common Puritanism and a love of outdoor life. By 1597 they were close friends, exchanging news and gossip and visiting each other's houses.[61] Another friend of the 1590s was Francis Bacon,[62] and that relationship too continued and prospered during James I's reign. Roger Manners of Uffington in Lincolnshire, a member of the great family of the Manners, earls of Rutland, was a friend who relied on Hickes for court news and gossip.[63] He complained in 1595 that he was merely a 'poor countryman', while Hickes lived among the best in London. He got little sympathy. Hickes told him that his senses must have grown dull not to be able to recognize his good fortune, but added that it was well known that no man was ever 'contented with his own estate, whatsoever it be'. He reinforced the point by offering to change places with Manners.[64]

Hickes lent money to Nicholas Beaumont of Coleorton in Leicestershire in 1565 and twenty years later, according to one of Beaumont's sons, was his best friend.[65] There were rumours that Nicholas Beaumont's death in July 1585 was caused by medicine prescribed by his physician, Dr Thomas Moffet, who wrote to Hickes indignantly refuting such slanders. From Moffet's letter it is clear that Hickes was with Beaumont at or just before his death. The family demanded a post mortem and Hickes himself asked for 'a plain information' of what was found in the body. Moffet obliged at length — his detailed description is not for the squeamish — and concluded by stating that the doctors had wanted to finish their examination by looking at the brain. One of Beaumont's four sons who was present, and had seen 'sufficient causes' of death, refused to allow them to proceed.[66] Francis and Thomas Beaumont, two of Nicholas's younger sons, remained on close terms with their father's old friend, corresponding frequently with him.[67] Francis spoke with gratitude of Hickes's kindnesses, 'both in descending divers times with me into my griefs and lending me at all times your best aid of counsel for every occasion'.[68] Thomas sent presents of cheeses, 'for I know your diet of old and I mean that you shall taste of my dairy anew'.[69] Hickes, in his turn, sent news from the capital. 'London indeed is the treasury of England for money and the storehouse for news,' he told Thomas in July 1586, 'and therefore you have better reason to look for it at my hands than I at yours, for the which cause, when you would have the one write, and when you want the other sign and seal, and you shall see somebody will send. But I know you will be sooner beholding to your friends for news than to the merchant for money.' He also made it plain that he was on the friendliest terms with the ladies of the family. 'Recommend me, I pray you,' he said, 'to your wife and tell her that after Michaelmas I mind to put her in remembrance of a mess of midsummer cream, and tell your sister [Dorothy] that rather than she should be slothful and her needle sleep she shall do well to busy herself about the performance of her old promise'.[70] Perhaps Hickes, then a bachelor, was considering the qualities of the unmarried Dorothy with more than casual interest!

In another, undated, letter to one of the male members of the family Hickes gave an interesting account of his appreciation of London, 'the only place of England to winter in'. He pointed out that there were three different types of life available, that of the Court, that of the city, and that of the country around. If a man tired of one, he could sample the delights of the others. 'When you are weary of your lodging,' he continued, 'you may walk into [St] Pauls, where you shall be sure to feed your eyes with gallant suits and fill your ears with foreign intelligences. In the middle aisle you may hear what the Protestants say, and in the out aisles what the Papists whisper, and when you have heard both believe but one, for but one of both says true, you may be assured.' The irony of the last remark is as typical of Hickes as is his concluding estimate of London as a place where 'you can want nothing ... if you want not money'.[71]

Hickes's gifts for friendship must have turned to a considerable extent on his ready wit and charm. We have seen the reputation which he acquired as excellent company in the 'merry circle' of which Cecil and he were members in the early 1590s, and it is clear that he was not often at a loss for words. On one very great occasion in his life, however, even he was completely bereft of speech. That was when the Queen visited him at Ruckholt in the autumn of 1597. On August 12th Henry Maynard informed him that he was to be the Queen's first host on her Essex progress,[72] and three days later he wrote again, reporting that he had been speaking with the Lord Chamberlain, George Carey, second Lord Hunsdon, about the state of Hickes's house. Hunsdon had been given to understand that Ruckholt was 'scant of lodgings and offices', whereupon, Maynard informed Hickes, 'I took occasion to tell his lordship that it was true, and I conceived it did trouble you that you had no convenient place to entertain some of her Majesty's servants.' Hunsdon replied that Hickes was not to worry about such trifles but advised that Mrs Hickes might present to the Queen, 'some fine waistcoat or fine ruff or like thing, which ... would be as acceptably taken as if it were of great price'. The visit was to be for 'two nights, as was first appointed'.[73] The Queen arrived on August 17th and left on the 19th.[74] Her stay was not a complete success. She got a favourable impression of the house itself and had words of praise for its mistress, but the usually voluble Hickes was overcome by the greatness of the occasion. He had intended to make an eloquent speech of welcome to his royal guest but, as he lamented to his friend Sir John Stanhope, Treasurer of the Chamber, 'the resplendence of her Majesty's royal presence and princely aspect did on a sudden so daunt all my senses and dazzle mine eyes as, for the time, I had use neither of speech nor memory'. He took some comfort from the fact that 'men of great spirit and very good speech have become speechless in the like case, as men astonished and amazed at the majesty of her presence'.[75]

A year after the Queen's visit Burghley died. It was a turning point in Hickes's life. His influence in Court circles from then on was based almost entirely on his friendship with Robert Cecil. That seems, on the whole, to have stood him in good stead in the years ahead, but after 1598 he certainly devoted much of his time to the offices which he acquired in local administration.

PART TWO

1598–1612
Country Gentleman and
Man of Affairs

6

The Government Official

Between 1598 and 1612, when he died, Michael Hickes held office in five different branches of local government. From 1598 until 1601 he was feodary of Essex; from 1603 to 1604 he was receiver-general of the revenues of the Crown lands in Middlesex, Essex, Hertfordshire, and London; from 1605 until 1612 he was a justice of the peace in Essex, and from 1609 until 1612 he held similar office in Middlesex; in 1606 he was appointed a commissioner for the assessment and collection of the subsidies granted by Parliament in that year; and from 1603 he was deputy chief steward and from 1608 chief steward of ten royal manors in Essex. These appointments gave him a wide experience of administration at grass-roots level at a time when local government, and especially the work of the justices of the peace, was far more important than the central administration to the vast majority of the population.

As feodary of Essex Hickes was an important cog in the machinery of the Court of Wards,[1] which had less than a dozen officials on its central staff but over forty representatives—the feodaries—in the localities. The officers in London were nominated by the Queen but the feodaries were appointed by the Master. In 1598 Burghley was at the very end of his long Mastership of thirty-seven years and after his death in August there was a bitter struggle between Essex and Robert Cecil for the vacant office, with all its resources of prestige and patronage. Cecil's victory in 1599, one of his most notable triumphs in his conflict with Essex, was followed by new policies in the Court of Wards, so Hickes's tenure of the Essex feodaryship came at a most interesting and important time in the history of the Court, the end of one Mastership and the beginning of another, which was to be an era of reform.

Hickes's role as feodary must be seen against the general background of the history and work of the Court of Wards as a whole. As we have already noted,[2] royal wardship, which had its original raison d'etre in the Middle Ages in the military services which tenants-in-chief owed to the king, had, by the sixteenth century, degenerated into a fiscal device which brought profits to both the Crown on the one hand and courtiers and officials on the other. In 1540 the Court of Wards was founded to control and exploit these profits and to carry out the necessary administrative and judicial functions connected with wardship. Upon the death of a tenant-in-chief the Crown immediately became entitled to take possession of his lands — the right known as *primer seisin* — and a writ was issued by Chancery ordering the taking of an *inquisition post mortem*, an inquiry which determined the location and quantity of the lands, put a valuation on them, and determined the name and age of the heir. If the heir was of full age he could sue out his 'livery', a process for which a fee was payable to the Court, and obtain possession of the lands. If he was a minor, control of his person and of at least a third of his lands passed to the Crown until he came of age at twenty-one (fourteen in the case of a female heir). Wards' lands were leased out in return for annual rents paid by the lessees to the Court, and the wardship of their bodies and the right to determine their marriages were sold to guardians who might or might not be the lessees of the lands. The guardianships of wards and leases of their lands only went to relations in a minority of cases; often they passed into the hands of influential courtiers or officials whose interest in their young charges was all too often confined to making as large a profit out of them as possible. Such profits could be made not only by ruthless exploitation of a ward's lands, but also by selling the ward in marriage to the highest bidder. It is hardly surprising that, by the end of Elizabeth's reign, wardship was very unpopular among the country gentry, who bore most of the burdens and enjoyed few of the profits.

It was by one of his last official acts that Burghley nominated Hickes to the feodaryship of Essex on July 15th, 1598.[3] A month later he was dead. His appointment, however, lived after him;

feodaries' patents were voided only by surrender or by the death of the reigning sovereign, although they could be cancelled at the discretion of the Court of Wards for neglect of duties or if a feodary became 'desperate and insolvent'.[4] Hickes's grant provided that he could exercise the office himself or by a sufficient deputy and he held it until July 1601 when it was granted, presumably on Hickes's surrender, to William Courtman.[5]

The office of wardship feodary probably began in 1513. In June of that year Sir Thomas Lovell, Treasurer of the King's Household, was appointed Master of the Wards, with the right to appoint feodaries and receivers of wards' lands. In August nineteen feodaries were appointed, most of them exercising the office for two counties.[6] By Elizabeth's reign there were forty-five and, with the exception of the combination of Rutland and Northamptonshire, they wielded authority in only one county, a sign of the extent to which their work had increased during the course of the century.[7]

The duties of feodaries were varied and numerous; and from 1599, with the appointment of Robert Cecil to the Mastership, a flood of orders poured from the Court, tightening up central control over them and setting out their responsibilities. In June 1599, just a month after he had taken office, Cecil ordered that no feodary was to exercise his authority until he had taken an oath before the Master to perform his duties properly.[8] In February 1600, among other provisions, he gave instructions that no feodary was to act by deputy unless that deputy was allowed by the Court and the permission placed on record. He also insisted that feodaries were always to be present at the taking of inquisitions, and that escheators, who were primarily responsible for the holding of inquisitions, were to give them notice twenty days beforehand.[9] Feodaries were required to survey the lands and property of wards, to certify vacancies in ecclesiastical benefices where the right of presentation belonged to a ward, to watch over wards' lands let out on lease, to search for concealed wardships, and, not the least important aspect of their work, to keep full accounts.[10] These are merely the more important of feodaries' many duties; they were the professional administrators of the Court of Wards in the localities, the men-of-all-work on whose efficiency and honesty its satisfactory working depended.

Hickes's patent of appointment granted him a basic fee of £2 per annum and he was also entitled to £1 for the 'portage' of every £100 which he brought up to London,[11] but these were trifling sums and it may be significant that when he himself drew up a list of the duties which he was required to perform and the additional fees which he might charge, he laid much stress on the fees. When, for example, he recorded his duty to collect, every six months, the rents reserved to the Crown from wards' lands let out on lease, he hastened to add that he was due 4d. from each lessee to whom he granted an acquittance for due payment of rent, and added—ominously perhaps from the point of view of Essex lessees—that 'some use to take 12d.'. He noted that he was to receive a fee of £2 for every inquisition held in the county, 'except it be a small matter', and that he might also be entitled to a further sum for 'charges and travail'. He could also expect an allowance from the Crown in proportion to the benefit which accrued to the Queen from his surveys of wards' lands, which might show that the lands were worth more and could therefore be leased for a greater sum than the values stated in the inquisitions. He added that the 'party'—it is not clear whether he meant the ward or the person to whom the lands were to be leased—could also be expected to pay for the work and charges of surveying, in proportion to the feodary's 'travail and pains'.[12]

Despite the importance of the feodary's survey, the *inquisition post mortem* was still, at the end of Elizabeth's reign, the pivot on which the whole work of the Court of Wards turned. It was the inquisition which determined whether or not any land was held of the Crown by knight service and whether or not the heir was a minor. If the heir was under age and held of the Crown by knight service in chief or by the unusual tenure of grand serjeanty then he was subject to the full rigours of wardship. If he was of age the findings were relevant in assessing the fine for livery.[13] There were three ways in which an inquisition could originate. If the lands of the heir were thought to be worth less than £5 per annum the escheator by virtue of his office (*virtuti officii*), could order the holding of an inquisition. For centuries, however, the common procedure had been for the inquisition to be held on the authority of a writ addressed to the escheator from Chancery. The result was a judicial inquiry, at which the escheator presided, before a jury empanelled by the sheriff. The jurymen, who were chosen because of their local knowledge, answered questions of fact about the deceased's lands and the age of his heir. The third system was to associate the escheator with a commission. The writ from Chancery was then addressed to the commissioners and not to the escheator alone, and it usually stated that certain named members of the commission must be present at the inquisition. The two scholars who have written most authoritatively on the Court of Wards attach great importance to this procedure by commission. Professor Hurstfield believes that it reflected the Crown's 'diminishing confidence in the authority and reliability of the escheator' and its increasing reliance on the feodary, who was 'invariably a member [of the commission]', and the late H. E. Bell also laid much emphasis on the growth of the feodary's, and the decline of the escheator's, importance by the end of the sixteenth century.[14]

It may be best to decide the importance of commissions on a statistical basis. Of the sixty-seven inquisitions held in Essex during the period November 1597 to November 1601, only three were held before commissions.[15] Of the other sixty-four, the escheator held one *virtuti officii*[16] and sixty-three on the authority of writs from Chancery.[17] We do not know how often the feodary was present when inquisitions were held by virtue of writs addressed to the escheator alone. Cecil's instructions of February 1600, which provided that feodaries were always to be present at the taking of inquisitions, implied that they had *not* always been in attendance before that date, and there is no means of telling how effective the new order was. Certainly, the Essex statistics do not suggest that the escheator was being pushed into the background. He was clearly still a very important figure at the beginning of the seventeenth century, which helps to explain the eagerness of local gentlemen to hold the office.[18]

It was notorious, at the end of the sixteenth century, that the valuations of lands in inquisitions were less than the real values, but the Master of the Wards had two other estimates of land values which he considered before determining the selling price of a wardship. He had 'particulars', estimates of the value of the inheritance prepared by suitors for wardships and, more important, he had the feodaries' surveys: valuations of the lands made by the feodaries or their deputies. A survey, however, dealt only with property in a single county, whereas an inquisition was supposed to take account of all lands. To compare inquisition and survey value, therefore, the master needed reports from the feodaries of all counties in which a deceased tenant-in-chief held land.[19] Eight feodaries' surveys have survived for Essex for the period 1599 to 1605. In five of these the values given of Essex lands were greater than the inquisition values.[20] In one case the values were the same.[21] In two cases, however, where some Essex lands which appeared in the inquisitions were omitted in the corresponding surveys, the total inquisition values for Essex were greater than the survey values.[22] All these surveys were made by Hickes's deputy feodary, John Meade, and the failure in two cases to include all the Essex lands must raise some questions about either his honesty or his capacity. The point is important because wards' lands were leased at annual rents equivalent to the values in the surveys.[23] The laxity or dishonesty of officials like Meade must have been especially irritating for Robert Cecil when, immediately after his appointment to the Mastership, he began a determined effort to raise the Crown's revenue from wardship. He did, however, have considerable success. The total net revenue of the Court for the year 1599–1600 was over £17,000, the largest since 1561–2. By 1601–2 it was over £22,000. A substantial part of this over-all revenue came from sales of wardships, which brought in £6,300 in 1560–1, but never again approached that figure during Burghley's Mastership. In fact wardship sales only once more realized over £4,000 during his lifetime. Within four years of his death they were bringing in over £8,500.[24]

The Master tended to relate the selling price of a wardship to the annual value of the ward's lands, though other factors were taken into consideration. At the beginning of Burghley's term of office over 80 per cent of wardships were sold at prices equivalent to not more than one and a half times the annual value of the lands. At the end of his Mastership just under 80 per cent were still sold at the same rate. Soon after Robert Cecil succeeded as Master more than 60 per cent of the sales were being made at three or four times the annual value of the lands.[25]

Turning from the general to the particular we can note that of the twenty-six Essex wardships sold between 1599 and 1605, twenty were sold at *three* or more times the annual value of the lands. We find, however, that the sale of the twenty-six wardships brought in £1,370, just over *double* the total annual value of the lands, which amounted to £656.[26] The reason was that some of the six wardships sold at less than the 'standard' rate were exceptionally valuable. Cecil's entry book of sales records that the wardship of Thomas Ayleworth, whose lands were valued at £154 a year, was sold for only £160 to Thomas Hibbots, to the use of Lady Scrope, 'because it was her Majesty's pleasure that she should have good benefit by it and not pay according to the rates now limited by my new instructions'.[27] An even more valuable wardship was that of Thomas Southwell, son and heir of Sir Robert Southwell, who had married Elizabeth Howard, daughter of Lord Admiral Nottingham. Sir Robert died when his son was only two years old and in November 1598 Nottingham, anxious about his grandson's wardship, sought Hickes's help. After noting that Hickes would have to survey all Southwell's lands in Essex Nottingham asked him 'to show unto my daughter the Lady Elizabeth ... for the easy values of the said lands and for her proceeding otherwise all the favour you may'.[28] We do not know how receptive Hickes was to this request from one of the greatest members of the Court circle, but it is certain that the other individual who was approached on Lady Southwell's behalf, the Queen herself, proved very accommodating. Young Southwell's lands were eventually valued at over £260 per annum but the wardship was sold to Lady Elizabeth in July 1599 for £400 'and no more, because her Majesty was pleased she should have one thousand pounds abated of all the fines'.[29] When it is noted that the wardship of John, son and heir of Edmund Fortescue, went to the Chancellor of the Exchequer, Sir John Fortescue, for only £30, although the lands were valued at £24 a year,[30] it becomes plain that the low rates in three cases benefited members of the Court circle. In two of these cases the wardship was sold at a low price by direct order of the Queen herself. In other words, Elizabeth was undermining her new Master's efforts to raise the revenue from wardship. She granted the earl of Nottingham's daughter a £1,000 reduction in price while the country gentry had to pay the increased charges. No wonder there were such loud and insistent demands for the abolition of wardship from country gentlemen in the House of Commons in the first Parliament of James I's reign.

The sale of wardships was one of two aspects of wardship revenue which could most conveniently be expanded. The other was fines for leases. Lessees of wards' lands, besides their annual rents, paid fines when they were first granted their leases. During Burghley's mastership the greatest amount brought in by these fines was between £1,200 and £1,300, in 1595–6. Within four years of his death they were producing a revenue of over £3,100 per annum.[31] An examination of fines for leases in Essex between 1596 and 1603, a period which includes the years of Hickes's feodaryship, shows this picture being reproduced at local level. Between 1596 and 1598 six out of nine fines were rated at between one and one and a half times the annual value of the lands, and the other three at between one and a half and two times the annual value. Between 1600 and 1603, in contrast, only one fine out of fifteen was less than twice the annual value and no less than eleven were three or more times greater.[32] These Essex figures are, therefore, another striking illustration of Robert Cecil's new policies.

When a ward's lands were eventually leased the local feodary had to collect and account for the rents due to the Crown from the lessee. During Hickes's three years as feodary of Essex he collected an average of £447 a year from these rents and paid to the Receiver-General of the Court of Wards an average of £356 annually, the difference between the two sums representing expenses of various kinds. His predecessor, Richard Glascocke, collected an average of £413 annually and his successor, William Courtman, an average of £389. Glascocke and Courtman paid to the Receiver-General average annual sums of £285 and £294 respectively.[33] Hickes, therefore, collected more money annually than either his predecessor or successor and paid out less than either in expenses. These figures seem to indicate that, from the Crown's point of view, he was a success as feodary. On the other hand, he was certainly a man who believed in looking to his own profits and the local gentry may have had reason to take a less favourable view of his years in office.

In May 1603, just under two years after he surrendered his feodaryship, Hickes was appointed Receiver-General of the Crown lands in Middlesex, Hertfordshire, Essex, and the City of London, an office which brought him an annual fee of £50, together with a portage allowance of £1 for every £100 which he collected.[34] He had been Receiver-General for just over a month when Lord Treasurer Buckhurst asked him to pay £10 a year to Dorothy Sotherton, the widow of one of his predecessors in the office. Mrs Sotherton had complained long before, during Burghley's Treasurership, that her husband had used her marriage portion to buy the position and then neglected to exercise it, allowing Smith, the man he should have replaced, to continue in office. After Sotherton's death Burghley had ordered Smith to pay her an annuity of £10 for the relief of herself and her four children. Buckhurst made it clear that if Hickes continued the payment it would be as a free gift, but, although we do not know Hickes's reaction, he can hardly have been pleased to receive such a request so soon after taking up his new office.[35]

During Hickes's receivership the Crown lands under his supervision produced a gross annual revenue of over £9,500.[36] He was thus responsible for a considerable sum of the Crown's money and he had an additional task laid on his shoulders on March 21st, 1604, four days before the feast of the Annunciation, when Buckhurst instructed him to receive the rents due at that feast from those of Queen Anne's lands which lay within the counties under his control. The extra work was assigned to him because the Queen's officers, in whose hands the duty of collection lay, were unable to perform the task by the appointed time. Having collected the money, Hickes was to hand it over to the Queen's Receiver-General.[37]

Although Hickes's appointment was for life he gave up the receivership after only a year. The reasons for his resignation after so short a time are unknown, but it may be guessed that, following common practice at the time, he sold the office to his successor John Davy, who was appointed in June 1604.[38] Hickes's period as Receiver was certainly brief but it must have added to that experience of the financial side of local administration which he had gained during his three years as feodary.

The significance of the position which Hickes held at the centre of the political world before 1598 and the fact that he was an important figure in local administration between 1598 and 1604 as feodary and Receiver-General make it rather surprising that he did not become a J.P. until 1605, when he was appointed to the Essex commission of the peace. Four years later he became a justice in Middlesex.[39] The unpaid office of J.P. was, of course, a medieval creation, but during the Tudor period there was a great increase in the work of the justices, who were required to assist in the enforcement of an ever-growing number of statutes. William Lambarde, in the 1599 edition of his *Eirenarcha*, the most famous sixteenth-century treatise on the justices' office, listed 306 such statutes, of which only 133 predated 1485. Some of the Elizabethan statutes in particular imposed on J.P.s complicated and vitally important roles in the administration of apprenticeship regulations, poor relief and the suppression of vagrancy, to mention only three of the most obvious and important categories. Statutes, however, represented only one source of the justices' powers and duties. The other, the commission of the peace, emphasized the judicial aspects of the office. It was issued annually and from 1590 came out in a new form which stressed the extensive powers of the justices both to inquire into and to judge breaches of common and statute law. Justices could deal with many matters singly or in small groups but some of their powers could only be exercised in quarter sessions, the meetings held four times a year at which all the justices in a county were supposed to be present. The number of justices grew very considerably during the sixteenth century, but this was not solely or perhaps even principally because of the great increase in their work-load. Throughout the period only a minority of J.P.s seem to have been active in any county and the initiative in increasing the size of the commissions of the peace seems to have come not from the Crown but from local gentlemen who regarded a seat on the bench as a mark of social prestige; it was considered a stigma for a man to be left out of the commission once he had achieved a certain standing in his locality.[40]

Hickes was certainly not one of the more active of the justices in either Essex or Middlesex. He was present at only one meeting of Essex quarter sessions during the entire seven years of his service on the Essex bench and did not attend a single meeting of Middlesex quarter sessions during his three years as a justice in that county.[41] Despite these failures to attend the regular meetings of the justices, Hickes did take cognizance of some of the multifarious duties which devolved outside quarter sessions upon Jacobean J.P.s. In November 1608 his friend and Essex neighbour Joseph Earth reported that his gamekeeper, who had long been troubled by poachers, had recently managed to catch up with them. He had got much the worse of the encounter, as the three culprits, 'armed with long staves and much malice', had beaten him about the body. The keeper had fled in terror and Earth asked Hickes to issue a warrant for the apprehension of the ruffians, and then, when they were caught, to punish them as he thought fit.[42] On another occasion Earth asked that one of his servants, who was to be brought before Hickes on a charge of fornication, might be dealt with lightly, as the woman in the case was a whore.[43] In the spring of 1609 Hickes was one member of a conference at which Essex justices aired the doubts which they felt about their powers to permit purveyors (the men responsible for supplying the royal household) to summon carts and carriages needed for the King's service from places far from where the supplies were to be loaded. They decided to seek a ruling from the early seventeenth-century legal oracle, Sir Edward Coke, who answered that only the officers of the Greencloth, the board responsible for the government of the royal household, had the right to summon carts from the farther parts of the county.[44] In May 1610 Hickes was asked to join with other justices in approving the building by John Hasenet, a bricklayer, of a new house near Ilford, a request which probably received sympathetic consideration from the bench, especially in view of the fact that another, now decayed, house had stood there only forty years before.[45] In May of the following year he was one of three Essex justices who met in London to discuss a petition from some tradesmen who lived near the city,[46] and in the spring of 1612 he was considering proposals to set up an inn at Ilford for the convenience of the grooms of the royal stables.[47]

In October 1611 the justices at the Michaelmas quarter sessions in Essex, at which Hickes was not present, issued directions to him and to two other justices to inspect 'certain decayed marsh bridges leading over Walthamstow and Leyton marshes'. These had been in constant use, time out of mind, by all those from the neighbouring towns and parishes who were in the habit of travelling on foot to the London markets. Hickes and his companions reported in the first instance in a letter of January 2nd,

1612, when they stated that twelve of the footbridges in question had decayed to such an extent that they could only be crossed with the greatest danger. Indeed, one man had already been drowned in attempting such a crossing and, just before the previous Christmas, two others had narrowly escaped a similar fate. They also certified that jurors whom they had called before them from several nearby parishes were unable to say who was liable to bear the cost of repairs. The justices considered the report at the Epiphany sessions of January 9th and 10th when they postponed a decision as to the measures to be taken until the Easter sessions following and, three days before the opening of the latter meeting, Hickes and the two other justices who had been directly concerned in investigating the problem submitted a suggestion that the whole county should be rated to bear the cost of repairs under the terms of a statute of Henry VIII's reign. Their letter is noted in the sessions records, but these make no mention of the decision finally taken.[48]

The evidence already cited of Hickes's work as a J.P., although it is slight, does give some idea of the range of duties which a paternalistic government heaped on the backs of these vitally important local agents. The remaining evidence about his activities as a justice relates to episodes in which he had personal as well as official interests. In June 1609 Sir Hugh Beeston and he, in their capacities as J.P.s, were commissioned to investigate slanders made against Salisbury — Cecil had been created earl of Salisbury in 1605 — by a certain Mr Wiseman.[49] As Beeston and Hickes were closely tied by bonds of service and affection to Salisbury and the Cecil family, Wiseman can hardly have had a pleasant interview. On December 16th, 1609, Hickes, together with his Essex neighbours and fellow justices Sir Robert Wroth and Thomas Fanshawe, examined Michael Pearson, an Essex husbandman who had seen service in the Low Countries. On December 9th Pearson had been in London, where he fell into the company of two soldiers. The three men made their way to a brewhouse 'to entreat the brewer to bestow some brew on them, and from thence to a cook's house at the Sign of the Ship to eat some victuals'. Later in the afternoon Pearson made his way out of London in the general direction of Hickes's house at Leyton, but was 'overtaken with drink' and slept under a hedge for some hours. When he woke up about ten o'clock he went to

Hickes's house. There, according to the charge against him, he broke into the stables. Pearson vehemently denied this, but on January 1st following he was indicted for being a sturdy rogue and vagabond. He was tried at quarter sessions on January 11th, and the verdict that he was 'a rogue but not an incorrigible rogue'[50] meant that he was liable to be whipped and then sent back to his birthplace. If he had been deemed incorrigible he would have been branded on the shoulder with a 'hot burning iron of the breadth of an English shilling, with a great Roman R upon the iron' and then banished from the realm and forbidden to return upon pain of death.[51]

As one of the leading local gentlemen, Hickes was appointed a commissioner in Essex for the three subsidies which were granted by Parliament to the Crown in 1606.[52] The duties of the commissioners were to supervise the assessment of those lay-men in the county who were not members of the peerage and to oversee the collection of the money. Subsidies originated in the reign of Henry VIII and became the main direct tax imposed by parliament. They were levied either on a man's income from land or on his personal property, whichever was of greater value, but Elizabeth and James I were unable to secure the co-operation of the local gentlemen in making realistic assessments, and the yield of these taxes slumped alarmingly during the Elizabethan and Jacobean periods. At the beginning of Elizabeth's reign a subsidy was worth nearly £140,000, whereas at the end of James's it was worth less than £70,000. This decline had already gone very far by 1606, when a subsidy was worth £75,000 or £80,000. These figures are even more dramatic than they seem at first sight because, owing to inflation, there was a substantial decline in the real value of the pound during the sixteenth and early seventeenth centuries. The commissioners, who constantly undervalued their neighbours' properties, were also notorious for the very low assessments which they placed upon their own lands and in 1594 the government threatened subsidy commissioners who were J.P.s and who assessed themselves at less than £20 with removal from the commission of the peace.[53] Throughout his career as commissioner Hickes was assessed at £20 in land,[54] thus complying with the letter if not the spirit of the government directive. There is little material in Hickes's private papers about his work as a commissioner. In

January 1607 arrangements were made for him to meet others among the commissioners to discuss the appointment of assessors, who fixed, under the commissioners' supervision, the values at which men were rated.[55] The commissioners could raise the rates fixed by the assessors and, even though such improved valuations might still be considerable under-assessments of the real value of the lands, the parties who were treated in this way could hardly be expected to see the matter in that light. Hickes himself received complaints from Nicholas Steward, a civil lawyer who had had his assessment raised.[56]

In June 1603, three years before Hickes was made a subsidy commissioner, his patron Robert Cecil was appointed chief steward of ten royal manors in Essex. The terms of the appointment permitted him to exercise the office by deputy,[57] and it is clear that he employed Hickes in that capacity. In the winter of 1603, when he passed the chief stewardship over to Charles Blount, earl of Devonshire, who had an Essex residence at Wanstead, he did so on condition that Hickes should retain his post.[58] Devonshire died on April 3rd, 1606,[59] and nine days later Salisbury received a new grant of the chief stewardship, which he surrendered again in July 1608, this time to Hickes.[60]

Hickes was responsible for the royal manors at a time when the Crown's serious financial difficulties led James I's advisers, particularly Salisbury, to make important efforts to increase the royal revenues, and the policies which Hickes was asked to pursue in Essex can only be understood against the wider background of the Crown's general financial position. In the sixteenth and early seventeenth centuries men drew a basic distinction between ordinary and extraordinary revenue and expenditure. In normal times the general assumption was that the Crown would 'live of its own', that is to say it would pay the everyday running expenses of government out of its ordinary revenue—the money coming to it year in year out from such sources as the Crown lands, customs duties, wardship, and the profits of justice. In times of emergency, principally in wartime, the Crown could ask the help of its subjects to meet extraordinary expenditure. That help was provided by parliamentary subsidies and, because of the political difficulties which the grant of subsidies often produced for the government, they have generally received a good deal more attention in textbooks than the Crown's ordinary revenue. In purely financial terms, however, it was ordinary revenue which was by far the more important. The parliamentary taxation which James I received between 1603 and 1621 totalled £913,000, an average of less than £51,000 per annum, whereas the ordinary revenue for these years probably averaged about £450,000 per annum. In any study of Elizabethan and early Stuart finance, therefore, it is the ordinary revenue and expenditure which is crucial. Elizabeth's policy was rigid economy in ordinary expenditure. Between 1590 and 1602, for example, she not only balanced ordinary revenue and expenditure but even carried a surplus to the extraordinary account; in the 1590s she was saving about £100,000 a year from her ordinary revenue, which she used to help the English war effort against Spain.

When James I came to the throne there was a vast increase in ordinary expenditure. This had averaged no more than £300,000 a year during Elizabeth's last five years, but in 1609 it was running at about £500,000 per annum. Ordinary revenue had also increased, but to nothing like the same extent. As a result the Elizabethan surplus on the ordinary account had been wiped out and instead there was a substantial annual deficit. This situation, of course, contravened the basic financial principle of the time: that the Crown was expected to live within its means except in wartime—and the war with Spain had come to an end in 1604. The reason for the huge rise in ordinary expenditure is clear enough. It was royal extravagance. James I spent money like water upon himself, his family and his favourites. Lucky courtiers were delighted by the change from the lean last years of the Elizabethan period, but the result for the royal finances was disastrous. Between 1603 and 1610 James's spending policies led the Crown towards an insolvency from which it could only hope to be rescued by huge parliamentary grants, by dramatic changes in royal land administration, or by a drastic cutback in expenditure. James, despite occasional good intentions, was incapable of carrying through the last. Parliamentary grants, however, seemed a possible solution and the financial history of the years 1606 to 1610 can be seen in terms of a coherent government plan to solve the Crown's financial problems, a plan which culminated in the Great Contract of 1610, by which the King, in return for a parliamentary grant of

£200,000 a year, was to give up wardship and purveyance and make various other concessions to Parliament. The Contract eventually failed because of the suspicions of both the King and the House of Commons of the other's good intentions; and its collapse was a disastrous blow to its principal protagonist, Salisbury, who lost much of his influence with the King, though he retained all his offices until his death in 1612.[61] Historians are still by no means agreed on the general significance of the Contract[62] and there is need also for more detailed investigation into the respective roles of Buckhurst (Lord Treasurer from 1599 to 1608) and Salisbury (Lord Treasurer from 1608 to 1612) in the financial history of the early years of James's reign. Certainly, when we turn to the policy adopted towards the Crown lands between 1603 and 1612, Buckhurst, just as much as Salisbury, appears as a reformer and innovator.

Many manorial tenants held their lands as copyholders, that is on terms stated in a 'copy' of the manorial roll. When a new tenant was admitted to copyhold land he paid a fine to the lord of the manor. Sometimes this was a fixed sum, but often it was 'arbitrable' or, as we would say, at the will of the lord, who, in the case of royal manors, was the King. On February 15th 1604, Hickes, then acting as Devonshire's deputy, received orders from Lord Treasurer Buckhurst about copyhold land which was subject to arbitrable entry fines. No new tenants were to be admitted to such land in the manor of Eastnewhall, one of the ten manors under Hickes's stewardship, except by special permission from Buckhurst, who also instructed Hickes to send him a certificate of all the annual copyhold rents of the manor together with details of the terms on which the tenants held their lands and estimates of the true value of one acre each of meadow, pasture and arable. In addition, Hickes was required to provide particulars of all timber standing upon copyhold land and to state whether there were any mines on the manor.[6] Hickes seems to have been forewarned of Buckhurst's instructions and demands because, the day before the latter's letter was written, he himself sent a questionnaire to his understeward William Waldegrave, asking about surveys previously taken of Essex manors and demanding information about technical matters relevant to the administration of the royal lands.[64]

It seems that these moves by Buckhurst and Hickes reflected

an intention on the former's part to institute a general survey of all the Crown lands,[65] which were often grossly undervalued and consequently let out at very low rents that, if they could be substantially raised, would bring a most welcome increase in royal revenue. Buckhurst's restrictions on the admission of new copyhold tenants seem to have applied to all royal manors, and Hickes had to get special permission to institute new tenants into copyhold land at Dovercourt and Barking.[66] It was not, in fact, until after Salisbury became Lord Treasurer in May 1608 that the general policy of prohibiting new admissions was reversed. In June 1608 Hickes received instructions to return to the practice in use before Buckhurst's orders.[67] It is not suggested that Salisbury's rejection of one of his predecessor's measures implied a general repudiation of Buckhurst's land policy. On the contrary, he took up and developed some of the most important of the latter's schemes. Buckhurst appointed commissioners to survey the royal lands in many English counties and it was his instructions which were responsible for the surveying of three hundred manors by John Hercy.[68] Salisbury too—in the summer of 1608—instituted a series of surveys which, like Buckhurst, he hoped to be able to use to raise Crown rents.[69]

A survey of the manor of Barking, one of the surveys ordered by Salisbury, was begun on May 25th, 1609, and continued for several days. Hickes, as chief steward, presided over the proceedings at the head of a commission of four. Nineteen jurors provided detailed descriptions of the holdings of the free and customary tenants and of the boundaries of the manor. The procedures adopted on the deaths of customary tenants and for the sale of copyhold lands were also discussed in detail, as were the rights of copyholders and the method of searching the court rolls.[70] The customary rents of the manor, which amounted to £103 a year, were less than one-sixth of the true annual value of £682.[71] These figures give some idea of the scope which existed for improving royal land revenues by charging something approaching market rents. In 1608 the net return from the Crown lands was about £87,000,[72] and while it would be absurd to suggest that this could rapidly have been increased by as much as 600 per cent, a considerably smaller percentage increase could have worked wonders for Crown finances.[73] That, of course, is making the admittedly large assumption that James I would not simply have squandered the extra revenue. In any event, it was a tragedy from the Crown's point of view that surveys were not completed for the whole country. It may be that Salisbury's preoccupation with the Great Contract pushed less immediately urgent matters to the back of his mind; and after 1610, when he was both a sick and a discredited man, he probably had little energy to spare for some of his earlier reforming projects. The abandonment of the policy of surveys meant that there was no hope of raising Crown rents to anything approaching an economic level. Many of the ancient rents persisted unchanged and by 1619, as a combined result of land sales made necessary by the failure of the Great Contract and lax Exchequer administration of what remained, the annual return from the Crown lands had dropped to £73,000.[74]

After Salisbury had made arrangements, immediately following his appointment to the Treasurership, to continue the series of surveys instituted by Buckhurst, he turned his attention to the problem of entry fines. We have seen that he reversed Buckhurst's policy of refusing new admissions to copyhold land and on December 20th, 1608, he explained his own policy to Hickes's deputy, William Waldegrave. Arbitrable entry fines, he stated, had generally been assessed at either twice or one and a half times the annual value of the lands. The Crown was willing to reduce such fines—he did not say by how much—provided some immediate payment ('composition' as he called it) was made to the Exchequer. He instructed stewards to assemble the tenants within the manors for which they were responsible and to explain the Crown's proposals. Several tenants were then to be appointed by their fellows to discuss the matter in the Exchequer Chamber on January 26th following with himself, the Chancellor of the Exchequer, and the Lord Chief Baron of the Exchequer.[75] In accordance with these instructions, courts were held at Copford, East Mersey, Dovercourt, Orsett, and Barking between January 9th and 17th, although it is not clear whether they were held before Hickes himself or before Waldegrave, acting as his deputy.[76] In each of these manors, with the exception of Copford, the reaction of the copyholders, when they were informed of the Crown's proposals, was to appoint representatives to discuss them in London on the stipulated

7 Sir Walter Raleigh, 1588 (*attributed to the monogrammist H.*)

8 James I (? by John de Critz)

day,[77] though this must not necessarily be taken to indicate that they approved of suggestions which would have meant heavy expenses for themselves as sitting tenants so that their successors could benefit from reduced entry fines. The tenants at Copford certainly opposed the proposals firmly from the start. Their immediate reaction was to draw up a petition asking that the system might continue as it then stood. Moreover, they did not appoint representatives to attend the meeting in London.[78] It seems unlikely that the resistance of the Copford copyholders was an isolated case of reluctance to comply with the scheme. The tenants of Clitheroe in Lancashire certainly adopted a similar attitude.[79]

The courts at which Salisbury's policy had been explained were exceptional meetings, but the manors in Hickes's charge did have their regular court days. At Barking two courts baron and one court leet were held annually.[80] In the courts baron Hickes, as steward, was the judge in all manorial cases among the copyhold tenants. In the annual court leet he exercised the jurisdiction of the sheriff's 'tourn', his principal duty being to see that the ancient frankpledge machinery, which associated each man with a group of his fellows in mutual guarantees of good behaviour, was in working order.[81] At Barking one of the courts baron and the court leet were held, at the same time, in the spring, and the other court baron took place in the autumn.[82] The courts were held in the manor's fine court-house, built during the years 1567 and 1568 at a cost of over £300. The tenants assembled in the spacious court-room, twelve yards in length, where Hickes presided from a dais which stood at the southern end, beneath the sculptured royal arms.[83] These courts may not have been too unpopular with the tenants, who were allowed dinner at the Crown's expense.[84]

Hickes's private papers reveal the wide range of manorial business with which he dealt. On August 23rd, 1608, he was asked to permit the holding of a special court of the manor of East Mersey to allow the entry of one of the bailiffs of Colchester into 40 acres of copyhold land. Three days later he granted permission.[85] In the summer of 1610, when he agreed to permit John Hayes, a yeoman, to act as guardian of the lands of a child of eight who held of the manor of Barking, he insisted that Hayes should provide adequate security to guarantee

E

honest administration of the property.[86] Although his understeward, William Waldegrave, was available to help with
manorial business,[87] Hickes was expected to deal personally
with some very trivial matters, such as a request from the vicar
of Barking for permission to buy two decayed trees on the
manor.[88] When Hickes was plagued by such demands he may
have consoled himself with the thought that his position as
steward enabled him, on occasion, to favour a relative. Sir
Thomas Lowe, husband of Hickes's sister-in-law, asked, when
he was admitted a tenant of the manor of Barking, that his
entry fine might be assessed leniently.[89] It is likely that his
request met with sympathetic consideration. On at least one
occasion Hickes was faced with potentially serious trouble. In
the spring of 1612 Hamlet Clark, one of the tenants of Barking
enclosed some of his lands, and this led to protests by 'sundry
people, who threatened violence. Hickes quickly issued a warrant instructing that disturbers of the peace were to be brought
before him.[90]

Many of the manors of which Hickes became steward in 1608
did not remain for long in the royal possession. The great land
sales of the early Jacobean period were a reflection of the extent
of the government's financial embarrassment—between 1605
and 1613 James sold lands worth £37,000 a year for £655,000.[91]
The sales which took place immediately before the Great Contract were undertaken on Salisbury's initiative in order to reduce the large Crown debt to respectable proportions before his
appeal to Parliament, and after the failure of the Contract in
1610 further sales were necessary in order to keep the Crown
solvent. These policies can be seen in operation, at local level
in Essex. It is true that Barking, the most important of the
manors under Hickes's control, did remain in the Crown's
hands until 1628,[92] but East Mersey and Copford were sold in
1609 and 1610 respectively,[93] and the sale of Dovercourt was
under discussion in the winter of the latter year.[94] In the spring
of 1611 Hickes was instructed to give notice to all within the
county of Essex who might be interested in purchasing land that
the Crown was prepared to sell[95]—a sad ending to Salisbury's
plans in 1610, at the time of the Great Contract, for preserving
and increasing the profitability of the remaining Crown lands.

During the last four years of his life, when he was a J.P.,

subsidy commissioner and a royal land administrator, Hickes must have spent a lot of his time on the problems of local government. In the same period, moreover, he had to devote attention to the central administrative office to which he was appointed in 1609, when he was made one of three deputies of the Lord Treasurer and the Chancellor of the Exchequer in the Alienation Office. The Alienation Office was set up in 1576, when Queen Elizabeth granted to the earl of Leicester the right to collect the dues — 'fines' as they were called — previously paid to Chancery by those who wished to sell freehold land or land held in chief of the Crown. After Leicester's death in 1588 the Crown took over direct control of the Office and in 1590 the right of supervising the collection of the fines was granted to the Lord Treasurer and the Chancellor of the Exchequer. In 1595 they were also made responsible for the fines paid by those who wished to sell entailed land.[96]

On May 11th, 1608, exactly a week after Salisbury became Lord Treasurer, letters patent were issued conferring control of the Alienation Office upon him and Sir Julius Caesar, Chancellor of the Exchequer. The terms of the patent permitted Salisbury and Caesar to direct the office through deputies, who were given extensive powers — two deputies acting together could even discharge any person absolutely from the need to pay a fine.[97] Hickes was made a deputy on January 17th, 1609,[98] and took up his duties within a few days.[99] He was one of a staff which consisted of the three deputies, a master in chancery, a receiver-general, and three clerks.[100] Each of these officials, with the exception of the master in chancery, was paid an annual fee which was deducted from the profits of the Office. In 1608 the deputies and the receiver-general were each paid £100, the chief clerk £26. 13s. 4d., and the two under-clerks £20 each.[101] The receiver-general, who handled all the money, was required to give security for his honesty.[102]

The fines which the staff of eight levied and collected were assessed as fixed proportions of the annual value of the lands concerned.[103] The decisive step in determining the amount of a fine was taken, therefore, when the annual value of the lands was assessed. To understand how these crucial valuations were made it is necessary to examine in more detail the procedure of the Office.[104] Land values could be assessed in either of two ways. They could be fixed by affidavit, a sworn statement made by the seller before the justices of assize or the chief justice of Common Pleas or the master in chancery, who was a member of the Alienation Office staff. Alternatively, they could be settled by an agreement known as a 'composition' made between the seller on the one hand and the Alienation Office deputies on the other. After the value of the lands was settled, whether by affidavit or composition, the receiver levied the appropriate fine and the second clerk of the Office entered the details in a book. After the entry had been made the deputies ascertained that the correct procedure had been followed at all stages in the making of the grant.

The importance of the complete discretion which the deputies had in assessing land values becomes very plain when it is noted that in the early years of James's reign almost all such values were agreed by composition rather than by affidavit.[105] Clearly it was open to those who had business in the Office to try to persuade the deputies to compound for a low annual value. Lord Danvers of Dantsey, Lord President of Munster, and Gilbert Talbot, earl of Shrewsbury, certainly asked for Hickes's favour in their business with the Office,[106] and it is improbable that they were his only suitors. Hickes usually expected some return for services rendered and we may doubt whether he shared the views of the anonymous official who wrote at the end of Elizabeth's reign that those deputies who took 'one penny besides their known allowance' bought such gratuities 'at the dearest price that may be ... the shipwreck of conscience and ... the irrecuperable loss of their honesties and credit'.[107]

Hickes's work at the Alienation Office was carried out while Salisbury was doing everything in his power to raise the royal revenue. Income from the Office rose from an annual average of £5,800 in the years 1604 to 1608, to an average of £7,250 per annum during the years from 1608 to 1612, the period of Salisbury's Treasurership.[108] No written orders from Salisbury to the deputies seem to have survived and we cannot be certain how Hickes and his colleagues obtained the extra money. It may simply be that much more land was changing hands between 1608 and 1612 than during the previous four years,[109] but it is also possible that Salisbury instructed the deputies to assess lands at higher values. He had, from 1600 onwards, tried to get feodaries to raise the values set upon wards' lands, since these formed the basis on which the selling prices of the wardships were calculated,[110] and he may have kept that precedent before him when he turned his attention to the Alienation Office. At any rate, whatever the reasons for the expanding revenue of the Office, it must have pleased Hickes and done his credit with Salisbury no harm at a time when, as we shall see, the personal relationship between the two men was probably a good deal less close and warm than it had been in earlier years.

7

Michael Hickes and Robert Cecil

When a Tudor minister died and his household was dispersed his secretaries sometimes passed into the service of other ministers where they could hope to continue with similar duties. This, as we have seen, is what happened to Henry Maynard who entered Burghley's service soon after the death of Lord Keeper Sir Nicholas Bacon.[1] In view of Michael Hickes's close personal friendship and political association with Robert Cecil before 1598, it might have been expected that he would become Cecil's secretary after Burghley's death. In fact, he did not. Cecil had a more elaborate secretarial organization than his father, with four secretaries in 1600 and no fewer than seven or eight during the years after 1608,[2] but Michael Hickes was never a member. He did do work for Cecil in the years after 1598, but this reflected the personal friendship between the two men rather than any more formal association.

In the anxious weeks after Burghley's death in August 1598 Cecil turned to Hickes for support. Hickes even made an offer of hospitality at that time to Cecil's children, but Cecil declined the favour because of his daughter's illness.[3] Cecil soon tired of the angry family bickering which followed his father's death. In a letter to Hickes he poured out his complaints, expressed weariness, and at the same time revealed the confidence which he had in his friend. Burghley had passed on to Cecil the guardianship of his two granddaughters, the Ladies Bridget and Susan Vere daughters of the earl of Oxford, and had bequeathed all the goods, money, plate, and valuables which remained in his bedchamber in Cecil House in Westminster to Robert Cecil and these two grandchildren. The goods were to be divided by his faithful steward, Thomas Bellot, and by the dean of Westminster.[4] These provisions led to much bad feeling. 'Be you sure my brother [Thomas Cecil] thinks so hardly to have none of the jewels,' wrote Robert Cecil to Hickes,

> as I fear now he will stand upon all advantages. But I will never consent ... to break my father's testament. For my private things at Theobalds, good Mr Hickes, end them, for I am weary of the noise of such beggarly things as they are and will be when they are at best. I commit all to you. Tell Mr Bellot [that], if the earl of Oxford should desire the custody [of his daughters], he can not have them of anybody ... Whether he that never gave them [a] groat, [and] hath a second wife and another child, be a fit guardian, consider you ... I wish Mr Bellot to have good care they be not stolen away by his means ... When you are there I pray you take order with my wardrober, that any stuff they want or anything else may be given them.[5]

For a time after 1598, indeed, Hickes seems to have attended to much of Cecil's personal business—he became a kind of extraordinary domestic supervisor. On one occasion in 1599 he was concerned, at one and the same time, with passing on instructions to Cecil's servant John Styleman; with negotiating successfully on Cecil's behalf for the lease of a house; and with conducting intricate negotiations for the renting of one of Cecil's deer parks.[6] In January 1600 he concerned himself about the killing of some of Cecil's deer.[7] In March of the same year he gave Styleman instructions about the conservation of Cecil's timber, ordered Cecil's factotum Amyas to finish his master's business in Rutlandshire, and busied himself with the task of procuring the lease of some parkland for Cecil. He was also concerned at that time with arrangements for bringing up to London some of Cecil's goods which had been 'laid by' at Theobalds.[8] Two months later, when he was on the point of undertaking another domestic assignment for Cecil, he was told that he need not trouble, as Styleman could do the job perfectly well.[9] From 1601 there is no evidence to suggest that Hickes acted as overseer of Cecil's personal affairs. The latter seems to have made use of other agents.

It is certain, however, that Hickes and Cecil remained close friends. In January 1603, when Cecil thanked Hickes for his New Year's gift, he told him, 'I can not write so much as I would if thanks be judged by many words ... I take your token as it is meant, and mean to you, as I say in few words, which is that I am your affectionate friend.'[10] Few words were needed between the two at that time. Their fondness for each other was not in doubt. Meanwhile, Hickes did not confine his presents to gifts at New Year. In April 1603 he sent rabbits and in the following month rabbits and asparagus. In July Elizabeth Hickes, not to be outdone by her husband, told Cecil that her apricots were beginning to ripen and promised him a supply as soon as they were worth sending.[11] In May 1605 Hickes again sent asparagus together with a letter congratulating Cecil on his elevation to the earldom of Salisbury. Cecil replied, 'I thank you for your congratulation and for your wish that I had *otium cum dignitate* ... though I fear I shall not be so happy ... If you be at London this week, I shall be there.'[12] Hickes's presents did not go unrequited. On one occasion Cecil sent him a hawk and promised to try to obtain some venison for him.[13] Cecil at times entrusted some of his valuables to Hickes's keeping. In December 1603 he wrote to him, 'You have a jewel of mine, with a pearl at it. I pray you, do me the pleasure to send me the pearl only by my servant, for I could now use it ... You may send it by my footman ... in a little box, as if it were no such matter, and, if he be robbed or lose it, I will discharge you.'[14] Cecil received the box safely.[15] Hickes and Cecil were both interested in bee-keeping and when the latter obtained details of a beehive 'project' Hickes borrowed the document. In October 1605 the original lenders ask for the return of their plan and Cecil wrote to his friend accordingly.[16]

After 1598 Cecil and Hickes had continued to find pleasure in each other's company. 'Mr Hickes,' wrote Cecil in September 1602

Being now come to the town and meaning to stay here for two or three days, because I would be glad of your company I have thought good to advertise you so much. But if you be not in good health, or that you have some extraordinary business of your own, my meaning is not to trouble you, for I have no other occasions with you but for matters of friendship.[17]

In October 1603 he wrote in similar terms. He had come up to London and wanted to see Hickes. 'Business I have none with you but to see you,' he told him, and concluded with a warning to avoid all villages on the journey for fear of the serious outbreak of plague which was causing so much alarm to all classes in the community at that time.[18] On another autumn day, two years later, when Cecil was planning to ride out of town, he asked for the pleasure of Hickes's company on the trip.[19]

It seems clear that in 1605 Hickes and Cecil were still firm friends. A letter of August 14th throws light on the relationship between the two at that time. Cecil had been invited by Sir Thomas Smith to be one of the godfathers of his son. He was willing, but business prevented him from being present in person. He therefore commissioned Hickes to be his proxy and asked him to obtain a basin and ewer worth about forty pounds and to present them on his behalf. Hickes was also to be sure to give the nurse £2 and the midwife £1. Cecil went on to tell his friend that he had bestowed a certain wardship upon the earl of Northumberland, who had given notice of its existence, 'when you were either sleeping with a handsome woman or bowling upon a fair green, which makes me fear that you and I shall never meet in heaven, seeing you have so pleasant a life upon earth'. He continued by asking Hickes to give his regards to their mutual friend Sir Hugh Beeston and to commiserate with him in his misfortune in being left behind in London when Sir Walter Cope, Hickes, and he himself were to meet at Oxford. He also told Hickes to be sure, before he set off for Oxford to join the Court, to pay a visit to the Tower to see the royal lion cubs, as the King was anxious to know how they were faring.[20]

After 1605 the number of letters which passed between Salisbury and Hickes seems to have declined. Fewer at any rate have survived. Salisbury was still anxious, on occasion, as in April 1606, to have Hickes's company.[21] In January 1608 he accepted the latter's New Year's gift with appropriate remarks about their mutual friendship and understanding and the following month asked him once again, provided his health was sufficiently good, to accompany him on a journey.[22] At the end of 1608 Hickes presented Salisbury with a piece of plate and told him that he sent it 'with the heartiest wishes both of health and happiness to your lordship this year and many'.[23] The two men, in short, remained on amicable terms. The tone of Salisbury's letters, however, underwent a change. August 14th, 1605 was the last occasion of which we have record on which he addressed Hickes in the terms of gay intimacy that had characterized his earlier correspondence.

Hickes continued to concern himself with Salisbury's wants and welfare. Sometime between 1608 and 1612 he provided Salisbury with some books which the latter required and, at the same time, drew up a prayer which reflected his concern for Salisbury's spiritual welfare.[24] In the autumn of 1609, when he visited his friend Sir Edward Suliarde, and found Suliarde's grapes 'as good as ever I tasted of for the relish and sweetness', his thoughts at once turned to Salisbury and he asked Suliarde to send some to the Lord Treasurer. In due course one of Suliarde's servants brought a basket of the grapes to Ruckholt for transmission to Salisbury. The letter which Hickes sent with them is touching. It shows the trouble which he obviously took over so trivial a matter and suggests that he still felt great affection for Salisbury.[25]

The warmth of Salisbury's own feelings by 1609 must be more in doubt. This becomes apparent when we turn to the 'political' aspect of the Hickes–Cecil relationship after 1598. Hickes continued, after that date, to receive a flood of letters[26] from clients, all as anxious to obtain his good offices with his friend Robert Cecil as their predecessors a decade before had been desirous of his word in Burghley's ear. Some of these letters concerned wardship, a reflection of the fact that in 1599 Cecil succeeded his father as Master of the Court of Wards. In 1604 Hickes's friend Roger Manners, a familiar figure in Court circles, asked him to move Cecil to bestow a wardship on his nephew, Sir Charles Manners. The letter contained a hint that Hickes would not be the poorer for his pains.[27] In 1610 William Vaughan, a servant of the earl of Worcester, approached Hickes with a letter from his master. The earl had heard that Hickes had the grant of a wardship which Vaughan wanted. Worcester asked that Vaughan might get preference before others and added that, if the wardship was of too little value to concern Hickes directly, he might pass Vaughan on to whoever was immediately concerned.[28] The last surviving letter in which Hickes was asked to deal with a wardship problem came from a man of a very different social standing, one John Tailer, who was outside the court circle. It was dated May 1611 and was concerned with the wardship of Tailer's grandson. Tailer wanted it to go to his daughter, the child's mother, and asked Hickes to further the suit.[29]

Hickes was not slow in advancing his own claims for wardships, but he was not always successful. In 1602 he angled for the wardship of Elizabeth Bassett.[30] On that occasion he certainly aimed high, as Elizabeth was a considerable heiress. In due course she married first of all a member of the Howard family and secondly William Cavendish, later first duke of Newcastle, to whom she brought an income estimated at £2,400 a year. It is hardly probable that Hickes expected to enjoy personally all the profits from such a prize. He may have been prepared to let a large part pass to Cecil. This possibility is reinforced by a statement made by Cecil when he refused Hickes's request. Cecil remarked that the Court was absolutely full of importunities for the wardship, and, he went on,

> though it b[e] not so much as fools do think it, yet it would stir too much envy f[or] me to give [it to you] or to father [it] upon [you]. In which respect, I have been driven to some other course to draw some benefit to myself ... but as if some great person had my grant for the mother and not ... any whom they would suspect so much to be but my figure, as they would do you.

Cecil was clearly determined to enjoy the profits himself and was quite prepared to deceive for his own ends. In fact, he found as 'front men' no less personages than Lord Cobham and Sir Walter Raleigh. He did hasten to assure Hickes that his refusal was not 'out of ... indisposition to do you pleasure, for I would be very glad to gratify where I love, but because I know you will in this particular see some circumstances which may vary from both our purpose'. He would do what he could to gratify him in 'some other matter'.[31] Cecil was as good as his word. In 1603, when he informed Hickes that the best way to obtain Lord Treasurer Buckhurst's favour was to offer Buckhurst's notoriously corrupt daughter, Lady Glemham, a bribe of £100, he promised to find Hickes a ward to pay for the bribe or else to give him twice the sum paid to Lady Glemham.[32]

In August 1604 Hickes was bidding for another wardship. The ward in question was the son of an old servant of Burghley. The dying father had written to Cecil, who had shown the 'pitiful letters' to other suitors for the wardship and had put them off with promises of future favour. 'This hath been my best answer,' he told Hickes, 'and if you look well into all our cases, yourself will think it hard not to be so respected if ever it should happen [to you], which I hope it shall not'.[33] The implication was that a relative was to get the wardship, and it says something for Cecil that he did not sacrifice past services to present importunities. On August 8th, 1605, Hickes's Essex friend Joseph Earth sent him word of an extraordinary 'accident' which had happened the previous day, when a Devonshire knight had wilfully run a man through with his sword. The man died, and thereupon the knight cast himself backwards upon his own sword and then ran himself through from the front. As a result, he was on the point of death. His lands were worth £800 a year and his heir was his five-year-old daughter. Earth thought that the wardship would be worth £1,000 and suggested that Hickes should ask Salisbury for it 'with all speed'.[34] Hickes clearly did so, but he was disappointed. Less than a week later Salisbury informed him that it had gone elsewhere.[35] In September 1610, on the last known occasion on which Hickes asked for a wardship for himself, Cecil again informed him that he could not meet the request, as he had already promised it to another.[36]

After 1598, just as before that date, Hickes was asked to further a wide range of suits, from requests to be taken into Cecil's service,[37] to a plea on behalf of Sir Anthony Dering for the lieutenancy of the Tower of London.[38] This last request was made in May 1604, in the expectation that the aged Sir George Harvey, who held the lieutenancy, was about to retire. In fact, Harvey continued to hold the office until 1605, when he was succeeded by Sir William Waad.[39] A man who appreciated Hickes's influence was Robert Fletcher, one of the King's cart-takers for the city of London. In the spring of 1604 Fletcher advised his fellow cart-takers to avoid commandeering any of Hickes's carts for the King's service. Hickes, he affirmed, was 'a gentleman that may pleasure any of us more in one hour than we can do him in seven years ... whereof myself have had good proof'.[40] In April 1607 the earl of Mar wrote on behalf of Mr Chadwick, who had previously been one of Salisbury's chaplains and now wanted the position again. 'Because your worth and desert hath made you gracious with my lord of Salisbury,' he told Hickes, 'I thought I could not make any choice of better means than yourself to recommend ... [the] suit.'[41] In September 1608 Pierce Pennant asked Hickes to help him to obtain the surveyorship of the Queen's woods,[42] and the following month Guy Godolphin wrote on behalf of his son, who had a debt due to him from the Exchequer. 'Two or three words of your mouth unto Sir Julius Caesar may easily procure him his money,' he told Hickes.[43] Godolphin may have exaggerated Hickes's ability to extract money from the notoriously slow-moving Exchequer machinery, but another client, Sir Robert Jacob, does seem to have owed a great deal to Hickes's efforts on his behalf. In April 1610 he asked Hickes to use his influence with Salisbury to obtain for him a grant of lands in Ireland, where, for some years, he had been Solicitor-General, a place which he had obtained on Hickes's recommendation.[44]

As Jacob's appointment shows, Hickes's clients sometimes obtained the posts they sought. John Shirley, a suitor for appointment as a serjeant-at-law, told Hickes, 'for any good you shall do me [in my suit] ... I will be very thankful'. He got the position and Hickes probably got the implied gratuity.[45] Some suitors were less fortunate. Sir John Morice tried, in 1606, to secure the appointment of his candidate for a serjeanty by Hickes's mediation.[46] He failed. In July 1607 Edward Bromley asked Hickes to help him obtain the surveyorship of the liveries, the most senior post in the Court of Wards after the Mastership itself. He did not get the job.[47] Another unlucky client was Paul Thomson. He was so eager to obtain the mastership of Trinity College, Cambridge, that he tried to secure Hickes's help before the post was vacant. Thomas Nevill, the master, who was seriously ill in January 1610, when Thomson asked for Hickes's aid, recovered and lived until 1615.[48]

Cecil's own servants did not hesitate to ask Hickes to intercede with their master on their behalf. When some of them heard, in the spring of 1608, that Cecil was to be elevated to the position of Lord Treasurer, they hastened to endeavour to turn the news to their own advantage. Cecil was not formally granted the office until May 4th, but by April 26th the appointment was sufficiently assured for Hickes to write,

It being now more than a bruit that your lordship shall be lord treasurer, and considering that your lordship hath been pleased heretofore to hear me always in such suits as some of your servants have desired me to move your lordship on their behalf, being now earnestly entreated by three or four of them to move your lordship in the particular suits following, I, having not opportunity to move your lordship verbally, am bold on their behalf to give you intimation of their humble request, leaving the granting or disallowing of their suits to your lordship's good consideration.

Mr Gerrard thinks your lordship will now have a gentleman of your horse. If your lordship shall think him meet for the place, he will accept it with his most humble thanks and seek no further, and serve your lordship with all duty, diligence and trustiness.

So like, your lordship's cook humbly prays your lordship to bestow on him the place of the cook for the Star Chamber, which belongs to your lordship to give. He will acknowledge it as an honourable favour and hope to discharge it very sufficiently, without any hindrance to your lordship's service otherwise.

The late lord treasurer bestowed on his steward the writing and keeping of the book of imposts of coins. If it please your lordship to bestow the place on your lordship's steward ... he shall be much bound to you for your favour in it and I think can very sufficiently discharge it.

Matthew Davies, sometime my man for twelve years whilst I served my lord, your lordship's father, and for these three or four years a messenger of the chamber, very earnestly besought me, which I have very unwillingly yielded unto, to move your lordship that, whereas your lordship is to appoint one to be your messenger, that it would please your lordship to grant it to him, if your lordship shall think him worthy ... If it please your lordship to bestow it upon any of your own servants that shall not execute it, he will give him good contentation for it.

This is written but to give your lordship overture of their desires, which in modesty they are backward to do for themselves.[49]

Clients often indicated to Hickes after 1598, as they had done when he was secretary to Burghley, that he could expect to profit for his pains. In July 1600 Sir William Russell, who was trying to obtain an office through Hickes's mediation with Cecil, told Hickes, 'my deserts hath been as great as any that standeth for the place, and my thankfulness shall be as great as any whosoever'.[50] In the autumn of 1606 Sir Josias Bodley, soldier and military engineer, sought Hickes's furtherance in obtaining payment of his pension. When Hickes agreed to help, Bodley, expressing appreciation, told him: 'You shall both bind me ... unto you and enable me withal to show the effects thereof.'[51] Other suitors promised gratuities openly. 'I will most willingly gratify you with forty angels for your favour,' wrote Sir Samuel Saltonstall in July 1608, when he asked Hickes to obtain, through Salisbury, the suspension of a Chancery decree against him.[52] In February 1605 Robert Kayle was anxious to secure Hickes's help in obtaining a Council clerkship which, it was believed, would soon fall vacant. Kayle felt it necessary to accompany his request for aid with a cask of 'sack' and to promise £40 in gold or plate if Hickes brought the suit to a successful conclusion.[53] In September 1611 Captain Humphrey Covert wanted Hickes to use his influence with Salisbury to obtain for him the post of mustermaster in Middlesex and Hertfordshire. He delicately refrained from offering a gratuity to Hickes himself, promising instead that, if he got the office, he would give Lady Hickes 'one hundred French crowns in gold, or a piece of plate to the same value'. Five months later he had abandoned that suit. He had by then decided that he wanted instead to be surveyor of the musters at the English garrisons at Flushing and Brill in the Low Countries. This time he promised Lady Hickes 'one hundred angels', and added that he would give 'one hundred more to any well deserving servant of my lord's he shall direct me unto', perhaps a disguised hint of a gratuity to Salisbury himself.[54] Covert and Kayle could probably afford substantial gratuities. Hickes did not hesitate to insist on payment from those less able to meet his demands. Lady Carr, writing on behalf of a poor widow, informed him that 'her estate is such as she is enforced to borrow the money that must be paid you'.[55]

Clients were occasionally prepared to pay very large sums. In October 1609 Dr Wyatt, one of the King's chaplains, had his ambitions fixed on the deanery of Salisbury, the place which 'of all the gifts in England he desired'. Wyatt mentioned his hopes to Hickes's nephew, Sir Charles Moryson, a prominent Hertfordshire gentleman. Wyatt asked, wrote Moryson to Hickes

> how I thought he might get the deanery of Salisbury ... to which I answered that, although he had named many great friends, yet, *sacra pecunia cuncta*, and that he was as well to pay as pray ... Then did I tell him how I thought I might persuade you to deal for him, but I did think it would be a suit of great trouble and by so much the more charge: to which he replied, 'I will give him a thousand pounds for his pains, so I may have it.'

John Gourden, dean of Salisbury since 1604, was alive when Moryson wrote, although he was believed to be on the point of death 'by reason of his years'. In fact, he deceived everybody by living until 1619.[56] Hickes did not get the opportunity to earn his thousand pounds. Moryson may, in any event, have been too confident about his uncle's ability to obtain the deanery. By 1609 there had been a considerable change in the Hickes–Cecil relationship.

In the pre-1598 period Robert Cecil was still a political apprentice. After the defeat of the Essex rising in 1601 his position as principal minister of the Crown was unchallenged. Between 1601 and 1603 he accomplished, in a masterly fashion, the delicate task of securing the Scottish succession. His increased power brought home to him a sense of the dignity of his position. This was reflected in a changed attitude to gifts from suitors. As early as January 1602 he made this clear when he wrote to Hickes,

I pray you, return to Mr Owen thanks for that [goodwill] whereof this New Year's gift is the sign, for, though these external things are welcome to many for themselves, yet [I] protest, to me they are only not unacceptable because I know they are not sent with opinion to purchase my goodwill, but to demonstrate theirs ... Otherwise I do take it rather unkindly of friends ... to have any such things given me.[57]

Cecil expressed, in this letter, a very different attitude from that which he showed in the 1590s, when he expected, even demanded, payment for his services.

In 1608 Hickes interceded on behalf of a young musician in Salisbury's service who had been involved in a kidnapping case. Hickes 'utterly' condemned the fault but pitied the young man, who had some good points. His youth and rashness might perhaps be regarded as extenuating the offence, though, of course, they could not excuse it. Above all, he had expressed sincere regret and desired pardon and another opportunity in Salisbury's household.[58] Salisbury's reply was harsh in tone. 'I can judge it fitter,' he told Hickes,

for me to quit my love of music which pleaseth mine ear, than to protect lewdness in this kind, where the offence is not to me ... but simply and originally to others, whose case may be yours and mine. To conclude, therefore, sir, I hate the fact so much to steal away any man's child as I am sorry it is not death by the law, seeing he that cuts my purse with fourteen pence shall be hanged. I am a master of wards, I am a councillor of state, and in my private conscience opposite to all fraud ... To yourself I say no more than I have said to greater persons.[59]

The Salisbury who wrote that letter with its admirable sentiments, high moral tone, and implied rebuke, had come a long way from the petty intrigues of earlier years.[60] Hickes's character seems to have remained unaltered and it may be that fact which explains the comparative coolness of Salisbury's attitude to him during the last years of their lives. Evidence of contact between the two, still relatively plentiful before 1608, declines considerably after that date.

In September 1610, in the last surviving letter which passed between Salisbury and Hickes, the former refused the latter's request for a wardship. [61] At that time Salisbury still had over a year and a half to live. The events of 1610, however, culminating in the failure of the Great Contract, lost him the confidence of both King and Parliament. His health was broken. The remaining evidence about the Hickes–Cecil relationship throws light only on the last days of the latter's life. Early in 1612 a multiplicity of distressing symptoms suggested that Salisbury was very seriously ill. His death could hardly have been long delayed. [62] Towards the end of April it was decided that he should take the waters at Bath, and he spent the first night of his journey, the night of Monday, April 27th, at the Kensington house of his friend, Sir Walter Cope. The following night he stayed with Lord Chandos at Ditton Park. He travelled with a train of about sixty, including three physicians, three surgeons, and two secretaries. Hickes accompanied him, while Cope followed him towards Bath on Friday, May 1st, planning to catch up with him on the way. [63] On the morning of Wednesday, April 29th, before the resumption of the journey, Hickes wrote to his own and Salisbury's old Cheshire friend, Sir Hugh Beeston. 'I commend me unto you,' he began,

but wherein I should commend you to any man else I know not. And though I know no cause, yet, as your countryman John Dutton was wont to say, 'Beeston, I love thee', so I say I know no cause except it be for old acquaintance. You went away out of town and never bid me farewell and, to fare the better by you I never could yet in forty years, nor never shall, though we should live forty years more together.

And yet you see my kind and generous nature in participating with you in your griefs, in rejoicing with you in your benefits, yea, and in soliciting your business for your profit. And that you may see that I continue my care to think upon you when there is any likelihood to do you good, I do at this time take this pain to write unto you, to give you knowledge that, albeit it hath been bruited in such remote countries as yours is, and therefore likely in yours also, that my lord was dead, yet, thanks be to God, his lordship at the writing hereof was at Ditton Park, in his journey towards the Bath, and in reasonable good state of body, only his legs a little swollen, as they were used to be, which we hope will also abate before we come to Bath. He eats well and sleeps well, and is as merry as a man may be in his case. And because I think he would be the merrier if he had such a merry man as your worship in his company, I have thought good to advise you, setting all your affairs for the country and his Majesty's service apart, to make your present repair to the Bath without any delay. In this advice of mine Sir Walter Cope doth join with me.

Now, to persuade you; besides your love and duty to my lord, the best argument I can use ... is *ab utili*, for, assure yourself, if my lord be in any case fit to play at tables [backgammon] we shall be sure to get £4 or £5 a piece from him and Sir Walter Cope, for you know, God wot, they can not play anything well, and you can, without cause, chaff, swear and brabble, and for a need, enter and bear a man falsely too. Therefore we have good advantage of them. But if this should fail, yet it is hard luck if you wring not one piddling suit or other from him, or at the least some velvet cloak or saddle not much the worse for the wearing ... Serjeant Goddins hath gotten a velvet pair of breeches already.

My lord is ready to take his coach for this day's journey, which is to Careham, at my Lord Knowles, and I am ready for my breakfast.[64]

In this, the last surviving letter from Hickes—written when nearly seventy—the character of the man appears very clearly: his irrepressible humour; his zest for life, even in old age; and, not least, his affection for Salisbury. All the chaff cannot conceal his concern for the latter and his anxiety that Beeston should come to Bath to help keep up the Lord Treasurer's spirits. Indeed, in the very last days of Salisbury's life, Hickes seems to have reverted to the role which he had filled so successfully some twenty years before. As a merry and affectionate companion he had shared the revels of the young Cecil. In 1612 he did what he could to brighten Salisbury's last hours.

The party reached Bath on May 3rd. Salisbury died on the

24th.[65] Hickes seems to have remained with him to the end. Certainly, during the first half of May he was sending a stream of reports on the course of the Lord Treasurer's illness to his own and Salisbury's friends, the earl and countess of Shrewsbury.[66] The funeral, poorly attended, took place on June 9th.[67] In the procession Hickes, carrying one of the banners traditional on such occasions, walked beside the dead man's cousin, Sir Francis Bacon—an honourable position.[68] Just over two months later, on August 15th, he himself died.[69]

8

Financial Expert

During the years after 1598 Michael Hickes extended his money-lending activities. He also continued to act as a loan-broker and financial adviser and engaged in some speculative property deals. The first of his speculative transactions took place in June 1603, when he bought from John Durninge, John Legate and William Drywood nearly 400 acres in Essex, part of the manor of Warley.[1] He paid £1,620 and promised a further £2,880 if Drywood would persuade his wife and mother to relinquish all their rights in the land.[2] He did not hold his new property for long. In September of the following year he obtained a licence to alienate it to Nicolas Fuller.[3] In June 1605, with Robert Jenkinson, a London merchant, he bought[4] the rectory of Irchester in Northamptonshire and the manors of Southrop in Gloucestershire and Snettisham in Norfolk from Peter Bradshawe, who had just before obtained them from the Crown.[5] These lands soon changed hands again as, in December 1607, they came into the possession of Salisbury.[6] Hickes's knowledge of the land market together with his general interests in the financial field may have persuaded him to act in 1606 and 1607 as an intermediary in the sale of the manor of Campes, situated in Cambridgeshire and Essex, to the enormously wealthy money-lender Thomas Sutton. The sale, for £10,800, involved complicated negotiations and necessitated a private Act of Parliament; Hickes was one of two mediators who helped to make the arrangements for Sir John Harrington and Sir John Skinner, both of whom had rights in the land.[7]

Hickes no doubt made his profits out of these deals; and the financial know-how which they suggest is confirmed by his work as a loan-broker. Great men in Government and official circles seem to have regarded him as an ideal link between the Court and the money market. In January 1601, when Francis Bacon needed £200 for six months, Hickes obtained the money for him from a friend.[8] In 1602 Robert Cecil made use of Hickes's expertise both to secure the renewal of existing bonds and to obtain a new loan.[9] In 1603 Fulke Greville, a prominent man in Court and Government circles, desperately needed a loan of £500 at short notice. Hickes obtained the money for him from city contacts within eight days, and Greville, who had been reluctant that his difficulties should be generally known, hastened to thank him for keeping his name out of the negotiations.[10] The earl and countess of Shrewsbury, who owed Hickes large sums, also used his services as an intermediary in obtaining loans from others. In the summer of 1609 they asked him to get a 'good sum' of money upon safe security. Hickes soon procured the loan and the countess wrote to thank him and to ask him for assistance in drawing up the necessary documents.[11]

Hickes's help was also much in demand, both by members of his family and others, in their more general financial problems. One man who sought his aid in 1604 was Sir John Garrard, a former lord mayor of London, who had received a government demand for a loan of £200 for six months. Garrard complained that the Crown already owed him £650 and that he had a 'great charge' of children, including four daughters, to be provided for. He then asked Hickes's advice as to how he might go about getting exemption from the present loan.[12] Michael Hickes's brother Clement wrote from Chester about his financial difficulties. In April 1612 he complained about his ill-usage at the hands of their Bristol cousin Gregory Sprint, who had owed him £35 for six years and refused to repay either the capital or interest. He asked Michael to attend to the matter for him, but evidently without success. Nearly three months later he still had not got his money and was forced to live 'in bare case', which, he told Michael pathetically, prevented him from sending him some cheeses which he would have liked him to have.[13] It was Michael's other brother, Baptist Hickes,[14] however, who really plagued him for help in money matters.

Baptist had already established himself as a money-lender before James's accession, but it was after 1603 that he became one of the most notable lenders in the country, both to private parties and to the Crown. On one occasion in 1603 or 1604 he asked for Michael's help in getting in two or three debts and complained bitterly about the ill-faith of debtors. He was, he said,

> so many ways disappointed of moneys at this present, being a time that I have always great payments to make in, as no day or night passeth me without care or trouble of mind for the discharge thereof, because thereupon depends my credit, and that makes me thus often to importune you, which I am loath to do, knowing your other business.

He found 'little truth in words ... and small assurance in bonds without great trouble, charge and unkindness'. Scotsmen were especially reluctant to pay up and he complained that they were 'fair speakers and slow performers. Being rid of them I will cross them out of my books.'[15]

Baptist often summoned Michael to London at short notice to help him with his financial affairs. In January 1608 he was involved in delicate financial negotiations in the city and wrote to Michael, 'come to London tomorrow though it be Sunday, so that on Monday morning we may take our best course in this business ... If your lodging be not ready aired for you after this foul weather, I have sweet chambers and a good fire ready for you.'[16] In November of the same year Michael received another summons. This was at a time when he had been very ill. 'If I had not heard this morning of your amendment,' wrote Baptist, 'I think I should have come unto you to have seen you.' This display of brotherly concern did not, however, prevent him asking Michael to 'repair to London this night or else if you could be here tomorrow morning with me before eight of the clock'. Baptist had important financial negotiations afoot and evidently considered Michael's advice more valuable than his health![17] Michael probably complied with these rather peremptory requests, for they continued. In February 1610 he was again summoned to Baptist's presence at eight o'clock in the morning, once more to help with weighty business affairs.[18] In April 1611 Baptist was hard pressed for ready money because of some land purchases which he had recently made. As a result, he was calling in some of his debts. The earl of Montgomery owed him two debts of £1,500 and nearly £1,700 and, though he was willing to defer payment of the larger sum, he insisted that he should get the smaller back, together with the interest due. He was reluctant to take legal action against Montgomery, but was quite prepared to do so if necessary, and he asked Michael, who was 'well conceived of' by Montgomery, to make this plain to him.[19]

Baptist's greatest difficulties in the early years of James's reign, however, probably rose from his efforts to recover debts owed him by the Crown. He had lent money to James even before the latter's accession to the English throne and in 1605 the King owed him about £16,000. In October of that year Baptist was very anxious to secure repayment of at least part of the debt, both to pay his own creditors and because he had to give 'good round portions' to his two daughters, who were soon to be married. 'I am enforced to use your help,' he wrote to Michael,

> and withal very earnestly to entreat you to take so much pains as to go yourself to my very honourable good lord, my lord treasurer [Buckhurst], to whose lordship I delivered a privy seal about ten months past for the payment of £4,000 unto me, parcel of the said debt … Albeit his lordship gave me very honourable and gracious speeches that I should be had in remembrance and receive satisfaction in reasonable time, yet since that time I have not received any, neither have I importuned or referred often to his lordship about it, so loath and fearful am I to give to his lordship the very least cause of offence therein.[20]

Michael seems to have made representations on his brother's behalf, but without effect, as two months later Baptist asked him 'again to repair unto my lord treasurer in my behalf at your coming to London'. He added bitterly, 'How exceeding ill I am dealt withal you see and I must bear. I pray God give me patience.'[21] A year later, in December 1606, Baptist had still not secured his money and wrote in despair to Michael, asking him to make further pleas to Buckhurst and bewailing 'the greatness of my whole debt, the unreasonable long time of my forbearance, my exceeding great loss and hindrance thereby, and my many and urgent occasions to use my money'.[22] By January 9th, 1607, he decided that it would be a good plan to enlist Salisbury's aid and asked Michael to bring the suit to his attention.[23] A week later he was able to write to Michael, 'you have eased my troubled mind at my lord of Salisbury his answer, for you tell me you make no doubt but I shall find him my honourable good lord in all right and equity'.[24] Baptist was certainly one for making the most of his troubles and it may be that his difficulties were never as great as he suggested. From 1607 onwards he lent further large sums to the Crown and, although this may have been largely because he saw further loans as the only chance of ultimately getting back the whole debt,[25] the fact remains that he was able to find the money. By the beginning of Charles I's reign he was an enormously wealthy man and in 1628 was raised to the peerage as Viscount Campden. Michael Hickes clearly spent a great deal of time and trouble on his brother's financial affairs during the first decade of the seventeenth century and Baptist himself acknowledged this in July 1608, when he asked him to try to persuade the Chancellor of the Exchequer, Sir Julius Caesar, to pay him the interest due on his loans. 'I pray you deal for me herein as for yourself,' he wrote, 'whereof I make no doubt, having always found you ready and willing to pleasure me with all your best favours, being within compass of your ability'.[26]

The patience which Michael Hickes showed in his dealings with his brother was at least as necessary when he tried to help an old friend, Vincent Skinner, with his very different financial difficulties. Skinner had, as we have seen,[27] been Hickes's colleague in Burghley's secretariat, but had left Burghley's personal service in 1593, when he was appointed to the auditorship of the receipt, an important Exchequer office.[28] Whatever his abilities at the Exchequer, he seems to have handled his own finances with the utmost ineptitude. In 1610 and 1611 he found himself involved in a financial crisis in the course of which he suffered indignity after indignity. In this crisis it is perhaps hardly surprising that he turned to Michael Hickes, a friend of fifty years' standing who was also something of an acknowledged expert in dealing with financial problems. Between July 1610 and October 1611 he bombarded Hickes with pleas for help.

No fewer than thirty-five[29] of these letters to Hickes have survived and we can only marvel at the care and trouble which
Hickes seems to have taken in the extremely complicated negotiations and discussions which took place. On July 25th, 1610,
in the first surviving letter which he wrote to Hickes about the
problem, Skinner explained how, during the past fifteen months,
he had sold land to pay off his debts. He had not managed,
however, to meet all his commitments and his remaining lands
had been extended to pay the money he owed to a Mr Orrell of
Lancashire. As an M.P., Skinner had been exempt from personal arrest while Parliament was sitting, but the fourth session
of James's first Parliament came to an end on July 23rd,[30] and
Skinner asked Hickes to secure Salisbury's protection from
imprisonment for him so that he could have an opportunity of
satisfying his creditors.[31] On August 8th, however, he was
arrested and imprisoned at the suit of two of his former clerks,
William Harrison and Alexander Glover, to whom he owed
money.[32] The fifth session of Parliament began on October 16th
and lasted until December 6th.[33] Skinner was released to attend
it, but from December onwards was in constant fear of re-arrest.
On January 27th, 1611, he informed Hickes that he would
fight to the death rather than suffer imprisonment again.[34] In
May he was still at liberty and Hickes was still doing his best to
help in what he described, very truthfully, as a 'tedious and
troublesome business'.[35] In his letters to Hickes Skinner constantly appealed for the use of Salisbury's influence to moderate
his creditors' zeal, and he also wrote directly to Salisbury himself.[36] In 1612 he was at last granted protection from arrest —
for one year.[37] Catastrophe, however, can never have been far
away. Despite the efforts of Hickes and his other friends,
Skinner's position was irremediable. He died in 1616 and was
buried 'out of Isaac Bringhurst's house in High Holborn', a
debtor's prison.[38] It was a sad end to the career of one of Hickes's
oldest friends.

Despite the considerable time which he must have spent on
his work as speculator, loan broker, and financial adviser,
Hickes's main interest in the financial world probably lay in his
own money-lending activities. In the draft[39] of a will drawn up
in August 1603 he spoke of the 'greatest' part of his estate being
in other men's hands — clearly a reference to his loans — and in

another draft,[40] composed nearly six years later, he noted that various sums secured by statutes, mortgages, and other obligations were owing to him. In nine cases between 1601 and 1612 in which gentlemen acknowledged in statutes that they were under an obligation to Hickes there is no independent evidence that these statutes represented security for loans.[41] It would be wrong, therefore, to assume that Hickes lent money in all of these cases, but even if only half of them involved loans— surely a conservative estimate—they must have represented an outlay by Hickes of two or three thousand pounds.[42]

In ten cases where it is known for certain that Hickes lent money we do not know what security he obtained. In January 1601 Francis Bacon owed him money. 'Your remain shall be with you this term,' he promised. In August of the same year, however, he was still in Hickes's debt, and we do not know whether the money had been repaid as late as July 1608 when, in a memorandum, he noted Hickes as a man from whom he could borrow 'upon any great disbursements'. In October 1609 he owed Hickes £200.[43] Another debtor was Dr Thomas White, canon of Windsor, who owed £200 in 1602.[44] The unfortunate Sir Griffin Markham, who was imprisoned for conspiracy against the Crown in 1603, wrote from the Tower to Cecil in December of that year praising Hickes as a man 'whose love I have many ways much tasted', and affirming that he was determined to leave himself 'worth nothing' rather than fail to repay a loan which he had obtained from Hickes.[45] Hickes's old friend Edward Suliarde acknowledged in August 1604 that he had often borrowed money from Hickes,[46] and in November of the same year Sir Walter Raleigh made it clear that he was one of Hickes's debtors.[47] In August 1605 Francis Bacon's brother Nathaniel owed Hickes money.[48] Sir Rowland Lytton was another debtor. He owed money in the summer of 1607.[49] A very distinguished borrower was William, Lord Compton, a peer who possessed great personal charm and a genius for high living. In 1599 he married, against her father's strong opposition, Elizabeth Spencer, heiress of the enormously wealthy merchant, Sir John Spencer. Compton got no money from his reluctant father-in-law, and financed his continuing reckless expenditure by selling his lands. By 1607 he had disposed of about one-third of his estates. In June 1608 he wrote to Hickes apologizing for his frequent failures to meet his day of payment. He was 'daily' expecting money and would send it to Hickes as soon as it arrived.[50] One wonders when Hickes did get his due. There can certainly be little doubt that he got it in the end, even though he may have had to wait until 1610. In March of that year Spencer at last died and his whole vast fortune — variously estimated at between £300,000 and £800,000 — passed to his daughter and her husband. Compton was temporarily unhinged by his good fortune. He 'fell mad', had to be removed to the Tower under medical care, and was even put in a straitjacket. Within a month, however, he had recovered, and in the next eight weeks, it was said, spent £72,000, 'most in great horses, rich saddles and play [gambling]'.[51] Later, no doubt, he found time to pay off his debts! Another, much less colourful, debtor was Hickes's Essex friend and neighbour Joseph Earth, who owed him an unspecified sum in the summer of 1609.[52] In March 1611 another borrower, Thomas Morison, promised to repay the sum which he owed.[53]

Many of these debtors may have owed Hickes quite small sums. If so, their debts were probably secured by bonds, the usual security for a small loan. It is also probable that bonds were the security for the substantial sums owed to Hickes by Gilbert and Mary Talbot, earl and countess of Shrewsbury,[54] although it was much more common for a creditor to insist on a recognizance, statute, or mortgage when lending a large sum. There are two reasons why Hickes may have been so accommodating to the Shrewsburys. One is that they were his close friends, and he probably trusted them. The other, perhaps more important, is that Shrewsbury, despite his continual lack of ready cash, was, in terms of his realizable resources, the wealthiest peer in England.[55] In November 1603 the earl and countess owed Hickes £600 but were unable to pay.[56] They sent £30 — the interest due for six months — and Hickes agreed to forego the principal for a further half year.[57] In August 1607 they were still in his debt and, on March 3rd, 1610, having only recently repaid him £1,000, asked for a further £1,000. He was unable to oblige, though he did send £100 which he had been retaining in hand for housekeeping expenses.[58] Two days later Shrewsbury wrote to him, gratefully accepting the £100 and promising to let him have it back, as requested, within two months.[59] In the summer of 1610 the Shrewsburys' debt was at least £700.[60] Seven months later, in January 1611, the countess asked for and received a further £120, for a month only,[61] and in the autumn of the same year she successfully negotiated for the renewal of loans of an undisclosed amount.[62] In May 1612 the earl and countess owed Hickes £1,575.[63] It seems probable that between 1603 and 1612, their debt to him was hardly ever less than £600 and often considerably more.

Another needy peer was the earl of Hertford, who is said to have spent £12,000 in excess of his allowance on an embassy to Brussels in 1605. It is hardly surprising that he had to borrow heavily both before and after his journey and in 1611 he was saddled with over £22,000 of debts.[64] Between 1600 and 1608 he negotiated seven loans, totalling in all £3,320, from Hickes, all of them upon bonds.[65] His capital wealth was a good deal less than Shrewsbury's,[66] and it seems very surprising that Hickes was prepared to lend such sums upon comparatively inadequate security. One possible explanation may be his family's long connection with the earl—we have seen that his stepfather, Anthony Penne, had been in Hertford's service in the 1560s.[67]

Hickes's other loans were upon statutes and mortgages. In June 1602 he lent a substantial sum, secured by a statute, to Lord Thomas Howard of Walden, who had Robert Cecil associated in the statute with him as extra security for Hickes.[68] A year later Cecil asked him to allow Howard to postpone repayment of the debt, which was probably £1,400, but stated that the interest due would be handed over.[69] Hickes agreed.[70] We do not know when the principal was repaid. Edward Blunt, a Derbyshire gentleman, was another who entered into a statute. In March 1604 he and Sir Thomas Pope Blunt of Hertfordshire undertook to pay Hickes £600 the following September. The penalty for failure to do so was £1,000.[71] Thomas Pope Blunt was not a principal in the loan, but was associated with Edward Blunt as further security.[72] Just before the end of the sixteenth century Hickes was lending large sums to Sir Henry Lee, Master of the Armoury, who was already heavily in debt, mainly due to his love of housebuilding.[73] Two loans which Hickes made in April 1598 and June 1599 were secured by statutes and were in the region of £2,000 and £500 respectively.[74] By 1606 Lee had reduced his debt to £300, which he was repaying at the rate of £100 a year. In 1606 he handed over £130, that is £100 plus £30 interest at 10 per cent, promising £120 the following year, and the remainder, £110, in 1608. He seems to have repaid the £120 at the promised time, but in July 1608 he wrote from his house at Ditchley, confessing his inability to pay the final instalment and asking for a year's indulgence. On that occasion he attempted to sweeten the request by sending Hickes a handsome 'nag', which he had promised him some time before.[75] Sir John Peyton, governor of Jersey, was another borrower. Between 1602 and 1612 he and his son John acknowledged their debts in five statutes and it seems clear that at any one time during these years they owed Hickes at least £1,000.[76]

Hickes also made loans to the extravagant and pleasure-loving William Herbert, third earl of Pembroke, who in 1604 married Mary Talbot, daughter of Hickes's friend and debtor Gilbert Talbot, earl of Shrewsbury. In May 1601, writing to secure forebearance of his debts, Pembroke made it clear that they were, at that time, secured by bonds.[77] By December 1604 Hickes was no longer content with such assurance and in that month Pembroke entered into a statute which bore a penalty of £2,000,[78] meaning that his debt was probably about £1,000. In June 1606 he asked for a further loan of £600.[79] This was granted, being secured in July by the mortgage of his manor of Knighton in Wiltshire.[80] From that date until 1612 he wrote to Hickes at regular intervals, requesting extensions of his loans and promising the payment of interest at appointed times.[81] It is clear from these letters that one of his debts, that for £1,000, continued to be secured by the statute of 1604, while the other, for £600, was assured by the mortgage of Knighton. In 1612 Pembroke still owed the £1,600 and it seems clear that between 1604 and 1612 Hickes obtained interest payments in excess of £1,100 — a very satisfactory return from a total outlay of £1,600.

We have record of two other loans by Hickes, both of them upon mortgages. In July 1606 Sir Edward Stanley of Shropshire borrowed £1,000, agreeing to repay the sum, plus interest at 10 per cent in six months. The bargain was secured upon the mortgage of two Pembrokeshire manors.[82] In July 1602 William Brydges, Lord Chandos, whose seat was at

Sudeley in Gloucestershire, obtained a loan of £1,000 upon the mortgage of the manor of Pirton in Wiltshire. The loan was originally for one year, but Hickes extended it until 1606, by which time William Lord Chandos had died, owing Hickes £200 in addition to the £1,000 lent in 1602. In July 1606 his son and heir Grey Brydges, in return for Hickes's agreement to cancel the mortgage and pay a further £50, sold to the latter 63 acres of the manor of Myntie in Gloucestershire.[83] In effect, Hickes had purchased 63 acres for £1,250.[84]

After Hickes's death, his widow and elder son carried on the family tradition as money-lenders. In December 1612, Elizabeth Hickes advanced £2,000, secured against the mortgage of his manor of Witcombe, to Sir John Chamberleyne of Presbury, Gloucestershire.[85] Two months later Edward Suliarde of Flemings, son of her late husband's old friend, obtained £3,000, his security being the manors of Claydons and Flemings, and other lands in Essex.[86] The earl of Montgomery was another of her debtors.[87] In the middle years of the seventeenth century William Hickes, heir of Michael and Elizabeth, was owed £2,500 by 'sundry men'. His ventures in the money-lending business were obviously on a smaller scale than those of his father. They also seem to have been much less profitable, even in proportion to their size: £2,000 out of the £2,500 was noted as bad debt.[88]

Money-lenders are not usually the most popular of men and at least one member of the Hickes family had a very bad reputation for his supposed harshness. At the beginning of James's reign Baptist complained bitterly to Michael that he was 'many times hardly thought of',[89] but Michael himself never seems to have acquired comparable unpopularity. Many of those to whom he lent money became or remained his close friends.

9

Michael Hickes and his Circle

By the early years of the seventeenth century Michael Hickes's previous religious radicalism was on the wane. In the prologues of draft wills drawn up in 1603 and 1609,[1] and in his final will itself, composed in 1612 on the day before his death,[2] he commended his soul to God in devout terms. None of these confessions of faith, however, indicated that their author had been a fervent Puritan. The impression which the reader obtains is of a conventionally religious man without extreme views. He employed the same kind of platitudes when he wrote to Salisbury, sometime after 1608, 'I beseech God [to] increase, confirm and strengthen you in the knowledge of his truth; inspire you with all Godly wisdom and counsel; arm you with true fortitude and Christian patience; protect you against all the wicked plots and practices of God's enemies and yours ... and preserve you this year and many to the advancement of God's glory.'[3]

As Hickes grew older his mind turned often to thoughts of the hereafter. In September 1611 he wrote to his friend Sir Hugh Beeston, who had just lost his only son.[4] As a summary of his attitude to life and death the letter could hardly be bettered. He expressed his most sincere sympathy to his 'ancient and loving friend', and told Beeston that he could offer some consolation and comfort. 'You complain and are grieved,' he went on,

for the death of your son ... I confess you have just cause so to be, but ... it is the way of all flesh and ... the term of our life is but at the will of the Lord ... He died in the flower of his youth. Consider that this also is common and usual and is but like an apple gathered whilst it is green or as a Michaelmas rent paid upon Midsummer day ... He died a sudden and an unusual death it is true, but our experience tells us that the one happens often and the other sometimes, but neither to be so grievously taken, for that they have [happened] and may happen to good and Godly men ... There is not a sparrow falls on the ground nor a hair from our head without his providence. He hath an oar in all our actions ... God who gives life may take it away again, both when he list and in what manner he list: *uno modo nascimus, multis morimur.*

Hickes continued on a more personal note,

... And now, Sir Hugh Beeston, to join in counsel myself with you; for as much as the glass of our life is almost run out and the light of our candle burnt to the socket, let us with David learn to number our days and to apply our hearts to wisdom, let us redeem the time past with an earnest apprehension and meditation of our approaching end ... To which end, let us cast off all worldly cogitations and cares, which are but ... thorns in our hearts, and being balanced and valued are nothing else but trash and transitory. And to conclude, let us by the example of your son take warning to ourselves and so be always prepared against death that it may never steal so suddenly upon us but, having oil in our lamps, we may with the wise virgins be ready to enter in at the gates of eternal bliss in the world to come.

Less than a year after he wrote these words Hickes was dead. The sincerity of the sentiments which he expressed to his bereaved friend bear witness to the deep faith in God that he shared with the vast majority of his contemporaries.

It is not sufficient, however, to paint a picture of Hickes as a fervent young Puritan who lost his early ardour. The piety which he retained to the end of his life must be reconciled with his attitude to ecclesiastical patronage. We have seen[5] that he was a prime mover in the dubious intrigues attending the elevation of Toby Matthew to the bishopric of Durham in 1595, and the words[6] of his nephew Sir Charles Moryson in 1609 seem to indicate that, three years before his death, Hickes was still demanding his own price for the use of his influence on behalf of suitors for ecclesiastical benefices. It would appear that we must condemn him as an odious hypocrite, full of pious sentiments but very ready to feather his own nest by intrigues behind the scenes in the negotiations attending ecclesiastical promotions. That, however, would be an unfair judgment. As secretary to Burghley and confidant of Robert Cecil a large part of Hickes's life was devoted to dealing with suits and suitors. He expected gratuities and was used to manoeuvring in order to obtain his client's desires. It is probable that he regarded suits involving ecclesiastics as no different in kind from those in which the clients were laymen.

One of the changes which took place in English religious life in the 1590s was an increased stress on the role of the household, and particularly of its head, in religious observances.[7] This may well have appealed to Hickes, who seems to have had a pleasant family life at his house at Ruckholt in Essex, where he spent more and more of his time after 1598.[8] There is little evidence about Hickes's relations with his wife. Only one letter[9] between the two has survived. It can be dated sometime between 1598 and 1602 and was written by Elizabeth Hickes while her husband was on a trip to London. She had been entertaining some friends during his absence. 'We drank to you and wished you here,' she told Hickes,

> but I cannot have it with wishing. If I could, you should not be from hence ... But if I had all that I would, I think I should be unwilling to leave the world ... I pray God bless you and give you health, for, I protest to you, it is the chiefest thing I desire in this world ... It freezes so hard that my ink will cease fall out of my pen. But that I write to you I should cease write in your counting house without a fire. But I will now bid you goodnight ... Your boy and girl is well, I thank God.

This seems to indicate that the marriage was a happy one and Hickes had high praise for his wife in 1603 when, in his draft will, he wrote of their love for each other and of his gratitude for her 'love and care' for their children.[10] As we have seen they had had a son and daughter before 1598[11] and a second boy, Michael, was born some time afterwards. The exact date is unknown, but, as he was admitted to Trinity College, Cambridge, in 1618,[12] it is likely that he was born about 1602. In 1613, a year after Hickes's death, his children were all involved in some branch of learning. William was at Cambridge, under the care of Francis Nethersole, a fellow of Trinity;[13] Michael was at school at Morteon in Essex;[14] and Elizabeth, then fifteen years old, had already been studying French for some time.[15]

During the early years of the seventeenth century Michael Hickes's brother Baptist was sometimes prevented by business commitments from accepting hospitality at Ruckholt. In January 1609 he was too busy to attend a masque which Michael was presenting,[16] but he did come when he could. In the summer of 1608, after spending some time at Ruckholt, he wrote to both Michael and Elizabeth, thanking them for their hearty welcome.[17] With his letter to Elizabeth he sent a present of some purple 'stuff' striped with gold, an offering which doubtless came from his mercer's shop. Michael Hickes was generous to his two nieces, Baptist's daughters. In December 1605 he gave a splendid party to celebrate the forthcoming marriage of the elder of these nieces, Juliana, to Sir Edward Noel.[18] A few days later the young couple were married from Ruckholt, the ceremony taking place in the nearby parish church of Leyton. Such was the success of the occasion that, a year later, the marriage of Mary, Baptist's younger daughter, to Sir Charles Moryson, was also held at Leyton.[19]

Michael Hickes seems to have been a good father to his wife's large brood of children by her first marriage, though it is clear that not all his stepsons made a good impression on contemporaries. In October 1608 Sir Oliver Manners complained bitterly from Rome about one of them, an 'idle fellow', Thomas Parvish, who had wronged both his master and Manners,[20] and the following year Thomas's brother Henry, then in Constantinople, was also in trouble. According to the English Ambassador, Thomas Glover, he had distinguished himself by his 'malapert insolency' and by the 'braving fashion' in which he spoke of Hickes's credit and repute.[21] Henry's youthful desire to brag of his stepfather's influence, though it did nothing to endear him to the English community at the Ottoman capital, was natural enough, and it is clear that he appreciated the good-will which Hickes had obviously shown him. In 1613, several month's after Hickes's death, Henry, then in Venice, wrote to tell his mother that he was 'praying daily' for his late stepfather. 'I did know him kind and honest towards you and yours,' he went on, 'and no doubt but he hath reached the fruits of an honest man'.[22] Hickes seems to have had a special affection for Mary Parvish, the only one of his stepchildren who was mentioned in his last, very brief, will, in which he left her £200.[23]

Hickes's family in the wider sense included his servants as well as his wife and children. Like all members of the aristocracy and gentry of the time, he found that there were plenty of men who were only too anxious to enter his service.[24] There was high unemployment throughout England during Hickes's lifetime, and this, together with the severe legislation against vagabonds (broadly defined as masterless men who had no obvious means of earning a living) meant that there was great competition to secure what were often comparatively comfortable and un-exacting jobs in the households of the upper classes. From the point of view of the gentry the servant problem of the time, there-fore, was the identifying and weeding out of undesirables in an effort to secure honest, well-behaved and competent staff from the large pool of applicants. It was a problem which caused Hickes a lot of trouble. He seems to have been a good master, careful of his servants' welfare; when one of them had ague in 1611 he corresponded with his own physician, Dr Palmer, about the man's treatment.[25] The servants themselves did not always appreciate their good fortune. Francis Ayscoughe only realized how lucky he had been in Hickes's service after he had left it under a cloud. When he asked, at length and in piteous terms, to be taken back, he was told that he must first confess his former faults and show himself sorry.[26] Sometimes a man might be required to give security that he would perform faithful ser-vice. Thomas Eastmeade, yeoman of Leyton, engaged by Hickes in 1602, was required to enter into a bond for £20 that he would fulfil satisfactorily the duties of gamekeeper of the Ruckholt estate.[27]

Cuthbert Bolton probably entered Hickes's service in the latter part of 1601. In September of that year he was employed at Knole, the Kent seat of Lord Buckhurst, but wanted to leave, because there were more of his 'quality in the house than were needful', and he hoped to make a change which would be to his advantage. Hickes, when told of Bolton's character and interests, replied that there was not a house in England where one might live more quietly and 'have better opportunity ... to practice ... music than in his house, only reserving times of service, which are at dinner and supper'.[28] The satisfaction which Bolton had given in Buckhurst's service was not repeated in his new job. He was soon asking his mistress not to dismiss him and to pardon his faults,[29] but it became evident that his misdemeanours were not of the kind which could be lightly excused. He eventually admitted stealing a large number of items, including sheets, ruff bands, handkerchiefs, a Bible, several books, a spoon, a pair of garters, and two jewels.[30] He was dismissed, probably early in 1604, for in April of that year he wrote to ask that a trunk might be bought to hold those of his possessions which were still in a chest at Ruckholt.[31] Hickes soon discovered, however, that two of his pistols were missing, and assuming, not unnaturally, that Bolton was the guilty party, detained the latter's effects. Bolton vehemently protested his innocence, but we do not know if he got his trunk.[32]

Theft was not the only problem with which Hickes had to deal. There seems to have been a good deal of fornication among his servants. In January 1603 he took down with his own hand the story of a pregnant maidservant, Dorothy Hoyd. She 'confessed before me and my wife', wrote Hickes, 'that Mark, my cook, did lie with her the first upon Marymas day ... a twelve-month [ago].' She got away, saying that there was somebody in the hall, but Mark followed 'and brought her back again'. The next episode in this domestic drama took place when Hickes and his household were at Putney, 'at which time she thinks she was gotten with chil[d] when she went up to make ... [Mark's] bed'. Dorothy protested that Mark had promised to marry her. That vow, if it was made, did not prevent her bestowing her favours in other quarters. She confessed that Matthew Davies, another servant, was 'very earnest with her many times and hath lain with her three times'. She also stated that Peter Makinson, the butler, 'did lie with her, and he promised to marry her if Mark did not, and yet if ... [Mark] did marry her to give her a piece of money'. Having admitted that Peter and she had been lovers

Dorothy then changed her tune and denied it, saying that Peter never lay with her, but that 'he had as good a will as the best of them, but that he was an old man, and she would not care of him'. She may have remembered that Peter had told her that she must, when questioned about the unborn child, lay the blame on Mark, 'for', Peter said, 'my master favours him and my mistress, and they will bear it better at his hands, for if they know it be mine they will send me to the jail'.[33] Makinson's ruse failed. He was held responsible and had to agree to place Dorothy in a 'convenient and fit' house, and to provide for her at his own expense until the child was born. After that, he was to provide for its future care.[34] Makinson seems to have decided that, in the circumstances, he might as well marry the girl. Unfortunately for him, her parents thought that he was a 'bare fellow ... [with] nothing but a little money', and would not permit the match.[35] We must assume that he provided for Dorothy and the child as promised. His pleasures had cost him dearly, as he seems also to have lost his job as a result of the scandal.[36]

Matthew Davies, one of the recipients of Dorothy's favours, had been in trouble before because of his attentions to women, with whom he clearly had a winning way. In August 1589, when he was already in Hickes's service, he confessed that he had corrupted two 'maidens ... Elizabeth Powell and Susan Scarlet, the one since married to one Sanderso[n], a player, and the other to one Daniel, a cutler, [and] very naughtily and wickedly did abuse their bodies, for the which I am very heartily sorry and do faithfully promise ... that, by the grace of God, I will never commit the like hereafter.'[37] Davies did, however, yield to the temptation of Dorothy's charms. After all, twelve years is a long time.

In dealing with these troublesome servants Hickes's well-developed sense of humour, which was such a notable aspect of his character, must have stood him in good stead. Other facets of his personality can be seen in the one portrait of him which has survived.[38] It was obviously painted when he was advanced in years, but the unlined face is full of vitality and life. The eyes sparkle beneath the skullcap which he wore to cover his bald head.[39] It is the picture of a man who lived a full life and enjoyed it. He combined the interests of a scholar with a wide range of outdoor activities. As the letter of March 1562[40] from his stepfather, Anthony Penne, shows, he was trying his hand at writing both prose and poetry while still in his teens, and he continued his literary interests in later years. The historian John Strype, writing well over two hundred years ago and drawing on evidence no longer extant, wrote of him that,

> He was well skilled in philological learning and had read over the polite Roman historians and moralists, out of which authors he had made large collections, especially of their moral and wise sentences, with which he filled divers paper books ... By his ingenious education and good parts he became very fit and agreeable to be admitted into the conversation of a society of the best learned and most eminent persons.[41]

Camden, the distinguished historian, was one of his friends.[42]

He had, too, a considerable interest in music. In 1608 he told Salisbury that, although he was not an accomplished performer himself, there were few that loved music better.[43] His friends were well aware of this, and sent him appropriate presents. Sir Francis Shane sent a harp in 1603,[44] and Henry Parker in 1609 sent an overture which he had composed.[45] In 1611 and 1612 friends in Ireland were searching for a 'fine Irish harp' for him.[46] Shortly before that Arthur Gregory had made him a viol.[47] In view of his own musical interests it is hardly surprising that Hickes took considerable trouble over his daughter's education in the subject. In 1611, when she was only thirteen, he was arranging for the composition of special exercises on the virginals for her benefit.[48] Another of Hickes's indoor pastimes was 'tables' or backgammon as we would call it, a game he often played with Robert Cecil and Hugh Beeston.[49] He also developed an interest in natural history. He made extensive extracts[50] from the works of Konrad von Gesner, an early sixteenth-century German–Swiss naturalist best known to his contemporaries as a botanist, but regarded by later scholars as the father of modern zoology.[51]

Hickes's interest in zoology and botany reflected his love of the outdoors. He enjoyed both archery and hunting,[52] but his great passion was bowls, a game which, he told his friend Roger Manners, 'I love better than my book, be it spoken without my praise and followed without my profit'.[53] His correspondence is full of references to the game,[54] and on one occasion a friend wished him fair weather for the 'better finishing' of the new bowling alley which he was having constructed at Ruckholt.[55] His nephew by marriage, Sir Charles Moryson, sometimes joined him in a match. In July 1609, when Moryson came to Ruckholt, they played for a stake of a crown.[56] Hickes sometimes played in very exalted company. On one occasion the earl of Shrewsbury, Lord Sheffield, and he played together in a match. They lost.[57]

Hickes, the extrovert of the bowling alley, had both serious and sensitive sides to his nature. The serious aspect can be seen in the need which he clearly felt to instruct and admonish the young. In a letter which he wrote in his vigorous euphuistic style to a Cambridge student, the son of a friend, he combined reproof with encouragement. 'It was my chance not long since,' he informed the young man,

> to light upon a letter written by you to your father ... [and] I found the letters so ill framed, the orthography so false, and the whole matter so slender, as I could devise no better excuse in your behalf than to think that your wit was, as we commonly say, a woolgathering and a wandering, whilst your hand was a writing; and had not ... the place from whence it was directed declared unto me that it came from the university of Cambridge, I would have judged verily that it had been written by some pelting Canterbury scholar.

Hickes went on to point out that, although a literary masterpiece could hardly be expected from so young a man, 'it is to be feared that that tree will bear no fruit in the summer that doth not bud and blossom in the spring time, for, as it is in the old proverb, it doth prick betime that will be a thorn'. Having made the student aware of his defects, Hickes suggested a remedy. The young man was to obtain from his tutor instruction in how to set down a logical argument. With diligent practice he would soon be able to express his thoughts quickly and lucidly. In order to improve his protégé's handwriting, Hickes sent him a book containing 'divers sundry sorts of hand', with a recommendation that the 'secretary' style was 'the fittest for your purpose'.[58]

Hickes, the stern but helpful critic of youthful literary efforts, showed his sensitivity when he was offered a knighthood in 1603. In July of that year Robert Cecil wrote that he would have him knighted at James I's forthcoming coronation.[59] In his letter of refusal Hickes made it clear that he had already turned the honour down once. 'I humbly thank you,' he replied,

> but since I refused it at Theobalds, where it had come with the greatest grace and credit to me as a mark of your honourable favour, I can be content to stay at this time. And if it shall happen ... that the King do come into the forest where I dwell to hunt and to come to my house, as it is not unlikely but he will, then, if it shall please him by your honourable intervention to think me worthy, it may be I will accept of it for my wife's sake, whom I think worthy to be a lady, though not myself fit to be a knight.[60]

It may be that, even in 1603, the memory of his blunder during the Queen's visit to Ruckholt in 1597[61] still rankled in Hickes's mind and that he was determined not to accept a high honour at the new sovereign's hand until he had made amends. His letter to Cecil certainly supports this interpretation, but the latter did not understand the reasons behind his friend's refusal. 'Good Mr Hickes that would not be Sir Michael,' he wrote mockingly.[62] On June 16th, 1604, however, James I paid a visit to Ruckholt.[63] He may have been better pleased with his reception than Queen Elizabeth had been and on August 6th Hickes accepted a knighthood.[64]

During the later years of his life, both before and after he was knighted, Hickes continued to find pleasure in meeting and in keeping in touch with his many friends. One of these was his old companion of Lincoln's Inn days, Edward Suliarde. During the first decade of the seventeenth century the two men were still on close terms,[65] and on one occasion, in the winter of 1603, Suliarde invited Hickes and his family to spend Christmas with him in Suffolk.[66] Another of the friends of his younger days who remained an intimate during later years was Hugh Beeston. Hickes and Beeston shared a common interest in and affection for the Cecil family[67] which must have helped to cement a friendship which had lasted for forty years by the time Hickes died.[68]

As secretary to Burghley and confidant of Robert Cecil,

Hickes was in constant contact with the great figures of Court and official circles, and he developed friendships with some of these important men. By 1601 he was well acquainted with Fulke Greville, Treasurer of the Navy,[69] and their friendship continued in the years ahead.[70] John, Lord Lumley, bibliophile, scholar, art collector and gourmet, was a notable member of the peerage who was on friendly terms with Hickes.[71] In June 1600 we find Lumley and Hickes dining together in London.[72] Hickes also had friends among the lawyers. James Altham,[73] a distinguished member of Gray's Inn, was one. In 1600 he invited Hickes to be his guest at the Inn for a fortnight.[74] Hickes also numbered prominent clergymen among his circle. Two of these were George Montaigne and Richard Neile, each of whom later became archbishop of York, Montaigne achieving the dignity in 1628 and Neile in 1631.[75] Montaigne's chaplaincy, during Elizabeth's reign, to the ill-fated earl of Essex did no harm to his career. He later filled the same office in Robert Cecil's service, and the wit and conversational facility which pleased James I and furthered his ecclesiastical career must have forged a bond between himself and the merry Hickes whom he was very anxious to secure as his supper guest.[76] Richard Neile, who filled successively the positions of chaplain to the elder and younger Cecil was also on terms of friendship with Hickes. On March 17th, 1601, he wrote[77] to apologize for his failure to visit him as arranged, explaining with disarming candour that the executions of Sir Christopher Blount and Sir Charles Danvers, two of the Essex conspirators, had been postponed and were due to take place the next day, 'which [event] I am loath to miss'.

Henry Maynard, Hickes's colleague in Burghley's secretariat, continued to be one of his closest friends after 1598, just as he had been before. In 1599, when a Spanish invasion of England was feared and a military camp was set up to oppose the possible invaders, Maynard was appointed camp secretary. He invited Hickes to pay him a visit, 'if Mrs Hickes will give you leave to go thither'.[78] It would clearly not have been suitable for Elizabeth Hickes to accompany her husband on that occasion, but she was not left out of the numerous invitations which Hickes received to visit Maynard and his family at Easton Lodge, Maynard's Essex home.[79] Maynard helped Hickes to find a suitable schoolmaster for one of his sons,[80] and did not neglect to provide him with a detailed account of an illness of a daughter-in-law, who, in the summer of 1608, was 'sick in her stomach'. The cause of the trouble was a 'surfeit of oysters' but she was so ill that a doctor had to be called in. His remedy was that sixteenth-century cure-all, a purge. Fortunately she was soon well again.[81] When, in June 1609, Maynard himself was seriously ill, Hickes wrote affectionate letters to his old companion,[82] who died the following year.[83] Shortly afterwards Henry junior, one of Maynard's sons, expressed to Hickes his appreciation of 'the long and faithful bond of friendship which I have seen and heard to have been between yourself and my father', and added the hope that, as Hickes's love had been 'truly affectionate to him, so it is hereditary to his'.[84] These hopes were not disappointed. Hickes corresponded frequently with Lady Susan Maynard, Henry's widow, and William Maynard, his eldest son, and each family seems to have kept open house to members of the other.[85]

Sir Robert Wroth was another Essex neighbour and friend of pre-1598 days whom Hickes continued to see during the first decade of the seventeenth century. Wroth and Hickes both enjoyed good company and were fond of outdoor sports and, until 1606, the date of Wroth's death, Hickes was a frequent visitor at his house at Loughton. Wroth always pressed him to bring as many of his own friends and relatives as possible and Hickes's brothers-in-law Alderman Thomas Lowe and Ralph Colston and their wives were singled out as especially welcome guests.[86] Wroth, who often addressed Hickes banteringly as 'Saint Michael',[87] provided such delicacies as 'very good oysters'[88] to tickle the palates of his guests. The favourite sports of the men were bowls and hunting[89] and, on one occasion, Hickes was reminded to be sure to bring his own set of bowls with him.[90] As a prominent member of the Essex commission of the peace Wroth was much concerned with the maintenance of law and order in the neighbourhood. In the autumn of 1599 he wrote to Hickes about bands of 'lewd fellows, sometimes horsemen, sometimes footmen, disguising themselves with beards, that they carry about them in their pockets', who were roaming the Essex countryside looking for opportunities to perpetrate mischief. Hickes was asked to remind his neighbours to keep a sharp look-out for these ruffians.[91] Wroth did not forget that his friend was the intimate of Robert Cecil. He was not slow to use Hickes's services to ingratiate himself with the powerful minister and expressed, in the most extravagant terms, his devotion to Cecil's interests.[92]

The many gratuities[93] Hickes received bear witness to his influence with the Cecils, while the presents he received from friends were, in contrast, marks of personal regard. The number of these gifts is an indication of the extent of his circle of acquaintances. Sir Rowland Lytton, a Hertfordshire man who had been captain of Queen Elizabeth's Gentleman Pensioners, her closest bodyguard, and was a dependant of the Cecils,[94] sent half a buck in 1606.[95] Sir Henry Glemham of Suffolk[96] and Sir Fulke Greville were others with Court connections who did not forget an old friend, sending respectively oysters and venison.[97] Sir Ralph Horsey, one of the leading members of the Dorsetshire gentry, sent geldings and a young horse,[98] while the wife of Zachariah Bethell of Hampshire favoured Hickes with a buck.[99] Others sent fish and fowl.[100] It is clear that the Ruckholt larder was seldom empty.

It is very striking that several of Hickes's closest friends were also his debtors. He seems to have been able to play the part of the money-lender without quarrelling with any of those friends who were in his debt—a considerable achievement. Sir Henry Lee was one who owed him money for years and yet remained on the most amicable of terms with him.[101] Lee expressed his feelings in quite unambiguous terms when he wrote in 1607, 'I have been ever careful to deal kindly with such as deal kindly with me. More kindness, more truth and plain meaning I never found than in Sir Michael Hickes.' He went on to say that, though his debts might have an end, yet his appreciation for Hickes's 'kind courtesy must end when I leave the world'.[102]

Other friends to whom Hickes lent money were Francis Bacon; Joseph Earth, servant of Charles Blount, earl of Devonshire; and Gilbert and Mary Talbot, earl and countess of Shrewsbury. Hickes and Bacon had, of course, been acquainted before 1598 and by 1606 their friendship was firmly established. In that year Hickes was one of the three chief guests at Bacon's wedding dinner.[103] In August 1610, when Bacon's aged mother died, he invited Hickes to the funeral and asked if he could have the comfort of his company for a few days afterwards.[104] It was possibly during a visit to Ruckholt that Bacon, who had a colourful taste in dress, borrowed a pair of carnation stockings from one of the ladies of the house. In January 1612, expressing regret that he could not remember whether the stockings had belonged to Lady Hickes or her daughter, he sent a pair to each, with his good wishes to all the family for the New Year.[105]

One of Hickes's closest friends during the early years of the seventeenth century was Joseph Earth, who spent a considerable part of his time at Wanstead in Essex, where his master, the earl of Devonshire, had a house. Earth, Hickes, and their families exchanged presents and visits and when Devonshire and Sir Robert Wroth quarrelled about some 'walks' at Wanstead—the details are obscure—Earth secured Hickes's services as mediator.[106] In June 1601 Gilbert Talbot, earl of Shrewsbury, invited Hickes to accompany him in his coach to visit a friend. At that time the two men had probably not been on friendly terms for long, as Shrewsbury had not then met Mrs Hickes, although he expressed a wish to do so as soon as possible.[107] By the autumn of 1603 the families were well acquainted, as the Talbots then spent some time at Ruckholt. Shrewsbury thanked his host in the most profuse terms and did not forget to send a present of a little 'nag' for Hickes's elder son, then seven years old.[108] In December 1603 Hickes provided Shrewsbury with a long report on the trial of Sir Walter Raleigh for conspiracy against the King.[109] The bulk of the evidence about his friendship with the Shrewsburys, however, covers the period 1608 to 1612. During these years the two families kept in close contact, exchanging news and presents.[110]

During the last year or two of his correspondence with Shrewsbury, Hickes's health was deteriorating. Although he did have illnesses in earlier years,[111] he seems to have kept generally well for most of his life. It is true that by 1594 he was troubled by deafness, but that was annoying rather than dangerous. It is doubtful if he obtained any help from the 'cure' prescribed by a friend who told him to

Make a loaf of the quantity of a twopenny loaf, of rye meal … and keep it hot until you go to bed … When you are in your bed cut it asunder in the middle and put the one half of the loaf to one of your ears and the other half to the other, as hot as you can suffer it ... Let them lie until they be cold and keep your head with double the warmth you were accustomed before. And when you have taken the loaves off, warm ... oil and drop two or three drops thereof into your ears lukewarm. And make two tents of fine lint ... and wet them well in the oil and tent your ears with them all night.[112]

By 1611 he had much more serious troubles. He seems to have been ill for much of the year,[113] and by the autumn his doctor was prescribing a remedy for kidney disease.[114] The Jacobean gossip and letter writer John Chamberlain reported his death at Ruckholt on August 15th, 1612,[115] at the age of sixty-eight, 'of a burning ague, which came, as is thought, of his often going into the water this hot summer, which, though it might seem to refresh him for the time, yet was thought unseasonable for a man of his years'.[116] He was buried in the nearby parish church of Leyton, where a fine monument, complete with an effigy, was erected over his grave.

Conclusion

At the time of his death Michael Hickes owned property in London, Nottinghamshire, and Gloucestershire.[1] In London he had a house on St Peter's hill and land in the parish of St Katherine Colman, inherited respectively through his mother and father, as well as a house, which he had bought himself, in Austin Friars. In June 1604 he obtained from the Crown a grant of over six hundred acres of land of the dissolved priory of Lenton in Nottinghamshire,[2] and in 1610 he bought the manor and castle of Beverstone in Gloucestershire,[3] the county from which his family had originally sprung. In his *inquisition post mortem* Hickes's land on St Peter's hill was valued at 50s. a year, his property in Nottinghamshire at £13.6s.8d. per annum, and Beverstone castle with appurtenances at £10 a year. Some idea of the extent to which these were undervaluations can be gained by noting that, forty years later, the annual values of these three properties were estimated — probably fairly reliably — at £50, £300, and £200 respectively. Not all the increase was due to inflation!

An inquisition, totally unreliable as to the value of the lands, might not record all the land actually held. The inquisition on Hickes did not mention the sixty-three acres of the manor of Myntie in Gloucestershire, which he held of the Crown by knight service,[4] or the Bristol lands which he had inherited from his father and which were still probably in his possession at the time of his death.[5] Ruckholt in Essex, his country seat, was the property of his wife Elizabeth, having been left to her for life by her first husband, Henry Parvish.[6]

Hickes's last will, a very short document, was drawn up on

August 14th, 1612. He appointed as his executors his wife, his brother Baptist and his brother-in-law Sir Thomas Lowe, asking them to distribute his movable goods among his wife and children according to their 'good discretions and wisdoms'. He also asked the executors to remember his brother Clement, his step-daughter Mary Parvish, and his servants. On the 15th—the day he died—he added a codicil, making his son William an executor and providing that the marriage portion of his daughter Elizabeth should be £2,000.[7] The lands and goods which Hickes left and the capital which in 1612 was tied up in his money-lending activities were the basis of the fortunes of the elder branch of the Hickes family which he founded and which is represented today by the earls St Aldwyn, just as the younger branch, founded by his brother Baptist, is now represented by the earls of Gainsborough.

During the course of his career Michael Hickes was a landowner, a money-lender, and an office holder, and he became the husband of a prosperous widow. A man could climb to fortune in any one of those four capacities. Hickes owed his success in life to luck in all of the last three. He did not inherit much land and in 1604 and 1610 he had to find the money—we do not know how much he paid—for his substantial land purchases in Nottinghamshire and Gloucestershire. It seems very unlikely that the revenue which he received from his own and his wife's lands could have paid for more than a fraction of the cost of these acquisitions. In other words, Hickes spent more money on land than he obtained from it. His landed property in 1612 was a sign that he and his family had arrived in society. The money which made that arrival possible came from other sources, one of which was almost certainly his wife, who brought with her at least £5,000 when he married her in 1594. That sum would have proved very useful in either money-lending or buying land. As Hickes's substantial land purchases did not begin for another decade, whereas his money-lending activities grew rapidly in scope from the 1590s onwards, it is likely that he employed his wife's money in the latter field.

Another source of money was office holding. As feodary of Essex Hickes received a basic annual fee of only £2, plus £1 of each £100 which he collected and brought up to London,[8] but he was also entitled to certain additional fees, including an allowance of £2 for every inquisition *post mortem* taken in the county. During his period in office between July 1598 and July 1601 fifty inquisitions were held in Essex, [9] and he must therefore have received £100, spread over three years, from that source. As some of the other allowances were assessed on the basis of the feodary's 'travail' in carrying out his duties, it is clear that his total earnings must have depended in part on his ability to stress the extent of his labours and thereby inflate his expenses. As receiver general of Essex, Middlesex, Hertfordshire, and London Hickes received a yearly fee of £50 plus £1 in each £100 collected.[10] As chief steward of Essex royal manors he received £12 per annum[11] and as a deputy in the Alienation Office £100 per annum.[12] As a justice of the peace he had a nominal fee,[13] and as a commissioner of the subsidy he was entitled to a share of the two pence which were divided among the commissioners out of each £1 paid into the Exchequer from subsidies.[14] Of course, it is a commonplace that Elizabethan and Jacobean office holders made much more out of their posts than the fees to which they were formally entitled and Hickes must have made larger sums out of the offices which he held than the fees enumerated above. He did not, however, hold any of the offices for very long and he never held an office which was of first-rate importance. It seems unlikely, therefore, that he could have made very large amounts from any of them. It is probable, on the other hand, that his position as Burghley's secretary and his role as Robert Cecil's confidant were of the greatest importance in helping him to accumulate capital. He normally expected gratuities for his services and, as we have seen, suitors were usually prepared to pay. Such gratuities might be as much as £100, and a few dozen 'gifts' of that magnitude would have given Hickes a large amount of money to invest in land or to lend to others. Once he had started money-lending on a fairly substantial scale in the 1590s this must have brought him considerable profits—the 10 per cent rate of interest ensured a rapid accumulation of capital.

Hickes's offices, both in central and in local administration, were, of course, much more than just a source of profit. They gave him a number of different roles to play in the government of the country. His only official post in the central administration was the deputyship in the Alienation Office which he held during the last four years of his life, but during the 1580s and 1590s, when he was Burghley's patronage secretary, much important government business passed through his hands. At that time he was simply Burghley's private servant. His work, and that of his colleagues in the secretariat, was organized by Burghley on whatever basis he thought best. This highly informal method of conducting important state business, which can be paralleled in the secretariats of other Elizabethan and early Stuart ministers, should remind historians of the danger of applying labels like 'bureaucratic' to the central administration of the time, and leaving it at that. Elizabethan and early Stuart government did, of course, operate to a considerable extent through state officials working the elaborate bureaucratic machinery of great departments such as Chancery and the Exchequer, but it also operated through private secretaries who had no official jobs and worked from the households of the Crown's leading ministers.[15] Elizabethan central government was a mixture of 'bureaucratic' and 'household' elements.

During the years after Burghley's death, with the exception of a period between 1601 and 1603, Hickes played an important role in local government in Essex. As feodary, receiver general, steward of royal manors, subsidy commissioner, and justice of the peace he occupied offices which gave him wide acquaintanceship with many aspects of local administration. This varied work, typical of that undertaken by many prominent gentlemen, reminds us that for the overwhelming bulk of the population in the Jacobean period it was local and not central government which was crucial in their lives. The poorer classes in particular might never come in contact with agents of the central government at all. For them it was local officials, especially the ubiquitous J.P.s, who determined their fate.

Hickes's governmental activities are historically the most important aspects of his career, but, for the biographer, much of the interest of his life lies in information in his personal papers which, combined with other material, allows insights into many elements of his character and enables us to see him among his family and friends. As a money-lender Hickes was capable of driving a shrewd bargain as he showed when, in his earliest recorded loan, to his friend Nicholas Beaumont, he obtained interest at a rate approaching 20 per cent. As secretary to Burghley he expected gratuities which clients sometimes considered excessive. Moreover, during the last years of Burghley's life he engaged with his friend Robert Cecil in intrigues which were at worst deplorable and at best hardly creditable. These facts suggest a picture of a hard and calculating businessman with an unscrupulous streak in his character. Other evidence reveals very different aspects of the man. As secretary to Burghley he had as much opportunity to offend as to gratify clients, and money-lenders are usually unpopular men. It says much, therefore, for his genius for personal relationships that he seems to have made few enemies, although he certainly had a multitude of friends. It is clear that he was a man of charm, with a ready wit and great human warmth, and this is nowhere better shown than in his relationship with Robert Cecil. As Cecil grew older he seems, to some extent, to have turned away from Hickes, the intimate of his youth, but there is no evidence that Hickes himself ever felt other than warm affection for his old friend. When he accompanied Cecil on the latter's final journey to Bath he did everything in his power to cheer the dying statesman's last days.

Hickes, so often the convivial extrovert, fond of games and hunting and the companionship of his friends, could also reveal sensitive sides to his nature. He did not marry until he was over fifty and his previous, unsuccessful, courtships suggest that he was often shy and inept with women. The story of how he refused a knighthood at the time of James I's coronation and only accepted the honour later, after a visit by the King to his house, also suggests a sensibility which might seem uncharacteristic of Burghley's grasping secretary. It is important to remember too, that, at least in his earlier years, he was a committed Puritan, the admirer of Thomas Cartwright and the friend of John Stubbe.

Hickes's character was a complex one and it would be wrong to minimize the contradictions which appear in the many facets of his personality. It is these contradictions which add interest to a study of the man and his work.

Abbreviations

and key to Public Record Office (PRO) call numbers

A7	PRO, Alienation Office, extracts from writs of covenant.
A9	PRO, Alienation Office, writs of entry in recovery.
Add MS(S)	British Museum Additional Manuscript(s).
APC	*Acts of the Privy Council of England.*
Assizes 35	PRO, records of Assizes.
BIHR	*Bulletin of the Institute of Historical Research.*
C2	PRO, Chancery Proceedings.
C54	PRO, Close Rolls.
C66	PRO, Patent Rolls.
C142	PRO, Chancery inquisitions *post mortem*.
CJ	*Journals of the House of Commons.*
CSP Dom	*Calendar of State Papers Domestic.*
DNB	*Dictionary of National Biography.*
E101	PRO, Exchequer, King's Remembrancer, Accounts Various.
E115	PRO, Exchequer, King's Remembrancer, Certificates of Residence.
E315	PRO, Exchequer, Miscellaneous Books, Augmentation Office.
EcHR	*Economic History Review.*
EHR	*English Historical Review.*
GEC	G. E. Cokayne, *The Complete Peerage*, new edition, 12 volumes (1910–59).
HMC	Historical Manuscripts Commission.
Lansd MS(S)	British Museum Lansdowne Manuscript(s).
LC4	PRO, Lord Chamberlain's Department, Entry books of recognizances in the nature of statutes staple.

LP	*Letters and Papers, Foreign and Domestic, of the Reign of Henry VIII.*
LR2	PRO, Exchequer, Land Revenue Department, Miscellaneous Books.
LR 6	PRO, Exchequer, Land Revenue Department, Receivers' Accounts.
MS(S)	Manuscript(s).
PCC	Prerogative Court of Canterbury.
PRO	Public Record Office.
Requests 2	PRO, Court of Requests, Proceedings.
SP 12	PRO, State Papers Domestic, Elizabeth.
SP 14	PRO, State Papers Domestic, James I.
SP 23	PRO, State Papers, Interregnum, Committee for Compounding with Delinquents.
SP 38	PRO, State Papers, Docquets.
SP 78	PRO, State Papers Foreign, France.
SP 84	PRO, State Papers Foreign, Holland.
Spedding	J. Spedding, *The Letters and Life of Francis Bacon,* 7 volumes (1861–74).
VCH	*The Victoria History of the Counties of England.*
Wards 5	PRO, Court of Wards, Feodaries' Surveys.
Wards 9	PRO, Court of Wards, Miscellaneous Books.
Wards 14	PRO, Court of Wards, Books of Orders.

Notes

Unless otherwise stated, all books referred to are published in London.

Chapter One
Young Michael

1. *Harleian Society Publications*, xxi (1885), *The Visitation of the County of Gloucester 1623*, ed. J. Maclean and W. C. Heane, 80.
2. S. E. Hicks Beach, *A Cotswold Family, Hicks and Hicks Beach* (1909), 29–33; PCC 9 Noodes.
3. *Harleian Society Publications, Registers*, xliv (1914), *The Registers of St Mary Le Bowe, Cheapside; All Hallows, Honey Lane; and of St Pancras, Soper Lane, London*, part 1 (Baptisms and Burials), ed. W. Bruce Bannerman, 128.
4. Ibid., 128, 285.
5. The memorial to Baptist Hickes in the church of Chipping Campden, Gloucestershire, states that he lived to the age of 78 and died on October 18th, 1629. See J. C. Jeaffreson, ed., *Middlesex County Records*, iv (1892), 343. It appears from Robert Hickes's will — PCC 9 Noodes — that Baptist was the youngest of the family. Clement must have been born in the interval between the births of Hilary and John or in that between the births of John and Baptist.
6. PCC 9 Noodes.
7. Ibid.
8. J. Stow, *A Survey of London*, ed. C. L. Kingsford, 1 (Oxford, 1908), 264–6. There is an excellent brief description of sixteenth-century London by Martin Holmes in *Elizabethan London* (1969).
9. In June 1561 lightning struck the spire and it burned down, never to be replaced. Stow, *Survey of London*, I, 331.

10. M. McDonnell, *The Annals of St Paul's School* (Cambridge, 1959), 94; J. Stow, *A Survey of the Cities of London and Westminster*, ed. J. Strype, I (1720), 288.
11. K. Charlton, *Education in Renaissance England* (1965), 98–117; McDonnell, *The Annals of St Paul's School*, 76–80.
12. PCC 9 Noodes.
13. After her death in 1592 both the land and the White Bear passed to Michael as the eldest son. He retained the land, but surrendered all his rights in the White Bear to Baptist. Hicks Beach, *A Cotswold Family*, 79.
14. A letter of William Cecil to Mrs Penne – Lansd MS 103 f 268 r – can probably be assigned to the year 1558.
15. W. W. Rouse Ball and J. A. Venn, eds., *Admissions to Trinity College, Cambridge*, II (1913), 36.
16. *CSP Dom 1547–80*, 121, 130, 131, 134.
17. H. C. Porter, *Reformation and Reaction in Tudor Cambridge* (Cambridge, 1958), 101, 104, 106–7; G. M. Trevelyan, *Trinity College* (Cambridge, 1941), 17.
18. For Blythe's career see J. and J. A. Venn, *Alumni Cantabrigiensis*, part i, vol. 1 (Cambridge, 1922), 171; C. H. and T. Cooper, *Athenae Cantabrigiensis*, 1 (Cambridge, 1858), 327; J. Fisher, *Alumni Oxoniensis 1500–1714* (Oxford, no date), 142; T. A. Walker, *A Biographical Register of Peterhouse Men*, 1 (Cambridge, 1927), 195–6.
19. For two very different views see Mark A. Curtis, *Oxford and Cambridge in Transition 1558–1642* (Oxford, 1959), ch. 4, and Charlton, op. cit., ch. 5.
20. Lansd MS 5 f 112 v.
21. Ibid., f 111 r.
22. Ibid., loc. cit.
23. *DNB*; Trevelyan, op. cit., 18; Porter, op. cit., 114–18.
24. *Athenae Cantabrigiensis*, II (Cambridge, 1861), 360; Trevelyan, op. cit., 18.
25. Lansd MS 69 f 101 r.
26. Lansd MSS 10 f 72 r, 841 f 2 r (Blythe); 18 f 35 r (Cartwright); 13 f 116 rv, 33 f 193 r (Skinner); 12 ff 117 rv, 217 rv; 21 f 26 r; 23 f 179 rv; 25 f 135 r; 31 f 40 r; 36 ff 212 r–213 r (Stubbe).
27. *Harleian Society Publications*, lii (1904), *Lincolnshire Pedigrees*, III, ed. A. R. Maddison, 887–8; Rouse Ball and Venn, op. cit., II, 33; H. M. Innes, *Fellows of Trinity College* (Cambridge, 1941), 23; M. M. Knappen, *Tudor Puritanism* (Chicago, 1939), 233–4.

28. *Athenae Cantabrigiensis*, II, 111.
29. Rouse Ball and Venn, op. cit., II, 45.
30. See Lansd MSS 75 f 88 r; 89 f 138 r.
31. See Lansd MSS 10 f 73 v; 12 f 117 v. These letters, from Blythe to Hickes and from Stubbe to Hickes, are dated 1568 and 1570 respectively, but, as their contents suggest that Blythe, Skinner, Stubbe, and Hickes were friends of long standing, each with the others, and as the four were contemporaries at Trinity College, it seems very likely that the intimacy which later certainly existed among them began to develop at Cambridge.
32. See Lansd MS 33 ff 14 r, 193 r.
33. *The Records of the Honourable Society of Lincoln's Inn, Admissions*, I (1896), 73.
34. There are accounts of the Grey–Hertford marriage in Mortimer Levine, *The Early Elizabethan Succession Question 1558–1568* (Stanford, 1966), 15–29; and in P. M. Handover, *Arbella Stuart* (1957), 27–39.
35. Lansd MS 4 f 180 r.
36. J. E. Neale, *Elizabeth I and her Parliaments*, I (1953), 90, 103–4; W. MacCaffrey, *The Shaping of the Elizabethan Regime* (1968), 124; HMC *Salisbury*, xiii, 66–7.
37. HMC *Salisbury*, i, 294.
38. Lansd MS 7 ff 210 r, 211 v.
39. MacCaffrey, op. cit., 124.
40. *CSP Dom 1547–80*, 306.
41. *The Records of the Honourable Society of Lincoln's Inn, The Black Books*, I (1897), 241.
42. *Lincoln's Inn Admissions*, I, 70, 71, 73.
43. Ibid., 73.
44. W. R. Prest, *The Inns of Court under Elizabeth and the Early Stuarts 1590–1640* (1972), 150.
45. Lansd MS 23 f 179 r.
46. *Lincoln's Inn Black Books*, I, 402.
47. Lansd MS 51 f 55 r.
48. *Lincoln's Inn Black Books*, I, xxxiii, 362.
49. *Lincoln's Inn Admissions*, I, 65; *Lincoln's Inn Black Books*, I, ii.
50. Lansd MS 43 f 6 r.
51. *Lincoln's Inn Black Books*, I, ii.
52. Lansd MS 90 f 97 r.
53. Lansd MS 101 f 138 v.
54. PCC 24 Daper.
55. Lansd MS 841 f 3 r.

56. Lansd MSS 46 f 29 v; 51 f 2 r; 108 f 147 r.
57. Lansd MS 103 f 268 r.
58. R. C. Barnett, 'Place, Profit, and Power. A study of the servants of William Cecil, Elizabethan statesman', *The James Sprunt Studies in History and Political Science*, li (Chapel Hill, North Carolina, 1970), 40–41, 128–9.

Chapter Two
Hickes in the Lord Treasurer's Household

1. It is possible that Hickes himself was the author. For the evidence see A. G. R. Smith, 'Sir Michael Hickes and the Secretariat of the Cecils, c. 1580–1612' (London University Ph.D. thesis, 1962), 316–20. See also a forthcoming volume of *Cecilian Documents*, edited by J. Hurstfield and A. G. R. Smith.
2. F. Peck, *Desiderata Curiosa*, vol. 1 (1732), book i, 29–30.
3. There is some information about the household in Richard C. Barnett, 'Place, Profit, and Power. A study of the servants of William Cecil, Elizabethan Statesman', *The James Sprunt Studies in History and Political Science*, li (Chapel Hill, North Carolina, 1970).
4. C. Read, *Mr Secretary Cecil and Queen Elizabeth* (1955), 119.
5. W. MacCaffrey, *The Shaping of the Elizabethan Regime* (1968), 295. This book contains much the best account of the Leicester–Cecil rivalry during the 1560s and of the significance of the crisis of 1568–72.
6. Peck, op. cit., 1, i, 45.
7. J. Clapham, *Elizabeth of England*, ed. E. P. and C. Read (Philadelphia, 1951), 80.
8. Peck, op. cit., 1, i, 47.
9. Ibid., 39.
10. HMC *Salisbury*, v, 191–2.
11. Salisbury MS 28/71.
12. Peck, op. cit., 1, i, 49.
13. Ibid., 47.
14. Read, *Mr Secretary Cecil and Queen Elizabeth*, 212.
15. For Burghley's policy as guardian, see J. Hurstfield, *The Queen's Wards* (1958), 241–59.
16. H. Chauncy, *The Historical Antiquities of Hertfordshire*, 1 (Bishops Stortford, 1826), 591; Barnett, 59–60.
17. Clapham, op. cit., 4–5, 71; HMC *Salisbury*, v, 191–2.
18. R. Somerville, *History of the Duchy of Lancaster*, 1 (1953), 579–

580; *Harleian Society Publications*, lii (1904), *Lincolnshire Pedigrees*, iii, ed. A. R. Maddison, 887–8; PRO List of Escheators, 80; Barnett, op. cit., 129.

19. F. Chancellor, *The Ancient Sepulchral Monuments of Essex* (1890), 82; account of the funeral expenses of Sir Nicholas Bacon, Raynham MS (I owe this reference to the History of Parliament Trust); Barnett, op. cit., 95–6.

20. J. Stow, *A Survey of London*, ed. C. L. Kingsford, ii (Oxford, 1908), 98; *Country Life*, December 3rd and 10th, 1953; J. Summerson, 'The Building of Theobalds, 1564–1585', *Archaeologia*, xcvii (1959), 107–26; E. K. Chambers, *The Elizabethan Stage*, iv (Oxford, 1923), 81–111; W. B. Rye, *England as seen by foreigners in the days of Elizabeth and James I* (1865), 44–5; C. Read, 'Lord Burghley's Household Accounts', *EcHR*, 2nd series, ix (1956–7), 343–8.

21. Lansd MS 108 f 147 r.

22. Lansd MS 107 f 166 r.

23. Lansd MS 108 ff 147 r–148 r.

24. Ibid., f 149 rv.

25. Peck, op. cit., i, i, 19–20.

26. Clapham, op. cit., 80–81.

27. Francis Bacon, Essay 'Of great place'.

28. The evidence is too scanty to build up a clear picture of Burghley's secretariat before about 1580.

29. R. Beale, 'A treatise of the Office of a Councellor and Principall Secretarie to her Ma[jes]tie', in C. Read, *Mr Secretary Walsingham and the policy of Queen Elizabeth*, i (Oxford, 1925), 427; 'Nicholas Faunt's Discourse touching the Office of Principal Secretary of Estate etc. 1592', *EHR*, xx (1905), 500.

30. T. Wilson, 'The State of England in 1600', ed. F. J. Fisher, *Camden Miscellany*, xvi (1936), 42.

31. Clapham, op. cit., 84.

32. SP 12/245/51.

33. Burghley's constant ill health after the end of 1591 is detailed by C. Read in *Lord Burghley and Queen Elizabeth* (1960), 477–546 *passim*.

34. *EHR*, xx, 501–2.

35. SP 84/48 f 76 v; Lansd MS 79 f 186 r.

36. For details see A. G. R. Smith, 'The secretariats of the Cecils, circa 1580–1612', *EHR*, lxxxiii (1968), 491–3.

37. Ibid., 485.

38. See e.g. HMC *Salisbury*, ii, 200; iii, 252.

39. See e.g. Lansd MS 58 f 180 r; HMC *Salisbury*, vi, 102.

40. See e.g. Lansd MS 77 f 170 r; SP 12/244/17.
41. *CSP Dom 1591–4*, 231.
42. HMC *Salisbury*, viii, 296, 298, 299, 339.
43. HMC *De L'Isle and Dudley*, ii, 403.
44. Lansd MS 61 f 145 r.
45. HMC *Bath*, ii, 37.
46. Lansd MS 77 f 172 r.
47. Lansd MS 80 f 168 r.
48. Lansd MS 82 f 188 r.
49. Lansd MS 85 f 57 r.
50. Vincent Skinner in 1584, 1586, 1589 and 1593; Henry Maynard in 1584, 1586, 1589, 1593 and 1597; Michael Hickes in 1584, 1589, 1593 and 1597; and John Clapham in 1597.
51. There can be little doubt that Burghley's influence, either direct or indirect, was primarily responsible for securing most of his secretaries' seats. Skinner sat in 1584, 1586 and 1589 for the Lincolnshire town of Boston, where Burghley held the office of recorder. Boroughbridge in Yorkshire, his constituency in 1593, was subject to Duchy of Lancaster influence and Burghley may have been able to bring pressure to bear on Chancellor Heneage in order to secure his return. Maynard sat, in all five of his Parliaments, for St Albans in Hertfordshire, where Burghley was high steward. Hickes sat in 1584 for the Cornish borough of Truro, where Burghley exercised influence through his relatives the Killigrews, but he probably owed his Dorsetshire seat at Shaftesbury in 1588 and 1593 to the earl of Pembroke. Burghley's influence probably obtained him his place at Gatton in Surrey in 1597. Clapham must have owed his Suffolk seat at Sudbury in 1597 to Robert Cecil, who exercised influence there through the office of Chancellor of the Duchy of Lancaster, which he held from 1597 to 1599.
52. Lansd MS 73 f 130 rv.
53. *Statutes of the Realm*, iv (1819), 847–9.
54. J. E. Neale, *Elizabeth I and her Parliaments 1584–1601* (1957), 363; A. F. Pollard and M. Blatcher, 'Hayward Townshend's Journals', *BIHR*, xii (1934–5), 20.
55. See HMC *Salisbury*, iv, 323; v, 360, 511; vi, 191, 527; vii, 266, 293, 378; viii, 205; xiii, 577; Salisbury MSS 28/71, 75; 32/30; 53/20; *CSP Dom 1591–4*, 370; Lansd MS 107 ff 72 r, 94 r.
56. Salisbury MS 28/75.
57. Salisbury MS 32/30.
58. HMC *Salisbury*, v, 360, 511.

59. A. Cecil, *A Life of Robert Cecil, First Earl of Salisbury* (1915), 16–17.
60. Lansd MS 107 f 76 r.
61. Lansd MS 65 f 192 r.
62. Lansd MS 107 f 74 r.
63. Ibid., f 75 v.
64. HMC *Bath*, ii, 37.
65. Lansd MS 107 f 107 r.
66. Ibid., f 83 r.
67. Lansd MS 85 f 36 r.
68. Lansd MS 68 f. 202 r.
69. Lansd MS 66 f 186 r.
70. GEC, xi, 404.
71. Lansd MS 107 f 65 r.
72. Ibid., f 66 r.
73. Ibid., f 80 r.
74. W. A. Shaw, *The Knights of England*, ii (1906), 88; *APC*, New Series, xxi, 358; xxvi, 7; A. Cecil, op. cit., 52, 58–9.

Chapter Three

The Patronage Secretary

1. There are general accounts of the Elizabethan patronage system by J. E. Neale, 'The Elizabethan Political Scene', *Essays in Elizabethan History* (1958), 59–84; W. MacCaffrey, 'Place and Patronage in Elizabethan Politics', *Elizabethan Government and Society*, ed. S. T. Bindoff, J. Hurstfield, C. H. Williams (1961), 95–126; A. G. R. Smith, *The Government of Elizabethan England* (1967), 57–69.
2. R. Naunton, *Fragmenta Regalia* (1808), 178–80.
3. E. Spenser, 'The Ruines of Time', ll. 449–53.
4. Spedding, vi, 6–7.
5. F. Bacon, Essay 'Of great place'.
6. E. Spenser, 'Mother Hubbard's Tale', ll. 895–906.
7. Lansd MSS 46, 51, 55, 59–61, 63–6, 68, 71–80, 82–7, 99, 107–109, 112 *passim*; HMC *Bath*, ii, 37, 42; HMC *Salisbury*, iv, 369; v, 158.
8. Lansd MS 77 f 168 r.
9. Lansd MS 85 f 4 r.
10. *DNB*; J. W. Stoye, *English Travellers Abroad 1604–67* (1952), 70; SP 78/55 f 80 v.
11. Stoye, op. cit., 47–9, 70–82.
12. Ibid., 70–74.

13. On the whole subject of wardship under Elizabeth see J. Hurst-field, *The Queen's Wards* (1958).
14. Lansd MS 71 f 180 r.
15. Lansd MS 68 f 29 r.
16. Lansd MS 84 f 164 r.
17. Lansd MS 87 f 37 r.
18. Lansd MS 77 f 114 r.
19. Lansd MS 82 f 46 r.
20. Lansd MS 77 f 180 r.
21. Lansd MS 64 f 92 r.
22. Lansd MS 85 f 55 r.
23. Lansd MS 77 f 102 r.
24. Lansd MS 108 f 121 r.
25. Lansd MS 75 f 100 r.
26. Lansd MSS 64 ff 97 r, 99 r; 75 f 101 r.
27. Lansd MS 75 f 100 r.
28. Lansd MS 68 f 72 r.
29. Lansd MS 72 f 209 r.
30. Lansd MS 77 ff 125 r, 151 r.
31. Lansd MS 107 f 48 r.
32. Lansd MS 108 f 17 r.
33. HMC *Bath*, ii, 37.
34. Lansd MS 78 f 76 r.
35. Lansd MS 72 f 195 r.
36. Lansd MS 82 f 138 r.
37. Lansd MS 109 f 132 r.
38. Lansd MSS 76 f 30 r; 85 f 10 r; 107 f 175 r.
39. HMC *Salisbury*, iv, 369; Lansd MSS 84 f 168 r; 86 f 28 r; 76 f 159 r.
40. Lansd MS 108 f 85 r.
41. Lansd MS 75 f 128 r.
42. Lansd MS 82 f 134 r.
43. Lansd MSS 71 f 190 r; 84 f 166 r.
44. Lansd MS 82 f 208 r.
45. Lansd MS 75 f 88 r.
46. Lansd MS 79 f 184 r.
47. Lansd MS 108 f 96 r.
48. Lansd MS 76 f 166 r.
49. Lansd MS 60 f 202 r.
50. Lansd MS 79 f 81 r.
51. Lansd MS 85 f 59 r.
52. Lansd MS 80 f 14 rv; *CSP Dom 1595–7*, 235–7, 239, 240–5; *DNB*.

53. Lansd MS 99 f 75 r.
54. Lansd MS 72 f 203 r.
55. Lansd MS 63 f 177 r; V. Pearl, *London and the Outbreak of the Puritan Revolution* (Oxford, 1961), 18–20, 26–7.
56. Lansd MS 61 f 62 r.
57. Lansd MS 98 f 215 r.
58. HMC *Ancaster*, 314.
59. J. F. Williams, 'An Episcopal Visitation in 1593', *Norfolk Archaeology*, xxviii, 79–82.
60. A. Pulling, *Order of the Coif* (1884), xv–xxvi, provides a list of all serjeants.
61. Lansd MS 76 f 30 r. Patents of appointments to customerships, controllerships and other customs posts in the gift of the Lord Treasurer were entered on the fine rolls. Thomas Ravenscroft's name does not appear. See PRO Indexes 17351, 17352. Index 17351 is a chronological calender of the fine rolls *temp*. Elizabeth–Charles I. Index 17352 is an index *nominum et locorum* to Index 17351.
62. See C 66/1468; C 66/1482. These contain the names of the justices of the peace between 1596 and 1598. Glaseour made his request in 1596; his name does not appear on the rolls cited.
63. Lansd MSS 82 f 134 r; 85 f 14 r.
64. *Haydn's Book of Dignities*, 3rd edn. (1894), 476–7.
65. *DNB*, *sub* Paulet, Sir Amias; *CSP Dom 1598–1601*, 457; A. J. Eagleston, *The Channel Islands under Tudor Government* (Cambridge, 1949), 90–98.
66. *Haydn's Book of Dignities*, 384.
67. See e.g. Lansd MSS 46 f 29 r; 66 f 187 r; 68 f 232 r; 72 ff 195 r, 209 r; 75 ff 115 r, 118 r; 82 f 140 r; 84 f 164 r; 108 f 46 r.
68. See pp. 70–72, 78–80.
69. Lansd MSS 75 ff 113 r, 124 r; 78 f 79 r; R. Somerville, *The Savoy* (1960), 239.
70. Lansd MS 78 f 79 r; Somerville, op. cit., 239.
71. Lansd MS 84 f 127 r; *CSP Dom 1598–1601*, 123.
72. Lansd MS 84 f 123 r; *APC*, New Series, xxvii, 39–40.
73. Lansd MS 85 ff 116 r, 118 r, 120 r.
74. Lansd MS 107 f 175 r; PRO Index 17351, 210.
75. MacCaffrey, 'Place and Patronage in Elizabethan Politics', 111.
76. Clapham, *Elizabeth of England*, ed. E. P. and C. Read (Philadelphia, 1951), 75.
77. Hurstfield, *The Queen's Wards*, 267–8.

78. SP 12/244/69.
79. L. Stone, *The Crisis of the Aristocracy* (Oxford, 1965), 489.
80. Lansd MS 107 f 162 r.
81. Lansd MS 76 f 180 r.
82. Lansd MS 82 f 134 r.
83. Lansd MS 75 f 153 r.
84. Lansd MS 108 f 19 r.
85. Lansd MSS 46, 51, 55, 59–61, 63–6, 68, 71–80, 82–7, 99, 107–9, 112 *passim*; HMC *Bath*, ii, 37, 42; HMC *Salisbury*, iv, 369.
86. Lansd MS 72 f 195 r.
87. Lansd MSS 108 f 46 v; 46 f 29 r.
88. HMC *Bath*, ii, 37.
89. Lansd MSS 66 f 161 r; 87 f 37 r; 86 f 77 r.
90. HMC *Bath*, ii, 42.
91. Lansd MS 75 f 30 r.
92. Lansd MSS 77 f 127 r; 108 f 96 r; 83 f 114 r.
93. Lansd MS 77, f 102 r.
94. Lansd MS 75 f 88 r.
95. Lansd MS 77 f 159 r.
96. Ibid., f 135 r.
97. Lansd MS 61 f 62 r.
98. Ibid., f 170 r.
99. Lansd MS 75 f 115 r.
100. Lansd MS 84 f 164 r.
101. Neale, 'The Elizabethan Political Scene', 76.
102. Lansd MS 75 f 134 r; HMC *Salisbury*, iv, 377.
103. Lansd MS 75 f 134 r.
104. Ibid., f 138 r.
105. Lansd MS 77 f 164 r.
106. Ibid., f 168 r.
107. Ibid., f 178 r; 82 ff 36 r, 42 r.
108. Lansd MS 74 f 216 r.
109. Lansd MS 75 f 134 r.
110. Lansd MS 77 f 164 r.
111. Ibid., f 178 r.
112. Lansd MS 82 f 42 r.
113. PRO List of Escheators, 141, 71, 124.
114. Lansd MS 107 f 78 r.
115. Ibid., f 81 r.
116. HMC *Bath*, ii, 37.
117. Lansd MS 107 f 77 r.
118. Lansd MS 77 f 137 r.

119. Lansd MS 61 f 210 r.
120. Lansd MS 64 f 147 r.
121. *Haydn's Book of Dignities*, 370, 399, 401.
122. Lansd MS 72 f 218 r.
123. Ibid., f 220 r.
124. HMC *Salisbury*, v, 7, 11, 31, 32, 35, 37, 41, 42, 46, 48 49, 51, 79, 84, 92, 95, 106, 112, 121, 128, 162, 174, 177, 215.
125. Lansd MS 77 f 36 r.
126. Ibid., f 153 r.
127. Ibid., f 147 r.
128. HMC *Salisbury*, v, 7.
129. Lansd MS 77 f 40 r.
130. Ibid., f 174 r.
131. Ibid., f 192 r. The letter is not precisely dated and Matthew's name is nowhere mentioned. It is, however, endorsed '1594' and, in view of the contents, there seems little doubt that it refers to Matthew.
132. HMC *Salisbury*, v, 121–2.
133. Ibid., 48–9, 79; *VCH Worcester*, ii (1906), 54.
134. Lansd MS 78 f 40 r.
135. Lansd MS 79 f 108 r.
136. Lansd MS 77 f 42 r.
137. Requests 2/70/49, document 1.
138. Requests 2/70/49, document 2.
139. PRO List of Escheators, 71.
140. According to Smith, Puckering was also deeply involved. Putto, however, makes no mention of Puckering undertaking an active role and his participation must, therefore, be regarded as not proven.
141. The best general discussion of the subject is by J. Hurstfield, 'Political Corruption in Modern England', *History*, lii (1967), 16–34, reprinted in his *Freedom, Corruption and Government in Elizabethan England* (1973), 137–62.

Chapter Four

The Money-Lender

1. R. H. Tawney, Introduction to *Thomas Wilson's Discourse Upon Usury, 1572* (1925), 22. Tawney's Introduction to this sixteenth-century classic contains much the best general account of contemporary attitudes towards money-lending.
2. Tawney, 'Introduction to Wilson', 31; L. Stone, *The Crisis of the Aristocracy* (Oxford, 1965), 505–6.

3. Ibid., 158, 542–3.
4. Ibid., 532–5.
5. Francis Bacon, Essay 'Of riches'.
6. On the role of the broker see R. Ashton, 'Usury and high finance in the age of Shakespeare and Jonson', *Renaissance and Modern Studies*, IV (1960), 14–43.
7. Francis Bacon, Essay 'Of usury'.
8. Tawney, 'Introduction to Wilson', 106–17.
9. 37 Henry VIII, c 9. *Statutes of the Realm*, iii (1817), 996–7.
10. 5 & 6 Edward VI, c 20. *Statutes of the Realm*, iv (1819), 155.
11. The point is made by Tawney, 'Introduction to Wilson', 131.
12. Stone, op. cit., 529–30.
13. 13 Eliz., c 8. *Statutes of the Realm*, iv, 542–3.
14. Tawney, 'Introduction to Wilson', 165–6; Stone, op. cit., 530–32.
15. There are good accounts of sixteenth-century security instruments in Stone, op. cit., 513–27, and R. T. Spence, 'The Cliffords, Earls of Cumberland, 1579–1646: a study of their fortunes based on their household and estate accounts' (London University Ph.D. thesis, 1959), pages xxiv–xlviii.
16. Lansd MS 103 f 268 r. This letter has been assigned to the last years of Henry VIII's reign by Conyers Read, who suggested that it was 'the product of a young man with hardly any claim to consideration' and argued that the Mrs Penne in question was either Sibilla Penne, nurse to Prince Edward, or Lucy Pen, wife of the King's barber (*Mr Secretary Cecil and Queen Elizabeth* [1955], 32). The fact, however, that the letter is found among Hickes's papers and that his mother was a money-lender makes it virtually certain that it was addressed to her. Her marriage to Anthony Penne cannot have taken place before 1557 and the reference to 'this troublesome time' makes it unlikely that Cecil wrote it after Elizabeth's accession in November 1558. It should, therefore, be assigned to the closing months of Mary's reign.
17. Lansd MS 108 ff 30 r, 31 rv, 33 r–34 v.
18. Ibid., f 30 r.
19. Lansd MS 68 f 255 r.
20. Ibid., ff 253 r, 257 r.
21. Ibid., f 207 r.
22. Ibid., f 209 r.
23. Lansd MS 39 f 116 r.
24. Lansd MS 108 f 43 r.
25. Lansd MS 79 f 197 r.

26. Lansd MS 107 ff 18 r, 20 r.
27. PCC 60 Nevell.
28. LC 4/193/32 (Between Hickes on the one hand and Sir Thomas Parry and Sir Henry Bromley on the other); LC 4/193/69 (Between Hickes on the one hand and Sir Robert Dormer on the other); LC 4/193/172 (Between Hickes on the one hand and Richard Corbett, Viscount Corbett, and Richard Wood on the other). A statute gave the amount not of the debt itself, but of the penalty for failure to repay the debt at the stipulated time. This was normally double the debt. The penalties in the three statutes cited totalled £4,000.
29. Lansd MS 109 f 129 r. Stafford had an income of less than £1,000 a year. Stone, op. cit., 760.
30. Spedding, ii, 28.
31. Lansd MS 34 f 44 r.
32. Lansd MS 109 f 113 r.
33. Lansd MS 77 f 158 r.
34. C 54/682.
35. HMC *Bath*, ii, 41 (the statute was for £400 representing a loan of £200); Add MS 4111 f 50 v; HMC *Salisbury*, viii, 559; Lansd MS 87 ff 87 r, 117 r.
36. LC 4/193/370. The penalty was for £4,000. It is virtually certain that this was a loan as there is independent evidence that Hickes lent money to Lee later on, in the early years of the seventeenth century.

Chapter Five

The Puritan Amidst his Family and Friends

1. The best account of Elizabethan Puritanism is by P. Collinson, *The Elizabethan Puritan Movement* (1967). See also P. McGrath, *Papists and Puritans under Elizabeth I* (1967).
2. Lansd MS 12 f 117 r.
3. Ibid., f 217 r.
4. Lansd MS 23 f 179 r.
5. Lansd MS 21 f 26 r.
6. Lansd MS 25 f 135 r.
7. *DNB*; C. Read, *Lord Burghley and Queen Elizabeth* (1960), 217; E. M. Tenison, *Elizabethan England*, iii (1933), 176–7; W. Camden, *Elizabeth* (4th edn., 1688), 270.
8. Lansd MS 107 f 170 rv.
9. Lansd MS 31 f 40 r.
10. Lansd MS 36 ff 212 v–213 r.

11. Lansd MS 107 f 168 rv.
12. Lansd MS 61 f 170 r.
13. There is a useful biography of Cartwright by A. F. S. Pearson, *Thomas Cartwright and Elizabethan Puritanism* (Cambridge, 1925).
14. Lansd MS 69 f 101 r (printed by Pearson, op. cit., 476).
15. Lansd MS 18 f 35 r (Pearson, op. cit., 432).
16. Lansd MS 64 f 59 r (Pearson, op. cit., 449–50).
17. Lansd MS 69 f 101 r (Pearson, op. cit., 476).
18. Lansd MS 79 f 174 r (Pearson, op. cit., 480).
19. Lansd MS 36 f 212 r.
20. Lansd MS 58 f 89 r.
21. Lansd MS 107 f 70 r.
22. Ibid., f 106 r.
23. HMC *Salisbury*, iv, 210–11, 221–2.
24. Lansd MS 72 f 213 r.
25. Salisbury MS 130/160.
26. Lansd MS 107 ff 100 r, 103 r.
27. Ibid., f 100 r.
28. C 142/261/59.
29. PCC 9 Noodes; C 142/261/59; S. E. Hicks Beach, *A Cotswold Family, Hicks and Hicks Beach* (1909), 65, 79.
30. Lansd MSS 78 f 52 r; 79 f 207 r; 82 f 128 r.
31. Lansd MS 78 f 52 r.
32. Lansd MSS 80 f 2 r; 107 f 162 r; 108 f 82 r.
33. Lansd MS 101 ff 138 r–139 r.
34. Lansd MS 43 f 6 r.
35. Lansd MS 101 f 129 rv.
36. Ibid., f 131 r.
37. Ibid., f 140 r.
38. Ibid., f 151 r; L. Stone, *The Crisis of the Aristocracy* (Oxford, 1965), 456–7, 609; GEC, xii, part ii, 678.
39. PCC 60 Nevell; C 142/236/74; D. Lysons, *The Environs of London*, iv (1796), 163.
40. Wards 9/158 ff 106 v–107 r; C 66/1447.
41. C 2 James I H 2/22; HMC *Salisbury*, vii, 113.
42. HMC *Salisbury*, xi, 549; *DNB*; R. Ashton, *The Crown and the Money Market 1603–40* (Oxford, 1960), 96.
43. Lansd MS 87 f 225 r.
44. Lansd MS 107 f 109 r.
45. Ibid., f 63 r.
46. Lansd MS 82 f 160 r.
47. Lansd MS 80 f 168 r.

48. Lansd MS 107 f 98 r.
49. A. Collins, *The Baronettage of England*, 11 (1720), 64.
50. Lansd MS 82 f 182 r.
51. Manuscript Register of Baptisms preserved in the parish church of St Mary the Virgin, Leyton.
52. Salisbury MS 62/51.
53. Francis Bacon, Essay 'Of friendship'.
54. Lansd MSS 10 f 72 r; 33 f 193 r; 841 f 2 r.
55. Lansd MS 21 f 24 r.
56. See pp. 26-7.
57. Lansd MS 109 ff 116 r, 114 r.
58. Ibid., f 111 r.
59. Lansd MSS 61 f 142 r; 68 f 220 r; 77 ff 149 r, 170 r, 172 r; 82 f 167 r; 85 ff 43 r, 45 r, 57 r; 87 f 71 r; 108 f 12 r.
60. Lansd MS 85 ff 43 r, 45 r.
61. Ibid., f 51 r; 86 f 79 r.
62. Spedding, I, 256–7.
63. Lansd MSS 80 f 2 r; 108 f 9 r.
64. Lansd MSS 80 f 2 r; 107 f 162 r.
65. Lansd MS 107 f 26 r.
66. Ibid., ff 22 r–23 r.
67. Ibid., ff 28 rv, 30 r, 32 r, 34 r.
68. Ibid., f 28 r.
69. Ibid., f 32 r.
70. Lansd MS 51 f 59 r.
71. Lansd MS 107 f 161 v. The letter – a draft – is addressed simply to 'Mr Beaumont'.
72. Lansd MS 85 f 47 r.
73. Ibid., f 49 r.
74. E. K. Chambers, *The Elizabethan Stage* (Oxford, 1923), IV, 111.
75. Lansd MS 108 f 86 r.

Chapter Six

The Government Official

1. For what follows on the Court of Wards see H. E. Bell, *An Introduction to the History and Records of the Court of Wards and Liveries* (Cambridge, 1953); J. Hurstfield, *The Queen's Wards* (1958).
2. See pp. 57-60.
3. Wards 9/275.
4. Bell, op. cit., 39–40.
5. Wards 9/275.

6. *LP*, i, part 2, 2055/104, 2222/12.
7. Hurstfield, *The Queen's Wards*, 238.
8. Wards 14/6/11.
9. *CSP Dom 1598–1601*, 394.
10. Bell, op. cit., 41; Hurstfield, *The Queen's Wards*, 235.
11. Wards 9/275; Bell, op. cit., 44.
12. Lansd MS 87 ff 119 v–120 v.
13. Bell, op. cit., 75–9.
14. Hurstfield, *The Queen's Wards*, 47; Bell, op. cit., 42.
15. C 142/253/73; 142/257/43; 142/262/106.
16. C 142/279/350.
17. C 142/252–266 *passim*.
18. See pp. 70-72, 78-80.
19. Hurstfield, *The Queen's Wards*, 83–5.
20. C 142/253/73; Wards 5/14/2346 (Inquisition value £4:13:4, survey value £6:13:4). C 142/261/91; Wards 5/13/2136 (Inquisition value £4; survey value £4:3:4). C 142/261/76; Wards 5/13/2185 (Inquisition value £2:5:0; survey value £2:13:4). C 142/262/106; Wards 5/13/2247 (Inquisition value £46:13:4; survey value £58:17:4). C 142/261/47; Wards 5/13/2082 (Inquisition value £5; survey value £8).
21. C 142/258/82; Wards 5/13/2226 (Inquisition and survey values £3:3:4).
22. C 142/258/73; Wards 5/14/74 (Inquisition value £7; survey value £6:13:4). C 142/256/27; Wards 5/13/2278 (Inquisition value £9:10:0; survey value £6).
23. Hurstfield, *The Queen's Wards*, 84–5.
24. J. Hurstfield, 'The Profits of Fiscal Feudalism, 1541–1602' *EcHR*, 2nd series, viii, 55–6.
25. Hurstfield, *The Queen's Wards*, 275–6, 312–13.
26. Wards 9/160 ff 39 v–45 r.
27. Ibid., ff 39 v–40 r.
28. Lansd MS 87 f 41 r.
29. Wards 9/160 ff 39 v–40 r.
30. Ibid., loc. cit.
31. Hurstfield, 'The Profits of Fiscal Feudalism', 56.
32. Wards 9/288, 191.
33. Wards 9/474, 484.
34. C 66/1608.
35. Lansd MS 88 f 117 r.
36. LR 6/70/1.
37. Lansd MS 89 f 15 r.
38. SP 38/7.

39. C 66/1682, 1822.
40. There is a brief account of the role of the Justice of the Peace in A. G. R. Smith, *The Government of Elizabethan England* (1967), 90–95.
41. Essex Record Office, Typescript Calendar of Sessions Records, xviii, xix; Middlesex Record Office, Manuscript Sessions Registers, i (1608–13).
42. Lansd MS 90 f 222 r.
43. Ibid., f 226 r.
44. Lansd MS 91 f 41 r.
45. Ibid., f 154 r.
46. Lansd MS 92 f 51 r.
47. Ibid., f 134 r.
48. Essex Record Office, Typescript Calendar of Sessions Records, xix, 58, 70 – 71. The relevant statute is 22 Henry VIII, C 5. *Statutes of the Realm*, iii, 321–3.
49. Lansd MS 91 f 110 r.
50. Essex Record Office, Typescript Calendar of Sessions Records, xviii, 308–9, 316.
51. 39 Eliz., C 4; 1 Jac. 1, C 7. *Statutes of the Realm*, iv, 899–902, 1024–5.
52. E 115/204/99; E 115/211/142: E 115/196/73.
53. F. C. Dietz, *English Public Finance 1558–1641* (New York, 1932), 382–93.
54. E 115/211/142; E 115/196/73.
55. Lansd MS 90 f 9 r.
56. Lansd MS 89 f 179 r. For Steward see J. and J. A. Venn, *Alumni Cantabrigiensis*, part i, vol. IV (Cambridge, 1927), 161.
57. E 315/320 ff 136 v–137 r. The manors were Orsett, Copford, Ramsay, Shawes, Little Thurrock, Harwich, Dovercourt, Eastnewhall and Le Rey, East Mersey, and Barking. The chief stewardship and its attached offices carried a fee of £12.
58. Lansd MS 88 ff 133 r, 183 r.
59. *DNB*.
60. E 315/323 ff 54 v–55 r.
61. W. R. Scott, *The Constitution and Finance of English, Scottish and Irish Joint Stock Companies*, III (Cambridge, 1912), 485–509; R. H. Tawney, *Business and Politics under James I* (Cambridge, 1958), 134 ff; R. Ashton, 'Deficit finance in the reign of James I', *EcHR*, 2nd series, x (1957–8), 15–29.
62. For sharply contrasting views of Salisbury and the Great Contract see Hurstfield, *The Queen's Wards*, ch. 15; M. Prestwich, *Cranfield* (Oxford, 1966), ch. 1.

63. Lansd MS 89 f 6 r.
64. Lansd MS 91 f 25 r.
65. In 1608 Lord Treasurer Salisbury and Chancellor of the Exchequer Sir Julius Caesar stated that Buckhurst's restrictions on the granting of copyhold estates had been designed to prevent loss to the King until a survey of all the Crown lands should determine their true value. Lansd MS 90 f 129 r.
66. Lansd MS 89 ff 21 r, 70 r, 72 r, 76 r.
67. Lansd MS 90 f 122 r.
68. SP 14/31/29; 14/32/85.
69. SP 14/37/103. Dietz, op. cit., 117, 297-8, does not give Buckhurst due credit for his part in promoting the surveys. His footnote (p. 298 n. 15), which implies that Hercy's surveys were the result of Salisbury's measures, is misleading. Hercy himself stated that they were undertaken on Buckhurst's instructions. See SP 14/32/85.
70. LR 2/214/ff 210-350.
71. SP 14/37/105.
72. Dietz, op. cit., 296.
73. Sir Julius Caesar, Chancellor of the Exchequer, thought that the 1608 surveys would raise Crown rents by between 200 and 500 per cent, Dietz, op. cit., p. 298 n. 15.
74. Ibid., 296.
75. Lansd MS 90 f 129 r.
76. Ibid., f 130 v.
77. Lansd MS 91 ff 4 v-5 r, 6 v-7 r, 8 v-9 r, 10 r-12 r.
78. Ibid., ff 2 v-3 r.
79. *CSP Dom 1611-18*, 43.
80. LR 2/214 f 351.
81. W. S. Holdsworth, *History of English Law*, i (7th edn., 1956), 181-2, 72, 135.
82. Lansd MSS 90 f 127 r; 91 ff 130 v-131 r.
83. A. W. Clapham, 'The Court House or "Old Town Hall" at Barking', *Essex Archaeological Society Transactions*, New Series, xii, 295-8.
84. LR 2/214 f 351.
85. Lansd MS 90 ff 124 r, 126 r.
86. Lansd MS 91 ff 133 v-134 r.
87. Ibid., f 23 r.
88. Lansd MS 89 f 189 r.
89. Lansd MS 91 f 29 r. Lowe was admitted a tenant of the manor in the autumn of 1609, ibid., loc. cit.
90. Lansd MS 92 ff 149 r, 132 r.

91. Dietz, *English Public Finance 1558–1641*, 298–9.
92. A. W. Clapham, 'The Court House or "Old Town Hall" at Barking', 295.
93. Lansd MS 91 f 19 r; P. Morant, *Essex*, II (1768), 195.
94. Lansd MS 91 f 132 r.
95. Lansd MS 92 f 10 r.
96. M. S. Giuseppi, *A Guide to the Manuscripts preserved in the Public Record Office*, I (1923), 258.
97. C 66/1787.
98. C 54/1956.
99. PRO Index 9981; A 7/19.
100. Lansd MS 648 f 10 r.
101. E 101/1/2. The whole income which the Master in Chancery received from the Office came from fees obtained from parties making conveyances.
102. E 101/1/1/34; SP 14/32/69.
103. SP 14/52/36.
104. The following account is taken from Lansd MS 648 ff 1 r–27 r, an account of the Alienation Office written between 1598 and 1603 by one of its officials. Procedure in the Office is described on ff 10 v–12 v.
105. See PRO Indexes 9981–9983 *passim*; A 7/19–22 *passim*; A 9/2 *passim*. It was always recorded in these entry books, which cover the period 1608 to 1612, whether the value of lands was assessed by composition or otherwise.
106. Lansd MSS 91 f 117 r; 90 f 112 r.
107. Lansd MS 648 f 20 v.
108. E 101/1/1/13, 19, 21.
109. This possibility is given credence by the work of L. Stone. See *The Crisis of the Aristocracy* (Oxford, 1965), 36–7, especially the graph on p. 37.
110. Hurstfield, *The Queen's Wards*, 312–13.

Chapter Seven
Michael Hickes and Robert Cecil

1. See p. 35.
2. On Cecil's secretariat see A. G. R. Smith, 'The secretariats of the Cecils, circa 1580–1612', *EHR*, lxxxiii (1968), 481–504.
3. Lansd MS 87 f 85 r.
4. B. M. Ward, *The Seventeenth Earl of Oxford* (1928), 332–3.
5. Lansd MS 87 f 96 rv.
6. Salisbury MS 75/74.

7. Lansd MS 87 f 176 r.
8. Ibid., f 178 r.
9. Ibid., f 206 r.
10. Lansd MS 88 f 99 r.
11. HMC *Salisbury*, xv, 45, 74, 164.
12. Lansd MS 89 f 82 r. Cecil was created earl of Salisbury on May 4th, 1605. GEC, xi, 403.
13. Lansd MS 88 f 133 r.
14. Ibid., f 191 r.
15. Lansd MS 89 f 2 r.
16. Ibid., f 98 r.
17. Lansd MS 88 f 87 r.
18. Ibid., f 159 r.
19. Lansd MS 89 f 94 r.
20. Ibid., f 92 rv.
21. Ibid., f 167 r.
22. Lansd MS 90 ff 102 r, 104 r.
23. Salisbury MS 126/114.
24. Lansd MS 108 f 151 r.
25. Salisbury MS 127/171.
26. Lansd MSS 87–92 *passim*.
27. Lansd MS 89 f 35 r.
28. Lansd MS 91 f 145 r.
29. Lansd MS 92 f 74 r.
30. The story of the Bassett wardship has been reconstructed in detail by Hurstfield, *The Queen's Wards* (1958), 301–4.
31. Lansd MS 88 f 91 rv.
32. Ibid., f 105 r.
33. Lansd MS 89 f 27 r.
34. Ibid., f 129 r.
35. Ibid., f 92 rv.
36. Lansd MS 91 f 139 r.
37. Lansd MSS 89 f 4 r; 90 f 36 r; 91 ff 91 r, 125 r.
38. Lansd MS 89 f 107 r.
39. *CSP Dom 1603–10*, 209; *DNB*, *sub* Waad, William.
40. Lansd MS 89 f 13 r.
41. Lansd MS 90 f 36 r.
42. Ibid., f 218 r.
43. Ibid., f 221 r.
44. Lansd MS 92 f 55 rv; *Haydn's Book of Dignities*, 589.
45. Lansd MS 108 f 63 r; A. Pulling, *Order of the Coif* (1884), xxiv.
46. Lansd MS 89 f 113 v.

47. Lansd MS 90 f 78 r; Bell, *An Introduction to the History and Records of the Court of Wards and Liveries* (Cambridge, 1953), 20–21.
48. Lansd MS 91 f 120 r; *DNB, sub* Nevill, Thomas.
49. Lansd MS 90 f 185 r.
50. Lansd MS 87 f 214 r.
51. Lansd MS 89 ff 173 r–174 r, 198 r.
52. Lansd MS 90 f 194 r.
53. Lansd MS 89 ff 62 rv, 105 r.
54. Lansd MS 92 ff, 117 r, 147 r.
55. Lansd MS 91 f 80 r.
56. Ibid., f 104 r; J. Le Neve, *Fasti Ecclesiae Anglicanae*, ii (Oxford, 1854), 617.
57. Lansd MS 88 f 56 r.
58. Salisbury MS 125/111.
59. Lansd MS 90 f 143 r.
60. There is no agreement among historians about Cecil's political morality during the course of his career. For very different pictures see Hurstfield, op. cit., *passim*; M. Prestwich, *Cranfield* (Oxford, 1966), ch 1. It is fair to note that Cecil was making gigantic profits from office during the last four years of his life. L. Stone, 'The Fruits of Office: The Case of Robert Cecil, First Earl of Salisbury, 1596–1612', *Essays in the Economic History of Tudor and Stuart England*, ed. F. J. Fisher (Cambridge, 1961), 89–116.
61. Lansd MS 91 f 139 r.
62. A. Cecil, *A Life of Robert Cecil, First Earl of Salisbury* (1915), 333–43, gives an account of Salisbury's last days.
63. J. Chamberlain, *Letters*, ed. N. C. McClure, i (Philadelphia, 1939), 346.
64. Lansd MS 92 f 203 r.
65. A. Cecil, op. cit., 336, 342.
66. See Lansd MS 92 ff 165 r, 171 r, 173 r, 175 r, 179 rv.
67. A. Cecil, op. cit., 344.
68. Salisbury MS 206/61.
69. C 142/327/132.

Chapter Eight
Financial Expert

1. C 66/1866.
2. Lansd MS 88 f 147 rv.
3. C 66/1632. See also C 66/1725.

4. C 54/1815. See also C 66/1670.
5. PRO Index 6802.
6. C 66/1737.
7. The act is 3 & 4 Jac. 1, number 45, preserved in the Record Office of the House of Lords in the Palace of Westminster. See also C 54/1827, 1854, 1904.
8. Spedding, II, 205–6.
9. Lansd MS 88 f 95 r.
10. Ibid., ff 123 r, 125 r.
11. Lansd MS 91 ff 49 r, 50 r.
12. Lansd MS 88 f 137 r.
13. Lansd MS 92 ff 191, r 209 r.
14. There is a good brief account of Baptist Hickes's activities in Robert Ashton, 'Government borrowing under the First Two Stuarts, 1603–42' (London University Ph.D. thesis, 1953), 592–6.
15. Lansd MS 89 f 60 r.
16. Lansd MS 90 f 118 r.
17. Ibid., f 224 r.
18. Lansd MS 91 f 127 r.
19. Lansd MS 92 f 68 r.
20. HMC *Salisbury*, xviii, 408–9; Lansd MS 89 f 142 r.
21. Lansd MS 89 f 146 r.
22. Ibid., f 205 r.
23. Lansd MS 90 f 6 r.
24. Ibid., f 8 r.
25. R. Ashton, *The Crown and the Money Market 1603–40* (Oxford, 1960), 158–9.
26. Lansd MS 90 f 202 r.
27. See p. 35.
28. HMC *Salisbury*, iv, 377. On the auditor of the receipt see G. R. Elton, *The Tudor Revolution in Government* (Cambridge, 1953), 253–4.
29. Lansd MSS 91 ff 159 rv, 162 r, 163 r, 165 r, 166 rv, 171 r, 174 rv, 178 v, 179 r, 180 r, 185 r, 198 r, 202 r, 207 r; 92 ff 14 r, 15 r, 17 rv, 19 rv, 21 r, 27 rv, 30 r, 34 r, 40 r, 42 r, 69 r, 71 r, 72 r, 77 r, 85 rv, 86 r, 95 r, 97 rv, 100 r, 121 r, 123 r.
30. *CJ*, i, 454. For the privilege of freedom from arrest at this time see G. W. Prothero, 'The Parliamentary privilege of freedom from arrest and Sir Thomas Shirley's case, 1604', *EHR*, viii (1893), 733–40.
31. Lansd MS 91 f 159 rv.
32. Ibid., f 163 r.

33. E. R. Foster, ed., *Proceedings in Parliament 1610*, II (New Haven, 1966), 295, 347.
34. Lansd MSS 91 f 207 r; 92 f 17 rv.
35. Lansd MS 92 ff 72 r, 73 r.
36. *CSP Dom 1611–18*, 17; Salisbury MS 129/52.
37. PRO Index 6804.
38. *Harleian Society Publications*, lii (1904); *Lincolnshire Pedigrees*, III, ed. A. R. Maddison, 888.
39. Lansd MS 88 f 147 r.
40. Ibid., f 149 r.
41. LC 4/194/401; 4/195/285; 4/196/94; 4/196/95; 4/196/118; 4/197/130; 4/197/191; 4/197/258; 4/197/328.
42. The total security represented by the statutes was £10,500. If all of them had involved loans the amount lent would therefore probably have been over £5,000.
43. Spedding, II, 205; III, 14–15; IV, 40, 87, 95.
44. Lansd MS 88 f 73 r.
45. Salisbury MS 102/97.
46. Lansd MS 89 f 34 r.
47. HMC *Bath*, ii, 54.
48. Lansd MS 89 f 136 r.
49. Lansd MS 90 f 82 r.
50. Ibid., f 150 r.
51. On Compton see L. Stone, 'The Peer and the Alderman's Daughter', *History Today*, January 1961, 48–55; GEC, IX, 677–9.
52. Lansd MS 91 f 86 r.
53. Lansd MS 92 f 155 r.
54. There is no evidence of the Shrewsburys being involved in recognizances, statutes or mortgages with Hickes.
55. Helen Miller, 'Subsidy Assessment of the Peerage in the Sixteenth Century', *BIHR*, xxviii (1955), 18; L. Stone, *The Crisis of the Aristocracy* (Oxford, 1965), 760.
56. Lansd MS 88 f 167 r.
57. E. Lodge, *Illustrations of British History*, III (1791), 221.
58. Lansd MS 91 f 119 r.
59. Ibid., loc. cit.
60. Lansd MS 92 f 8 r.
61. Ibid., f 12 r.
62. Ibid., f 62 r.
63. Ibid., f 207 r.
64. Stone, *The Crisis of the Aristocracy*, 461–2.
65. HMC *Bath*, iv, 347.

66. Stone, *The Crisis of the Aristocracy*, 760.
67. See pp. 23-4.
68. LC 4/195/111. The penalty in the statute was for £2,800.
69. Lansd MS 88 f 127 r.
70. Salisbury MS 103/17.
71. LC 4/195/254.
72. In another statute of the same date Edward Blunt undertook to pay Hickes the £600 at the stipulated date or else forfeit £2,000 to Thomas Pope Blunt. LC 4/195/254.
73. On Lee see E. K. Chambers, *Sir Henry Lee* (Oxford, 1936).
74. LC 4/193/370 (penalty £4,000); 4/194/165 (penalty £1,000).
75. Lansd MSS 89 f 160 r; 90 ff 72 r, 74 rv, 196 r.
76. LC 4/195/73; 4/195/316; 4/196/137; 4/197/238; 4/197/243. Peyton refers to his debts to Hickes in a letter of July 1612. Lansd MS 92 f 211 r.
77. Lansd MS 88 f 23 r.
78. LC 4/195/360.
79. Lansd MS 89 f 169 r.
80. C 54/1872.
81. Lansd MSS 90 ff 2 r, 42 r, 67 r; 91 ff 45 r, 63 r, 143 r; 92 ff 59 r, 64 r, 163 r.
82. C 54/1840.
83. C 54/1711, 1847.
84. Hickes's land at Myntie was omitted in his inquisition *post mortem*, although it was still in the family in 1613, the year after his death. See C 66/2013.
85. C 54/2125.
86. C 54/2191.
87. Lansd MS 93 f 4 r. Her brother-in-law Sir Thomas Lowe made references to her money-lending activities in his letters to her. See Lansd MS 93 ff 34 r, 35 r.
88. SP 23/236/153.
89. Lansd MS 89 f 60 r.

Chapter Nine

Michael Hickes and his Circle

1. Lansd MS 88 ff 147 r, 149 r.
2. PCC 110 Fenner.
3. Lansd MS 108 f 151 r.
4. Lansd MS 92 f 113 r.
5. See pp. 75-7.
6. See p. 144.

7. C. Hill, *Society and Puritanism in Pre-Revolutionary England* (1964), 501.
8. After 1598 proportionally more letters were addressed to Hickes at Ruckholt. Lansd MSS 76–92 *passim*.
9. Lansd MS 93 f 48 r.
10. Lansd MS 88 f 147 r.
11. See pp. 104-5.
12. J. and J. A. Venn, *Alumni Cantabrigiensis*, part i, vol. II (Cambridge, 1922), 365.
13. Lansd MS 93 ff 13 r, 32 r, 42 r, 44 r.
14. Ibid., ff 11 r, 20 r, 27 r, 36 r, 38 r, 51 r.
15. Ibid., f 29 r.
16. Lansd MS 90 f 229 r.
17. Ibid., ff 198 r, 189 r.
18. Lansd MS 89 f 146 r.
19. J. Kennedy, *A History of the Parish of Leyton, Essex* (Leyton, 1894), 107–8.
20. HMC *Rutland*, i, 412.
21. Lansd MS 91 f 74 r.
22. Lansd MS 93 f 46 r.
23. PCC 110 Fenner.
24. Lansd MSS 88 f 74 r; 89 f 119 r.
25. Lansd MS 92 f 115 r.
26. Lansd MS 107 ff 8 r, 9 r, 11 r.
27. Lansd MS 88 f 65 r.
28. Ibid., f 36 r.
29. Ibid., f 109 r.
30. Lansd MS 89 f 57 r.
31. Ibid., f 18 r.
32. Ibid., f 23 r.
33. Lansd MS 88 f 195 rv.
34. Ibid., f 199 r.
35. Ibid., f 196 r.
36. Ibid., ff 196 r, 197 v.
37. Lansd MS 60 f 80 r.
38. This is at Witcombe Park, Gloucestershire. It is undated.
39. On Hickes's baldness see Lansd MSS 64 f 147 r; 107 f 66 r.
40. See pp. 20-21.
41. Quoted by A. Collins, *The Baronettage of England*, II, (1720), 55.
42. Ibid., loc. cit.
43. Lansd MS 90 f 178 r.
44. Lansd MS 88 f 119 r.
45. Lansd MS 91 f 95 r.

46. Lansd MS 92 ff 143 r, 145 r.
47. Lansd MS 91 f 129 r.
48. Lansd MS 92 f 105 r.
49. Salisbury MS, Estate and Private MSS, Accounts 6/13; Lansd MS 92 f 203 r.
50. Lansd MS 98 ff 256 r–262 r.
51. Gesner (1516–65) produced his *Historia Animalium*, the starting-point of modern zoology, in 4 volumes, between 1551 and 1558. His main botanical works were *Enchiridion Historiae Plantarum* (1541) and *Catalogus Plantarum* (1542).
52. Lansd MSS 68 f 31 r; 88 f 145 r.
53. Lansd MS 107 f 162 r.
54. See, for examples, Lansd MS 90 ff 85 r, 213 r.
55. Lansd MS 85 f 41 r.
56. Lansd MS 91 f 89 r.
57. Lansd MS 101 f 159 r.
58. Lansd MS 107 f 164 rv.
59. Lansd MS 88 f 127 r.
60. Salisbury MS 103/17.
61. See p. 108.
62. Lansd MS 88 f 153 r.
63. J. Nichols, *The Progresses of King James I*, 1 (1828), 439.
64. Ibid., 454.
65. Lansd MSS 841 f 41 r; 88 f 179 r; 89 f 175 r; 90 f 97 r.
66. Lansd MS 88 f 179 r.
67. Lansd MS 92 f 114 r.
68. Ibid., f 203 r.
69. Lansd MS 88 f 2 r.
70. Lansd MSS 90 f 15 r; 91 f 214 r.
71. On Lumley see L. Stone, *The Crisis of the Aristocracy* (Oxford, 1965), 560, 705–6, 714, 716; GEC, viii, 276–9.
72. Lansd MSS 87 f 193 r.
73. For Altham see R. J. Fletcher, ed., *Pension Book of Gray's Inn 1569–1669* (1901), 149 n. 1.
74. Lansd MS 87 f 216 r.
75. For Montaigne and Neile see *DNB*.
76. Lansd MS 92 f 141 r.
77. Lansd MS 88 f 10 r.
78. *CSP Dom 1598–1601*, 282; Lansd MS 87 f 164 r.
79. See, for examples, Lansd MS 89 ff 130 r, 132 r, 138 r.
80. Lansd MS 91 f 17 r.
81. Lansd MS 90 f 203 r.
82. Lansd MS 91 f 82 r.

83. C 142/319/195.
84. Lansd MS 91 f 155 r.
85. Lansd MSS 91 ff 103 r, 122 r, 147 r, 181 r; 92 ff 37 r, 76 r, 79 rv, 96 r, 159 r (letters of Susan Maynard); 91 f 172 r; 92 ff 66 r, 153 r, 193 r, 195 r, 199 r (letters of William Maynard).
86. Lansd MSS 86 f 79 r; 87 ff 218 r, 220 r; 88 ff 75 r, 89 r, 187 r; 89 f 36 r.
87. Lansd MSS 87 f 218 r; 88 ff 59 r, 89 r; 89 f 36 r.
88. Lansd MSS 88 f 187 r; 89 f 36 r.
89. Lansd MSS 87 ff 218 r, 220 r; 88 f 89 r; 89 f 36 r.
90. Lansd MS 87 f 218 r.
91. Ibid., f 167 r.
92. Lansd MS 89 f 127 r.
93. See pp. 67-71, 143-4.
94. J. Chamberlain, *Letters*, ed. N. C. McClure, I (Philadelphia, 1939), 200.
95. Lansd MS 89 f 197 r.
96. Glemham married the daughter of Lord Treasurer Buckhurst. W. C. Metcalfe, ed., *The Visitations of Suffolk, 1561, 1577, 1612* (Exeter, 1882), 140.
97. Lansd MSS 92 f 36 r; 89 f 140 r.
98. Lansd MS 90 ff 120 r, 205 r.
99. Lansd MS 88 f 81 r.
100. Lansd MSS 93 f 2 r; 107 f 136 r.
101. Lansd MSS 88 f 185 r; 90 f 87 r.
102. Lansd MS 90 f 95 r.
103. Spedding, III, 291.
104. Spedding, IV, 217–18.
105. Spedding, IV, 246–7.
106. Lansd MSS 88 ff 67 r, 69 r, 113 r, 143 r, 169 r, 171 r, 173 r, 175 r, 183 r; 89 ff 46 r, 54 r, 123 r, 164 r; 91 ff 70 r, 72 r.
107. Lansd MS 88 f 25 r.
108. Ibid., ff 135 r, 136 r, 141 r, 155 r.
109. E. Lodge, *Illustrations of British History*, III (1791), 214–21.
110. Lansd MSS 90 ff 157 r, 165 r, 167 r; 91 ff 53 r, 57 r, 59 r, 61 r, 65 r, 68 r; 92 ff 61 r, 135 r, 137 r, 161 r, 165 r, 169 r, 171 r, 175 r, 179 rv, 181 r, 183 rv, 185 r, 189 r.
111. See e.g. Lansd MSS 12 f 117 r; 21 f 26 r (illnesses of 1570 and 1575).
112. Lansd MS 77 ff 213 r, 215 r.
113. Assizes 35/53.
114. Lansd MS 92 f 103 r.

115. C 142/327/132.
116. Chamberlain, *Letters*, I, 379.

Conclusion

1. C 142/327/132.
2. C 66/1645.
3. J. Maclean 'Pedes Finium or Excerpts from the Feet of Fines, in the County of Gloucester, from the 30th Elizabeth to 20th James I', *Transactions of the Bristol and Gloucestershire Archaeological Society*, xvii (1892–3), 253; C 66/1958.
4. C 54/1847; C 66/2013.
5. He certainly still owned the lands in 1603. Lansd MS 88 f 147 v.
6. C 142/236/74.
7. PCC 110 Fenner.
8. Wards 9/275.
9. C 142/254–79 *passim*.
10. C 66/1608.
11. E 315/320 ff 136 v–137 r.
12. E 101/1/2.
13. In theory he was entitled to 4*s*. for cach day he attended at Quarter Sessions. In fact, the Justices' fees were often used to provide them with a dinner. VCH *Wiltshire*, v (1957), 90.
14. See the Subsidy Act of 1606. *Statutes of the Realm*, iv, 1122–3.
15. There has been much controversy among historians about the nature of Tudor administration. See G. R. Elton, *The Tudor Revolution in Government* (Cambridge, 1953) and the discussion between G. L. Harriss, P. Williams, and G. R. Elton in *Past and Present*, numbers 25 (July 1963), 29 (December 1964), 31 (July 1965) and 32 (December 1965). See also A. G. R. Smith, 'The secretariats of the Cecils, circa 1580–1612', *EHR*, lxxxiii (1968), 481–504.

Index